Kmart's Ten Deadly Sins

Kmart's Ten Deadly Sins

How Incompetence Tainted
An American Icon

MARCIA LAYTON TURNER

WILEY

John Wiley & Sons, Inc.

Published by John Wiley & Sons, Inc., Hoboken, New Jersey.
Published simultaneously in Canada.

For general information on our other products and services, or technical support,
please contact our Customer Care Department within the United States at
800-762-2974, outside the United States at 317-572-3993, or fax 317-572-4002.

Wiley also publishes its books in a variety of electronic formats. Some content that
appears in print may not be available in electronic books.

For more information about Wiley products, visit our web site at www.wiley.com.

Library of Congress Cataloging-in-Publication Data

Turner, Marcia Layton.
   Kmart's ten deadly sins: how incompetence tainted an American icon /
Marcia Layton Turner.
      p. cm.
Includes bibliographical references.
   ISBN 0-471-43593-7 (Cloth)
   1. K-Mart Corporation—Management.   2. Business failures—United
States—Case studies.   I. Title.
   HF5429.215.U6T87 2003
      381′.141′0973—dc21   2003006632

Printed in the United States of America

10 9 8 7 6 5 4 3 2 1

Contents

Acknowledgments

Without the help of retail experts, industry veterans, knowledgeable insiders, business analysts and specialists, this book would have been far less interesting. A heartfelt thanks goes to Theo Addo of San Diego State University; Dennis Altman of the University of Kentucky; Will Ander of McMillan Doolittle LLP; Paul Argenti of the Tuck School of Business at Dartmouth; Kurt Barnard, publisher of Barnard's Retail Trend Report; Britt Beemer of America's Research Group; Don B. Bradley III of the University of Central Arkansas; Tony Camilletti of JGA, Inc.; Peter Fader of the University of Pennsylvania; Lynda Falkenstein "the Niche Doctor" of the Falkenstein Learning Corporation; Eugene Fram of the Rochester Institute of Technology; Rob Gelphman of Gelphman Associates; Mark Goldstein; Steven Greenberg of The Greenberg Group; Cathy Halligan of Prophet; Jim Harris of Seneca Financial Group; Stephen Hoch of the University of Pennsylvania; Barbara Kahn of the University of Pennsylvania; Don Longo of Retail Merchandiser; Al Napier of Rice University; John Parham of Parham Santana; Lars Perner of the University of California-Riverside; Mike Porter of Morningstar; Al Ries of

Ries & Ries; George Rosenbaum of Leo J. Shapiro & Associates, LLC; Biff Ruttenberg of Atlas Partners, LLC; Mark Scheinbaum; Mark Shinderman of Munger, Tolles & Olson LLP; Sandra J. Skrovan of Retail Forward, Inc.; Roger Valdez of Kmartsucks.net; Bart Weitz of the University of Florida; George Whalin of Retail Management Consultants; Ulysses Yannas of Buckman, Buckman & Reid; and the top notch local reporting teams at the Associated Press, *Detroit Free Press, Detroit News, New York Times,* and *Wall Street Journal.*

Thanks also to my group of long-time women business owner friends, Dana Abramson, Betty Andelman, Sandy Beckwith, Mary Anne Brugnoni, Elaine Lotto, and Mary Anne Shew, who cheered me on and encouraged me to write this book.

Likewise, my sincere appreciation goes to my agents Susan Barry and Lisa Swayne who helped create the opportunity for this book's existence, and to my editor, Jeanne Glasser, who shepherded the book along, despite numerous twists and turns in the plot along the way.

Finally, I will always be indebted to my husband, Charlie, for taking over many of the day-to-day responsibilities within our family so that I could bring this story to light.

Where did Kmart go wrong? That is the central question I try to answer in *Kmart's Ten Deadly Sins,* for myself and others seeking to understand how an industry pioneer became a laggard.

The answers I found are varied. Some reasons for the company's poor financial health are due to troubles decades ago, while others are very recent. Some can be traced to a particular CEO's misstep, while others appear to be related more to miscommunication throughout the organization. Some reasons are due to pure stupidity, while others might have made perfect sense at the time.

In the end, Kmart went wrong in a number of areas. I've identified ten that I believe account for a large portion of the company's challenges, but those ten are not all-encompassing. They are a framework, however, for evaluating other decisions, initiatives, and moves the company has made.

Through interviews with industry veterans, retail gurus, financial analysts, thought leaders, professors, former employees, supplemented with thousands of pages of reports from newspaper articles, magazine articles, books, websites, newsletters, case studies, and reports, I've tried to dig for the real answers—the real reasons Kmart is struggling for its survival.

By reading Kmart's story, you'll learn about greed and corruption, as well as the dangers of empire-building, arrogance, and poor decision-making. You'll hear about the major players throughout Kmart's history, as well as the minor ones that could have had an even bigger impact if given the chance. It's an interesting tale that I hope you'll both enjoy and find instructive.

Discount Retail Timeline*

1879   F.W. Woolworth opens its first five-and-dime.

1899   S.S. Kresge Company founded by Sebastian S. Kresge.

1912   S.S. Kresge incorporates with 85 stores and sales of more than $10 million.

1918   S.S. Kresge Company becomes a publicly traded company on the NYSE.

1962   The first Kmart discount department store opens in a Detroit suburb, followed by 17 more that same year; Sam Walton opens first Wal-Mart store in Rogers, Arkansas.

1966   Sebastian Kresge dies at age 99; Kmart has 162 stores.

1968   Wal-Mart begins opening stores outside of Arkansas.

1970   Wal-Mart opens first distribution center and headquarters in Bentonville, Arkansas; chain has 38 stores.

---

*Adapted from Kmart corporate web site, Wal-Mart corporate web site, CNN/Money timeline from January 22, 2002.

1972   Robert Dewar named chairman and CEO, following Harry Cunningham, Kmart's chief architect; Wal-Mart added to NYSE.

1975   Wal-Mart has 125 stores in operation generating $340 million in sales.

1976   271 Kmart stores opened this year alone; total stores = 1,206.

1977   Company name changed from S.S. Kresge Company to Kmart Corporation to reflect that 94.5 percent of sales from the company in 1976 came from Kmart units; Wal-Mart acquires 16 Mohr-Value stores.

1978   Wal-Mart acquires Hutcheson Shoe Company and introduces its pharmacy, auto service, and jewelry divisions.

1979   Wal-Mart has 276 stores with more than $1 billion in sales.

1980   Bernard Fauber elected chairman and CEO.

1981   By year end, there were 2,055 Kmart stores in the U.S., Canada, and Puerto Rico; Wal-Mart buys 92 Kuhn's Big K stores.

1983   Wal-Mart acquires Woolco stores in U.S.; opens first Sam's Club.

1984   Kmart buys Walden Book Company and Builders Square; David Glass named president at Wal-Mart.

1985   Jaclyn Smith apparel collection debuts at Kmart; Wal-Mart has 882 stores with sales of $8.4 billion.

1986   Joseph Antonini succeeds Fauber as chairman, president, and CEO; Martha Stewart brand introduced.

1987   Wal-Mart has 1,198 stores with $15.9 billion; completes satellite network linking all of company's operating units.

1988   David Glass named CEO of Wal-Mart; first Wal-Mart Supercenter opened; 90 percent of Wal-Mart stores use bar-code scanning.

1990   Kmart purchases The Sports Authority; Kmart's logo changed from red and turquoise to red and white; company buys 22 percent interest in Office-Max; Wal-Mart becomes nation's top retailer; Wal-Mart acquires McLane Company.

1991   Kmart raises $1 billion in equity through convertible preferred stock offering; company raises its stake in OfficeMax to 90 percent; Wal-Mart's Sam's American Choice brand products introduced.

1992   Kmart acquires Borders, Inc., a chain of bookstores; Kmart enters the European market; Sam Walton passes away.

1993   Kathy Ireland apparel line introduced; Wal-Mart acquires 91 Pace Warehouse Clubs.

1994   Kmart opens stores in Mexico and Singapore; a portion of The Sports Authority and OfficeMax sold off; Wal-Mart acquires 122 Canadian Woolco stores.

1995   Floyd Hall named chairman, president, and CEO; spins off Borders and sells remaining stake in The Sports Authority and OfficeMax; Wal-Mart has 1,995 Wal-Mart stores, 239 Supercenters, 433 Sam's Clubs, and 276 international stores with sales of $93.6 billion.

1996   Kmart completes $4.7 billion in new financing; Route 66 brand introduced.

1997   Big Kmart store format introduced; Martha Stewart Everyday line introduced; Builders Square and Kmart Canada sold off; Sesame Street brand introduced; Wal-Mart acquires OneSource nutrition centers.

1999   Martha Stewart brand expands into garden and patio products and Martha Stewart Baby Baby for infants; BlueLight.com web site debuts; Wal-Mart has 1,140,000 associates, becoming the largest private employer in the world.

2000	Martha Stewart line extended into kitchenware and plants; Charles Conaway takes over as chairman and CEO; H. Lee Scott named president and CEO of Wal-Mart.
2001	BlueLight Special reintroduced after 10 years; Martha Stewart introduces organizing and home decorating lines; Kmart signs $4.5 billion exclusive agreement with Fleming to distribute food and consumables to its stores; BlueLight.com acquired by Kmart from SOFTBANK, its partner; Wal-Mart has biggest sales day ever—earning $1.25 billion on the day after Thanksgiving.
1/22/02	**Kmart files for Chapter 11 bankruptcy protection.**
3/08/02	Kmart announces that 284 underperforming stores will be closed.
3/11/02	James Adamson is appointed CEO, Julian Day, president and chief operating officer, as former CEO Chuck Conaway leaves the company.
4/18/02	Karen Austin is promoted to senior vice president and chief information officer.
6/19/02	Kmart relaunches its Internet site, renaming it Kmart.com.
1/14/03	Kmart announces that it intends to close 323 more stores.
1/19/03	Julian Day is promoted to CEO as James Adamson continues to serve as non-executive chairman during the reorganization process.
1/24/03	Kmart files its plan of reorganization with the bankruptcy court, setting its target exit date as 4/30/03.
2/04/03	Kmart and Fleming end their supplier relationship.
4/22/03	The U.S. Bankruptcy Court approves the company's reorganization plan, allowing Kmart to proceed.
5/06/03	Kmart emerges from Chapter 11 bankruptcy with a new chairman, Edward Lampert, a major shareholder in the new Kmart, and new stock.

"How did you go bankrupt? Gradually, then suddenly."
—*The Sun Also Rises,* Ernest Hemingway

For years, Kmart's financials had been lackluster, but until 2002, the company had never filed for bankruptcy. Sure, there had been rumors, but it had never actually happened. Why now? What caused the company's prospects to become so bleak that bankruptcy protection was the only answer? Some say the answer is Chuck Conaway, who began his tenure as CEO in 2000, and his "frat boy" management team.

Out of what looks like pure greed, former managers pushed Kmart into bankruptcy by draining the corporate coffers, in the process giving themselves extensive compensation packages and embarking on ill-advised price wars. The extent to which executives and managers went to conceal their ill-gotten financial gains is impressive. One newspaper report called it a "two-year program of deceit, intimidation and unauthorized spending,"[1] in which "former Kmart managers altered information submitted to the board of directors about a controversial $24 million loan program for key executives in December 2001,"[1] This indicates that their minds definitely were not on helping Kmart improve its market position. If they had been, Kmart would be better off for their leadership, not worse.

Finally, employee whistleblowers could stay quiet no longer and began sending anonymous letters on Kmart letterhead about accounting irregularities and wrongdoing within the company to local media and government investigators. Those letters prompted the FBI, the U.S. Attorney's office, and other government agencies, as well as Kmart itself, to cull through its corporate records for answers.

According to the stewardship review that the company performed and reported in its bankruptcy reorganization plan in 2003, it appears that Kmart was financially stable, although not immensely profitable, when Chuck Conaway took over. But it was under his leadership that executives began exploiting the company for all that it was worth.

Many of the executives were new to the company, hired during Conaway's massive push for more staffers. However, Conaway didn't feel it necessary to follow the company's hiring guidelines or requirements. No formal applications were requested of many new management hires, no background checks were completed, nor were any interviews conducted with the new hires, according to Kmart's review.[1] Instead of consulting the company's human resources department for salary guidelines, certain former executives doing the hiring determined the compensation packages offered all on their own. Reports *The Detroit News,* the executives "set contract terms of these new hires, authorizing excessive compensation packages. Not only did these hiring packages go beyond what Kmart would normally have given its employees, they also were far larger than what the new hires had received from their previous employers."[1]

Comments Kmart retiree Nathan Menoian regarding employee salaries, "When I was there, they made a valid point that you had to pay good salaries to attract and keep talented people. But somewhere along the line, it just became outrageous. They (executives) just wanted to take as much as they could get."[2]

Jeffrey Boyer, a Conaway pick and Sears veteran, was CFO for just seven months, but pocketed more than $1 million in cash, bonuses, and severance on his departure. Mark Schwartz, the brash president Conaway instated, earned more than $2 million in fiscal 2000, of which he only worked about five months,[2] and received more than $1.2 million just for housing in 2001. Conaway earned millions in salary and bonuses on top of the perks that included more than $500,000 for housing and other personal expenses in 2000 and 2001, plus another $122,000 for personal use of the company jet.[2] Buying corporate airplanes was another Conaway initiative, and with other managers he spent $12 million of Kmart's money on them without getting proper authorization. The planes then were used for both business and personal trips by management, with Kmart footing the bill.

The BlueLight Always program that Conaway and Schwartz devised, however, was what really broke the bank. In the summer of 2001, to gear up for Kmart's planned price war against Wal-Mart, executives bought $850 million in new merchandise for its stores without talking to Kmart's treasury officials about whether the company could afford such a buying spree, without consulting its suppliers about the practicality of such a program, and without any kind of internal analysis to verify that such a strategy was one Kmart could adequately support. When the program failed, as most observers—including Kmart's board—fully expected, the company lost millions and quickly ran into liquidity problems.[1]

To try and cover up the cash flow shortage, managers began shuffling vendor payments—"allowances"—Kmart receives from suppliers for premium shelf space, attributing $92 million in payments to different time periods to improve its accounting records. Two Kmart executives were also later charged with fraudulent reporting of revenue, arising from a secret arrangement with American Greetings Corp in 2001. The execs agreed to make American Greetings its sole source of greeting cards and received a $42.3 million payment from the company at a time when it was struggling to meet Wall Street earnings expectations. Although American Greetings indicated to auditors that there were "no strings attached" to the payment, there was actually a side agreement with Kmart that if their exclusive contract was rescinded, the payment had to be returned. That fact made it improper for Kmart to include the payment as revenue when it did.[3] Kmart's financial statements from the first three quarters of 2001 were impacted by these maneuvers, which made the company's financial health seem stable when it clearly was not.

In addition to covering up the company's current cash flow shortage, executives also sought to continue the charade by falsifying projections. *The Detroit News* reported that "Executives began to force Kmart's merchandising personnel to use outrageous and unattainable goals in Kmart's forecasts and financial reports. When these staffers resisted, they were demoted or transferred."[1] And in September 2001 executives initiated a payment slowdown to make up for the cash shortfalls, dubbed "Project Slow It Down," or "Project SID,"[4] reducing or stopping payments to vendors and then avoiding explanations for the slowdown when questioned.[1]

Despite the obvious financial problems executives knew the company was having, they took the opportunity to request additional financial compensation from the board. And the board, seeing the strong forecasts for the future that the executives had prepared, approved nearly $29 million worth of "retention loans" for 25 top-level executives[5] in December 2001. However, unbeknownst to the board, loans then were doled out to two additional, lower layers of employees, far beyond the scope of the agreement.[4] To cover up that additional loan activity, "management created purported committee documents that varied materially from the loan program documents submitted for approval, and these documents were inserted in the company's official board files after the fact," according to the stewardship review.[1]

When the company's 2001 holiday sales failed to materialize and the company suffered a catastrophic $2.42 billion loss, suppliers stopped shipping product due to nonpayment, its bonds were downgraded to junk status,[6] and a Prudential Securities financial analyst predicted a bankruptcy filing,[1] Kmart's future was sealed. With suppliers unwilling to provide product on credit and a growing cash shortfall making prepayment for product impossible, the company had few options.

The Announcement

Kmart's bankruptcy filing was the largest-ever for a retailer. Most industry analysts weren't caught off guard by Kmart's bankruptcy announcement on January 22, 2002, a situation that was reversed in May 2003. In fact, many had expected it. But what had forced Kmart to take such steps at that particular time?

Few outside Kmart knew of the treachery and greed that had brought the company down, but over the next year, with the help of the Justice Department and the Securities and Exchange Commission, the company and its customers finally started to get some answers. Then-CEO Jim Adamson conceded the stark reality of the situation in a statement issued about Kmart's bankruptcy: "These results reconfirm the significant difficulties Kmart experienced last year, including unsuccessful sales and marketing initiatives, an erosion in supplier confidence, and below-plan sales and earnings performance in the fourth quarter—all of which were factors in the decision to file for Chapter 11 bankruptcy protection."[7]

This statement is interesting given Adamson's cushy compensation package. During his stint as CEO, Kmart was contractually bound to provide him with similar luxuries, such as access to weekly private plane service from his residences in Detroit, New York, and Florida, a car and driver in Michigan and New York, and temporary accommodations near Kmart's headquarters,[2] while the company claimed bankrupt status. That's on top of the $2.5 million "inducement payment" to convince him to take the job *and* his $1.5 million salary.[2] Meanwhile, laid-off Kmart employees received a severance package consisting of a wave goodbye.

Comments Patrick McGurn, special counsel for Institutional Shareholder Services, which advises big investors on corporate governance and CEO pay, "Kmart boggles the mind. At least Tyco (another company hit by corporate scandal) still has some value for shareholders. You can't say that for Kmart. It's really a pay-for-failure situation."[2]

To get past its troubled times and get the company back on track, Kmart's new leadership let go most of the executives in place prebankruptcy and terminated any managers who had received retention loans. Fearful of any continuing questions about its compensation processes, Kmart elected to start over.

The government's investigation is not over, however, and it has been suggested that past executives could end up facing criminal charges or being sued by creditors. In February 2003, two former senior executives were indicted by a federal grand jury on charges that they inflated Kmart's revenue by misrepresenting vendor payments and a third has been subpoenaed to give testimony about former management. If there is evidence against Conaway and he ends up being sued, it is likely that his director's and officer's liability insurance policy, paid for by Kmart, will cover any required payout although that issue has not yet been decided.[2] It appears that Kmart continues to foot the bill for the past misdeeds of its executives, but can it afford to?

The Aftershocks

In marked contrast to Kmart's 2002 losses, Wal-Mart reported first quarter 2002 results showing nearly 20 percent earnings growth and sales increases of more than 14 percent, despite increasing inventory only 3 percent.[7] As Kmart's sales have slid, Wal-Mart and Target are picking up the slack, gaining market share. But since the three discount retail powerhouses account for 88 percent of the $206 billion U.S. market,[8] any major gains will likely be at Kmart's expense. However, according to Cathy Halligan, a director at Prophet, a strategic brand and marketing consulting firm, "Three players can survive in a market. Three players can do well if each company has a distinctive, relevant, and compelling brand and marketing strategy. The problem is that Kmart has nothing that differentiates it from the other two major competitors in the same space." Its identity overlaps with both Target and, to a greater degree, Wal-Mart. The result is that the company is getting squeezed out of the industry, and its financials show it.

Proof that three players can survive and thrive in the discount mass merchandise category is the emergence of Kohl's, a strong competitor, points out Halligan. "Kohl's is coming on strong, is expanding rapidly, and has posted excellent financials," she says. Three-some Wal-Mart, Target, and Kohl's are evidence that three companies can do well in a competitive category.

Both Wal-Mart and Target have higher sales per square foot, with Wal-Mart achieving $440-per-square-foot and Target $275, while Kmart earns just $245. Its 2.0 to 3.0 percent gross margins are also at the bottom of the barrel, while Wal-Mart achieves 5.5

to 6.5 percent and Target hits 5.5 to 7.5 percent.[9] Kmart, however, is determined to regroup and recapture its lost customers.

Kmart's Roots

Many of Kmart's troubles are rooted in its former life as the S.S. Kresge chain of five-and-dimes. Kresge was the powerhouse of its day but recognized a cultural shift in the 1960s away from variety stores, as they were also known, toward discount shopping. To remain ahead of the pack, in 1962 Kresge introduced the Kmart discount store, which later eclipsed the Kresge stores in terms of growth and sales. Over the next 25 years, all of the Kresge stores were sold or converted into Kmart-format stores.

With the financial resources of the well-established Kresge Corporation and the expertise of its employees, Kmart was well positioned to own the discount retailing industry. For almost 20 years it did. And then came 1980, a pivotal year for Kmart. Around 1980, Kmart's always-rising sales started to fall. It was the year the company's past strategies began to catch up with it. It was the year that then-CEO Robert Dewar recognized that the company's growth through expansion had to change; more than 800 new stores had been opened in the past four years, with little positive impact on the company's bottom line.[10] Although new store openings had fueled the company's growth for many years, that strategy was not working anymore and Kmart had to devise a new plan. Dewar stepped down and was replaced by Bernard Fauber. This also was the year Wal-Mart really started gaining steam, following record sales of $1 billion in 1979.

Never having faced declining sales, Kmart's management was not equipped to respond. Over the next two decades, Kmart tried a variety of strategies to reverse its downhill course, few of which seemed to work. Some boosted sales, others worked in the short term but damaged the company's long-term prospects, and others drained the company's resources altogether. Meanwhile, Kmart's board and shareholders grew impatient for the turnaround. That turnaround came thanks to Floyd Hall, who essentially saved the company from the threat of bankruptcy. So when Hall was ready to step down, in came fair-haired Chuck

Conaway to take the reins and leverage Kmart's strengths even further. As it turns out, he leveraged more than its strengths. He leveraged its future.

Kmart Today

The Kmart of 2003 looks little like the Kmart of 1962, or of 20 or even 10 years ago. Decimated by nearly 600 store closings in 2002 and 2003, close to 67,000 job cuts, and financial losses in the billions, Kmart is down for the count. What's left is approximately 1,500 stores, 180,000 employees, and an unknown quantity of die-hard Kmart customers. How much more the customers are willing to endure on behalf of the retailer also is a big unknown.

Store closures were expected to generate approximately $500 million in cash flow for the company in 2003, but the cost of bankruptcy has been heavy, with Kmart recording about $1.7 billion in restructuring charges[11] in connection with its filing. Although many bankruptcies drag on for more than a year, Kmart emerged in little more than 15 months. Due to the high cost of remaining in bankruptcy, from attorneys fees, consultant fees, court fees (estimated at about $145,000 in billable hours a day, or more than $114 million in professional fees and expenses since its bankruptcy filing[12]), and the negative impact bankruptcy presumably has on sales, Kmart pushed aggressively to exit at the first opportunity.

Summarizing management's feelings on the subject, former CEO James Adamson stated, "We do not want to remain in bankruptcy a day longer than necessary."[11] Of course, he has the added incentive of several million dollars in bonus compensation if the company exits before July 30, 2003, that also nudged the company's progress. Adamson led Kmart for little more than a year—from 2002 to 2003.

After regrouping under Chapter 11 bankruptcy protection, which eliminated most, if not all, of its obligations to continue operating underperforming stores, the company emerged with a stronger balance sheet (eliminating $7.8 billion in debt), improved cash position, and a head start toward profitability, which it anticipates as soon as 2004. But is its plan to position the company as "the store of the neighborhood" a smart one? And can it really become "the authority for moms?" Will Hispanic and African-American consumers be its ticket to profitability?

Perhaps of more immediate concern, will customers be willing to venture back into Kmart stores now that the company's survival looks more assured? And will they come back a second time after seeing that not much has changed at the store level? Although these are critical present-day issues for Kmart, some of its biggest problems lay in its past, and continue to haunt the company today.

The Ten Deadly Sins

Depending on whom you talk to, Kmart's fall from grace could be due to any number of factors. Some analysts believe Kmart has been focusing on the wrong demographic group, targeting younger blue-collar workers making less than $40,000 when it's the middle-income customer with kids who is doing all the buying. Focus has been a weakness for the company and its leaders, who have shifted the company's objectives and brand strategy time and again. Others argue that throughout its history, Kmart's strategy has been to grow by opening new stores, rather than keeping its existing stores looking fresh and inviting.

The truth is that Kmart has made a number of errors throughout its 40-year history, some that seemed like good decisions at the time, and others that were obviously off-base even then. By taking a look back at Kmart since its establishment in 1962, you begin to see patterns.

Yes, the names of CEOs change every few years, but in some cases, the decisions they make are often course reversals from previous leaders—almost a cycle that all Kmart policies face. Its approach to information technology management is a case in point; successive CEOs vow to overhaul the system and end up just throwing out portions developed by former leaders. Other strategies are just flawed, plain and simple, such as its decision to engage in a pricing war with Wal-Mart. Some realities are mind-boggling, such as how Kmart virtually could have ignored Wal-Mart as it made serious inroads into its market. Instead of making great strides forward, Kmart often has found itself playing catch-up, with some CEOs undoing the damage done by prior leaders and others simply making the situation worse. Its poor supply chain management system is an area where the company has consistently been weak, but why it is still today is more puzzling.

The point of this book isn't simply to point fingers, it's to identify how such a retail pioneer could have fallen so far behind its upstart competitors. By studying its inconsistent past, readers will get a sense of where Kmart went wrong, as well as what it needs to do now to succeed in the postbankruptcy future.

The recent scandal involving past Kmart executives is a very small part of the story. It explains a little of why a relatively stable company could fall so far so fast, but it doesn't account for all of the company's problems. Although greedy managers ultimately caused the cash crunch that precipitated Kmart's bankruptcy filing, Kmart was already at a disadvantage. It had no clear market position, no niche, no inviting stores, no state-of-the-art technology, and no focus. It did have a tendency to switch strategies with the wind. On the positive side, it did have—and continues to have—a remarkably loyal group of customers. Those customers want a better Kmart. Management now has a chance to give it to them. Will they? That's the big unknown.

Through phone interviews with dozens of financial analysts, retail consultants, former employees, former suppliers, researchers, strategists, professors, and industry observers and leaders, a picture of Kmart management's thinking emerged. When coupled with the review of thousands of pages of articles, SEC filings, news reports, and background data, a clearer image emerged of what exactly went on—and why.

Let's hope there's a lesson in there for each of us.

Notes

1. "How 'frat boys' drove Kmart to ruin," by Karen Dybis, *The Detroit News*, January 26, 2003.
2. "Greed-mart," by Nelson Schwartz, *Fortune*, September 30, 2002.

3. "Feds indict 2 Kmart execs," by David Shepardson, *The Detroit News*, February 27, 2003.

4. Kmart reorganization plan, filed with the U.S. Bankruptcy Court, Northern District of Illinois, Eastern Division, Hon. Susan Pierson Sonderby, Jan. 24, 2003.

5. "Kmart files plan of reorganization," Associated Press, January 24, 2003.

6. "Vendors stand behind Kmart—and its $2B bailout," *TWICE*, www.twice.com, January 24, 2002.

7. "A study in contrasts," by Greg Jacobson, *Mass Market Retailers*, May 27, 2002.

8. "Big discounters turn warlike in fight for customers," by Anne D'Innocenzio, Associated Press, August 25, 2001.

9. Figures from an Atlas Partners presentation to the Kmart Shareholders Committee, June 14, 2002.

10. "Can Kmart come back again?" by Stephen Taub, *Financial World*, March 31, 1983.

11. "Kmart to dismiss 37,000 workers, close 326 stores," by Shirley Leung, *The Wall Street Journal*, January 15, 2003.

12. "Legal fees plague Kmart," by Karen Dybis, *The Detroit News*, April 20, 2003.

1

Brand Mismanagement

"The issue is, who is Kmart?" stated former CEO Jim Adamson in early 2002 shortly after taking the helm, bluntly stating the question Kmart has been trying to answer for more than a decade,[1] and admitted that "we're not at our best right now."[2]

Or, as Wally O'Brien of the International Advertising Association put it, "Kmart is a brand that lost its way."[3] Consumers became confused when the store with cheap prices began selling upscale goods like Ralph Lauren paints and Martha Stewart–branded merchandise.

In the meantime, as it was negotiating high-profile exclusive licensing deals, Kmart ignored most of the other aspects of its brand image. Stores were messy, products were often out of stock, checkout lines were long, and no one seemed to care—or notice. Only too late did management realize that its inattention was costing the company in sales.

Kmart broke the "golden rule of retailing," as Tony Camilletti explains it. Camilletti is senior vice president of JGA, a brand strategy and design firm headquartered in Kmart's neighborhood, in Southfield, Michigan. "The golden rule is that you don't wait until something is broken to fix it. Kmart never believed this. They thought they could get by just with maintaining their brand." "If anything," he says, "aside from the failed attempt at reviving the Blue Light, its marketing efforts of the past decade have diluted and confused the core essence of the Kmart brand." Unfortunately for Kmart, as its brand name faltered, so did its sales. Since nearly two-thirds of most customer purchases are driven by the brand, as brands weaken, so do purchases. Turning this around requires attention from every functional area of the company.[4]

Lack of a Strategic Approach

"What I find fascinating about Kmart," says Cathy Halligan, a director at Prophet, a brand-building firm in San Francisco, "is the lack of a strategic approach to brand development." Instead of defining where Kmart wanted to be as a brand, assessing its strengths, and then conducting a gap analysis to determine how it could get to where it wanted to be as a brand, Kmart simply decided to sign on more private label brands.

To develop a cohesive brand strategy, says Halligan, a company like Kmart must ask how many individual brands they need, what the identity of each is, and what the relationship is between each individual brand. Rather than creating a brand platform, as Target has done, for example, Kmart simply identified new brand names to "plug in the assortment," or fill a particular need that it perceived. Kmart's brand strategy is based on a collection of branding deals—like puzzle pieces that correlate to certain market demographics—rather than a cohesive link that underlies many of its labels. Kmart "didn't have a brand strategy" observes Halligan.

Losing Sight of Its Value Proposition

According to marketing communications consultant Rob Gelphman, Kmart had a perfect understanding of its core value proposition during its early days—Kmart was a low-cost, commodity goods provider. Its value proposition, a series of words or phrases regarding tangible results achieved through the use of its products or services, was clear. "Buy decent goods at great prices" could have been its stated value proposition, and its marketing reflected that. "Its BlueLight Specials and 'Attention Kmart Shoppers' style of retailing, although widely lampooned by late-night comics, served as their own marks of distinction," he says.[5]

While the company was growing unchallenged during the first 10 or 15 years, "it didn't have to refine its core value proposition and tighten its focus; Kmart didn't move beyond its original vision," Gelphman notes. By the time it had to, in the late 1970s and 1980s, it was too late to make a move. By then Wal-Mart and Target had taken Kmart's value proposition and kicked it up a notch, adding service and product depth and leaving Kmart empty-handed.[5] According to Gelphman, "Kmart also made the mistake in thinking that [its] long-term leadership as a discount retailer translated into a value proposition."

Poor Positioning

Although Wal-Mart and Target have positioned themselves at the low and high end of the market, respectively, "Kmart is more of a blank slate," says John Parham, president of Parham Santana, a brand strategy design firm. "They hadn't defined what [consumers] were supposed to think about them. I think the only meaning [Kmart] has now is that it's an American institution." What Parham says Kmart needs to do is define a position that is different from the competition. "It's not about being better," he says. "It's about being different." Determine what it is that makes Kmart unique, in a good way, and then communicate that clearly to customers. Drill that difference into consumers' minds.

According to Kmart's bankruptcy reorganization plan, it hopes to define itself as "the store of the neighborhood," drawing on its convenient locations in urban markets and combining that strength with inventory tailored at each store to better match its local customers' purchase preferences. Unfortunately, that position is still right in the middle between Target and Wal-Mart, where it has been all along.

No Meaning

Summarizing Kmart's current image dilemma, *The Detroit News* quipped, "On a good day, it lacks an identity. On a bad day, it's a tacky out-of-touch discounter whose merchandise just gathers dust in its big-box stores."[6]

Finding out what it stands for in the customer's mind is Kmart's challenge now, says Britt Beemer of America's Research Group. The company could become the discount home store, for example, and may need to rely on Martha Stewart more. But it can't continue to try and be good in all categories, he indicates.[7]

The Kmart brand name doesn't stand for anything in the consumer's mind any more, lament the experts, which virtually eliminates any value associated with it. Unfortunately, without a positive emotion or perception attached to the Kmart moniker, there is little the company can do to leverage the brand name. The Kmart name emblazoned on a particular product or service will do more harm than good, most branding experts would agree, which is presumably why in the 1980s the company began pursuing licensing deals with brand names not previously associated with the company—fresh names, fresh approaches, and a fresh new reason for consumers to come to Kmart. That's what Jaclyn Smith, Martha Stewart, and, later, JOE BOXER, have done—become a tool for enhancing the Kmart label when it could no longer stand on its own.

"Kmart used to have a private label that had a K in front of it. In lawn and garden, for example, they would have KGrow," explains Professor Stephen Hoch of The Wharton School. Thus, when Hoch met with a former Kmart president five years or so ago, he asked why Kmart no longer put its name on its private label goods. The president responded that putting the Kmart name on products had bad results. Says Hoch, "That really is a total indictment that you can't even put your own label on a product. That your brand equity is so pathetic that you can't even brand your own products." As a result, Kmart began to explore putting other brand names on the products it sold, leading to some of the celebrity licensing deals it has now.

By giving these brands a leg up, however, has Kmart done itself a disservice? Is Kmart as a company and a brand now over-shadowed by the persona that is Martha Stewart, for example? Yes, says brand strategy specialist John Parham.

Needing More Marthas

Despite Kmart's many mistakes, the decision to license the Martha Stewart brand wasn't one of them. In fact, it was genius. Where they faltered was in not pursuing more celebrity licensing deals.

Sure, they had Jaclyn Smith, and later Kathy Ireland, but it wasn't until very recently that the company decided to replicate its success with other strong brand names. Disney, Sesame Street, and JOE BOXER brands have brought much-needed sales revenue and customers into Kmart stores. But could they have had more? Yes, says Mark Goldstein, former consultant and CEO of Kmart's web site, bluelight.com. While working for Blue-light.com, Goldstein recommended signing seven licensing deals similar to the agreement with Martha. Kmart opted to move slowly, only picking up speed with respect to its licensing deals as it approached bankruptcy.

In 1985 Kmart created the Jaclyn Smith clothing collection at Bernard Fauber's direction, later signing Martha Stewart as a spokesperson and consultant in 1987 after Joe Antonini had taken over. But Kmart didn't leverage its access to Martha Stewart for many years. In the meantime, it introduced a line of swimwear and bodywear by Kathy Ireland in 1994 and debuted the Route 66 brand of casual apparel for the whole family in 1996.

Finally, in 1997, the Martha Stewart Everyday line was intro-duced following Martha Stewart's skyrocketing prestige and celebrity in the media. The Martha Stewart Everyday line was an immediate hit. That same year, under Floyd Hall, the Sesame Street line of clothing for newborns, infants, and toddlers was launched under a long-term agreement with the Children's Television Workshop, and in 1999 Martha Stewart Everyday ex-pands into garden and patio products, as well as Martha Stewart Baby Baby. On the heels of those launches, in 2000 Martha's garden line adds live plants and seeds, as well as a new Martha Stewart Everyday Kitchen collection. Chuck Conaway continued the Martha Stewart brand extensions with organizing products in 2001, called Martha Stewart Everyday Keeping, and Martha Stewart Everyday Decorating, a line of home decorating items. But two new brands were added shortly thereafter, with licensing agreements signed with Disney for a line of children's clothing and with JOE BOXER for clothing and home fashions. Those agreements were modified in 2002, giving Kmart exclusive rights to the two fashion lines,[8] and a new deal with Latin pop star Thalia was inked at the end of 2002. But so far, no brand has passed Martha Stewart in popularity or sales.

Today, sales of Martha Stewart products are a collection of more than 5,000 exclusive items ranging from home decor to bedding to garden accessories and baby goods.[9] The Martha Stewart brand is a merchandising powerhouse, making up 4 percent of Kmart's revenues and bringing in $1.5 billion in sales each year. Even in 1999, Martha Stewart Everyday accounted for 70 percent of Kmart's domestic offerings.[10] With the new holiday line, as well as future concepts, Martha Stewart sales are expected to grow at least 20 percent a year.

Interestingly, those figures are exactly in line with the estimates former CEO Floyd Hall made back in 1999. He believed at that time that Martha Stewart Everyday could grow to represent as much as 4 percent to 5 percent of Kmart's gross revenues, which equates to $1.5 to $2 billion,[10] exactly where the brand stands just three years later, at the end of 2002. In fact, one retail guru believes Kmart owes its existence today to Martha Stewart. "The only reason they're in the game is because of Martha [Stewart]," says Howard Davidowitz, chairman of Davidowitz & Associates in an *Ad Age* article.[11]

Despite her recent stock trading scandal, the Martha Stewart name is currently the biggest single branding program within Kmart and continues to grow through brand extensions. The secret to the brand's success at extensions is a three-season rollout program and a three-tiered product line. Sharon Patrick, president and COO of Martha Stewart Living Omnimedia, explained in a *Discount Store News* article that new Martha Stewart lines are introduced and filled in over three seasons. The first season is a teaser to build interest, followed by a second season that fills in the bulk of the product line, which is finished in the third season with remaining products to fill in any gaps. "It's a three-season rollout that gives us the time we want to do what we want," said Patrick.[10]

Martha Stewart Everyday also has three price points corresponding to good-, better-, and best-quality products. Kmart and Martha Stewart aim to move customers along on the product quality continuum as they educate consumers about the benefits of each level of quality, such as why 250-count sheets are better than 180-count. Presumably, Martha Stewart's visibility in such media as her magazines *Martha Stewart Living, Martha Stewart Weddings,* and *Martha Stewart Kids*; her television show; her syndicated newspaper column; her radio show, broadcast on nearly 300 stations in the United States, covering 93 percent of the total U.S. market;[4] and her new magazine, *Everyday Food,* also serve to educate her target audience on "good things" at Kmart they should aspire to own.

However, there are some product categories that Martha Stewart will never enter, says Sharon Patrick. "We have areas in which we are experts, and we stick to those,"[10] which means, don't look for a line of Martha Stewart clothes any time soon. Fortunately, Kmart's recent alliance with Windsong Allegiance netted the company a clothing brand with 87 percent name recognition.[12]

Kmart's five-year exclusive licensing agreement with Windsong for a JOE BOXER line of clothing targeting teenagers and college students is looking like the next home run for the retailer. JOE BOXER represented the "biggest one-day launch in Kmart history,"[13] according to former CEO Adamson, and generated $200 million in sales in its first three months, and is anticipated to sell $1 billion its first year.[12] Windsong believes that those sales should double by 2005.[12]

Although Windsong may have had ultimate confidence in its brand, Kmart was apparently taken by surprise by the immediate demand for its newest line. At a launch fashion show in New York, JOE BOXER products were selling so quickly that employees had to set some aside for the launch ceremonies. Store managers feared that there would be none left for the festivities.[13]

In addition to swift-selling apparel, however, the JOE BOXER home line also delivered better-than-expected results right off the bat—even better than Martha. The JOE BOXER basic bed was the best-moving home segment shortly after its release, reported Adamson.[13] But Martha needn't be worried—Kmart sees the lines coexisting rather than competing. "In home, JOE BOXER versus Martha Stewart is very complementary," said Adamson. "The customer base is very different."[13] With an 87 percent brand recognition among customers between 12 to 34 and price points that go no higher than $26.99, JOE BOXER seems to be the perfect draw for younger, trendy shoppers.[13]

All of this brings up the question of why Kmart doesn't pursue more deals with niche celebrities, as Martha Stewart is for home decor and entertaining? The company has done well with celebrity apparel lines, but how about expanding into new territory, beyond clothing and softlines? For example, a line of Jeff Gordon automotive accessories, Lance Armstrong sporting goods, Sammy Sosa sportswear, and Nigella Lawson cooking appliances would continue to link the Kmart brand name with well-known and well-liked personalities.

The Silver Bullet

"Kmart blew a golden opportunity" when it limited its perception of the Martha Stewart brand, says Cathy Halligan of brand and business strategy firm Prophet.[14] According to Halligan, Kmart saw Martha Stewart as access to branded products, rather than as a much more lucrative and strategic silver bullet—a brand that significantly enhances the image of another brand through a partnership or affiliation. "Target," she explains, "developed a compelling value proposition and viewed the Michael Graves Design collection not only as access to a branded assortment, but as a potential silver bullet brand." Of course, Graves did become the silver bullet that enabled Target to position itself as a more design-savvy merchandiser.

However, brand strategist Tony Camilletti disagrees, stating that "Martha Stewart *is* Kmart's silver bullet and always has been, long before Target found Michael Graves." According to Camilletti, "Much like Graves, Kmart took the risk of building a brand around a relatively unknown celebrity (back in the 1980s when [its] relationship with Martha first began) and helped establish her into a national authority." But it took nearly 10 years before Kmart apparently recognized that Martha was a powerhouse. Says Camilletti, "The only flaw I see in Kmart's strategy with Martha is that they didn't integrate her taste and influence into the culture of the organization earlier on."

Why did Kmart resist the positive impact that the Martha Stewart brand was having on the company at the store level? Camilletti says, "I can only chalk it up to the political culture that was steering Kmart's future, the many guard changes they endured and Martha's overbearing style of micro-managing her brand assets." The fact is that Martha Stewart's and Kmart's images became ever more intertwined in the 1990s as sales of her products rose. It appears that Kmart resisted allowing her influence to carry over at the corporate level, even turning down an overture Martha made in the late 1990s to join the Kmart board. "What seemed to be an ideal opportunity to welcome her influence on a strategic level was denied," comments Camilletti. Fortunately, it seems that Kmart's resistance may be waning and the new regime may even be looking for Martha's input; Martha herself had a hand in designing the new prototype store.

Says Camilletti, "Target may grow the Michael Graves brand into a similar multi-lifestyle brand (and is doing so as we speak), but it will be a while until it achieves the powerful lifestyle presence to rival Martha. Because of the narrow aspect of his product's styling, I don't believe his line will ever achieve the middle-America mass appeal Martha's merchandising has developed." Michael Graves has not yet achieved household name status along the same lines as Martha Stewart, notes Camilletti. Even if Kmart was slow to pull the trigger, Martha seems to be the ultimate silver bullet for Kmart.

An Overpowering Label?

Others argue that the Martha Stewart brand may actually be too strong for Kmart. Instead of drawing shoppers into Kmart stores to buy a range of goods, says Wharton School's Hoch, Kmart simply created demand for Martha Stewart products. "I think people just went into [Kmart stores] and bought the Martha Stewart [products] and got out of there without buying that much more stuff." Which means that Kmart misses out on ancillary purchases because the Martha Stewart brand, in and of itself, becomes the destination—rather than the Kmart store.

For other customers, Martha may not be a fit with their lifestyle and preferences. For example, many Hispanic consumers prefer bold colors, points out graphic designer Marjorie Crum. Martha's color are frequently subdued, she says, while many Latino consumers look for brighter hues when buying clothing or home fashions. And the increasing interest in ethnic patterns when it comes to clothing or furnishings does not jibe with Martha's image, which is probably one of the reasons Kmart sought out singer Thalia to design a clothing line, and is currently searching for an African-American celebrity to tackle a line better suited for its black customers.

Lack of a Niche

"One of the key problems of Kmart is that they have not created a niche outside of pricing. The only major difference between Kmart and their competitors, on the positive side, is Martha Stewart, Sesame Street and some of the other private label apparel products," says Eric Beder, formerly of Ladenburg Thalmann, in an online interview.[15] "For the department store group in general, a lack of different fashion looks drives consumers to specialty chains that are focused on only one specific niche . . . what used to be a large positive (the ability to satisfy all customers) now has become a negative," says Beder.[15] That is, Kmart's rather generic-looking fashions may actually be detrimental to its image and its sales.

Kmart never defined a niche for itself because it didn't need to initially, says Professor Lars Perner of the University of California at Riverside. "Early on [Kmart] defined itself broadly because there wasn't a need for a niche." Until competitors began cropping up, Kmart was the dominant discount retailer. It didn't need to differentiate itself because there was no other company like it. Now, however, Kmart has been overrun with competition all fighting for the same consumers. The challenge now is developing a brand image that truly reflects what makes Kmart different. The "Kmart Difference," as the folks at Kmart refer to it.[16]

Without a clear strategy, explains Retail Forward's Sandra J. Skrovan, Kmart hasn't had a clear marketing and merchandising message. "Consumers understand that Wal-Mart stands for low prices. Target stands for trendier, fashion-forward types of merchandise—exclusive labels—at a value price. But what does Kmart stand for? Its marketing message is really unclear in the marketplace," she says. "I've always wondered why companies want to target the masses," says Rob Gelphman. "There's no margin in targeting the masses," unless you're a super-efficient Wal-Mart or Target, which Kmart is not. Instead of being a generalist, Kmart needs to become a specialist—or at least to develop a specialty, says Gelphman.

So Kmart decided to specialize in moms. Former marketing chief Brent Willis stated that Kmart's goal was to be the "value, quality, authority Moms can trust," with an emphasis on home and kids.[16] But stating a specialty doesn't make it so, especially when there is no history or action to support it. How does Kmart intend to become the authority for moms? What strengths does the company have that benefit this particular customer group? Is Kmart's inventory and level of service superior to its competition when it comes to satisfying moms? And most importantly, says the "Niche Doctor," Dr. Lynda Falkenstein, author of *Nichecraft*, "Is the niche intentional? Does it take the business where you want it to go? Do customers want it? And does it have the capability to evolve and grow?" Without consistent "yes" answers, you've carved out a weak niche.

At Kmart, the selection of serving moms as a niche is intentional. Moms probably would like a retailer that puts their needs first, and it surely has the capability to evolve and grow, but it's unclear that such a niche can take Kmart where it wants or needs to go. Martha Stewart's strong brand presence boosts the image of Kmart's home decor products and selection, and the Martha Stewart Baby Baby line, along with licensed Sesame Street and Disney lines, are aimed squarely at kids, but what's the draw for moms? The company's clothing lines are lacking when it comes to young moms; Brent Willis saw the Jaclyn Smith brand to be targeting more mature women and Kathy Ireland to be for young women. The new JOE BOXER brand is clearly for juniors, so what's left? Not much.

Why doesn't Kmart pursue a niche in an area where it already has a leg up—in home decor? With the Martha Stewart Everyday brand already strong in that arena, and Wal-Mart and Target without a stand-out presence there, it seems a natural. Said Britt Beemer of America's Research Group in a *Wall Street Journal* article, "The category of home is the best and only opportunity Kmart has to shine vis à vis its two discount-store competitors."[9] It also may be more profitable than the higher-margin apparel category, which has been in a slump for the last few years.[17] Betting Kmart's future on new apparel lines is risky. But building up the company's home decorating offerings may help Kmart improve its numbers and win new customers.

In 2002, Kmart also launched another extension of the brand, creating the Martha Stewart Everyday Holiday collection, which was expected to generate sales of $80 to $100 million during the holiday shopping season.[9] Analysts indicate that the line performed even better than expected. With families spending more time at home following September 11, sales of home decor and home improvement products have been rising steadily. As travel expenditures have dipped, consumer spending on home improvement has risen.[18] Home improvement product sales were expected to reach a record-high $200.7 billion in 2002, with annual growth of more than 5 percent forecast for the 2003–2007 time frame.[19] Interest in home decorating can be seen in the growing number of decorating and home improvement shows on television, which are drawing record audiences. Americans are investing more money in their homes to make them more comfortable and attractive, giving a boost to home-related brands such as Martha Stewart.

Of course, since Stewart became embroiled in a scandal surrounding the sale of stock in ImClone Systems Inc. and is being investigated for insider trading, how much Kmart should promote the Martha Stewart brand becomes touchy. Sales of her merchandise were actually up by 21.4 percent for the three months ending September 30, 2002, due primarily to higher royalty revenues from Kmart.[20] Then-CEO Adamson stated in

November that "We're seeing that the product is actually doing better than last year, on a per-store basis."[21] But a consumer study conducted by America's Research Group that same month, weeks after Martha Stewart's legal problems began, found that slightly more than 17 percent of those interviewed said that "they were less likely to buy Martha Stewart products because of the investigation into her sale of ImClone shares."[9] Whether Martha Stewart the brand can weather the storm from Martha Stewart the person's activities is unclear. At the moment, Kmart and Martha Stewart remain solid partners.

Lack of Communication

Perhaps because of its size, Kmart was not known for its efficient communication, either internally or externally. Poor communications between corporate headquarters and the stores resulted in more autonomous stores and ill-informed employees. And poor communication with the public may have hastened its bankruptcy.

As Eric Beder explained in an online interview, "Many times in retailing, fear of bankruptcy can become a self-fulfilling prophecy . . . in Kmart's case, management did a terrible job of soothing investor (and more importantly) supplier fears. We can compare Kmart's reaction to Saks' when their debt was downgraded by the ratings agencies. Saks immediately responded with a fact-filled press release which provided concrete information about their financial condition, while Kmart said nothing. As such, this vacuum of information from Kmart spooked nervous vendors and eventually led to suppliers cutting off shipments. When suppliers and factors stop supporting a company, bankruptcy becomes the only alternative."[15]

In addition to communicating poorly with its suppliers and shareholders, Kmart also has done a poor job of communicating to its target audience. A recent slate of ads, produced by Spike Lee in early 2002 and introducing the new theme "Stuff for Life," does nothing to explain why consumers should shop at Kmart. Instead of leveraging the impact of using brand names in third-party advertising, Kmart makes no mention whatsoever of brand names at all, points out *Ad Age*.[22] Nor does it hype the one advantage Kmart often has over Wal-Mart—"there's one around the corner."[22]

However, what Kmart communicates internally is much more important than what the company says to its shareholders, customers, or suppliers, argues Dennis Altman, associate professor of advertising at the University of Kentucky. "It seems to me that Kmart's problems can't be fixed by what they say to the public, but by what they say to themselves. The malady stems from their cultural DNA."[23] Changing the corporate culture is the only way to make wholesale change within the company that will result in any meaningful change for customers, says Altman. Altman cites the example of typical shopping experiences at Kmart and Wal-Mart in which a customer asks where a particular item is located and then is either told "somewhere in automotive" at Kmart, or walked over to the particular display by a Wal-Mart associate. "The difference is enormous," says Altman, "and something that no media message can correct."

BlueLight Bomb

The BlueLight Always fiasco, although described in other chapters on store appearance and mistakes, is at its heart a branding issue. The fact that Kmart management thought reintroduction of the BlueLight Special in the year 2001 was a smart idea suggests a disconnect with the buying public of today.

"The return to the BlueLight Special was an attempt to go back to their roots, thinking there was some value there," says Wharton's Professor Fader.[24] "But in fact there wasn't anything about the new BlueLight Special that gave people a warm and fuzzy feeling and offered them a reason to visit the stores." "What is the BlueLight associated with? Just things being cheap," says Fader. "And cheap isn't good. Kmart is positioned as cheap. Period. And the whole BlueLight thing is emphasizing the wrong stuff, not to mention the fact that it harkens back to an era when the whole buying process was very different. . . . The BlueLight is just a bad thing."

In its heyday, says Fader, the BlueLight Special was a "novelty" for consumers, providing "an element of surprise to the shopping experience and made shoppers feel connected to Kmart. But that was a different generation. Shoppers today have different habits. They are directed; they go into a store to buy certain things," and are much less likely to linger in the store awaiting a potential sale on an item they may or may not need. But former chief marketing officer Brent Willis heard that the BlueLight "brand" had 80 percent awareness and a positive association and believed that was reason enough to reintroduce it. He explains that the reason it was discontinued back in 1991 was that "stores lost discipline" and used BlueLight promotions to dump defective merchandise or out-of-season washouts.[16]

Willis's vision of the BlueLight revival of 2001 involved promotions that would be announced in-store every hour on the hour and last for 25 minutes featuring one product per day, two on weekends.[16] In Willis's plan, a manager would get on the public address system to make the announcement as music fills the store. At that point every employee was to stop whatever they were doing, clap twice, and pump their fists in the air twice shouting "BlueLight, BlueLight."[16] The entertainment value of the BlueLight Special, combined with the "ridiculous" deals Willis intended to offer, was supposed to make customers say "Wow."

In Willis's world, shoppers would leave the store, cart filled, giddy with excitement about the amazing bargains they had just snared, eager to tell their friends. Radio talk-show hosts would be picking up on stories of hard-to-believe bargains, telling listeners "about what the fools at Kmart" sold at ridiculously low prices that day, or the day before.[16] Sadly, Willis's world never came to be. Just as in 1991, stores seemed to lack the "discipline" to carry out the BlueLight Special campaign consistently. There have been no reports of employees shouting "BlueLight, BlueLight," at the start of a special promotion, or even of an actual BlueLight Special in progress—although it's possible some stores actually followed through.

Slashing Its Source of New Customers

Chuck Conaway's decision to cut the marketing budget and save money on its legendary ad circulars during the economic downturn in 2001 was, in his words, "a mistake."[25] In a conference call to analysts later that fall, Conaway stated, "There's no doubt we made a mistake by cutting too much advertising too fast. Clearly, we've learned where the threshold of pain is in advertising." In fact, his mistake was a big step back for the company at a time when it needed to be moving its brand forward. The upshot was that Kmart had lost far more in sales than it had saved in advertising costs and many of its customers had turned to Wal-Mart and Target for solace.[25] Historically, Kmart has printed more than 70 million glossy, four-color, 10-page booklets that are inserted in Sunday papers each week nationwide.[26]

Kmart needs to be paying more attention to current customers than new ones anyway, although the company seems to have only recently realized this. Existing customers turn to Kmart for a range of goods, including sale and nonsale, low and high margin, which is financially better for the retailer. New and infrequent customers generally shop at Kmart in response to a special sale price on an item, which may be the only thing they buy during a trip to the store. Since most sale items yield low margins for Kmart, focusing its attention on getting more of these customers in the door seems financially disastrous. Instead, improving the company's relationship with its current customers can mean higher profits simply by giving these shoppers a reason to come to Kmart more often, and to buy a wider range of products. Introducing new brands, ensuring inventory is in stock and on the shelves, and improving the store environment are the foundation for a more profitable relationship with the customers who are already shopping there.

The fact that Kmart lost so much business when it shifted its advertising expenditures in 2001 suggests the company has been directing too much attention and money at fair-weather shoppers when its future lies with its diehard regulars. Wal-Mart's and Target's aggressive campaigns to win Kmart customers over are another reason to keep its eyes on its 30 million weekly shoppers, rather than the millions of other shoppers[27] who are out there.

Lead with Kmart

What differentiates Kmart is its brands. Consumers can't buy Martha Stewart Everyday, Jaclyn Smith, Kathy Ireland, JOE BOXER, Sesame Street, or Disney anywhere else. That's a key strategic advantage. "These brands really have resonance," asserts John Parham of Parham Santana. "They mean something to someone." He says, "Line up 100 Americans in a room and I'll bet you that 99 of them will know who Sesame Street is," whereas only three or four will know Phillippe Starck or Todd Oldham, Target's houseware brands. That's a big benefit to the Kmart brand name.

In promoting its licensed brands, Kmart needs to be sure that its name is not overshadowed, cautions Parham. "Kmart is the umbrella, so it has to lead the charge." That means that instead of telling customers, "Martha Stewart is at Kmart," the lead has to be "Kmart, the company that brings you Martha Stewart" or "Come to Kmart. We've got the brands you love." The retail brand has to lead, states Parham.

Advertising

Kmart's annual advertising budget of approximately $500 million has remained flat for the past few years, according to Eric Beder.[17] And most of those funds have been invested in newspaper inserts rather than national broadcast campaigns, as had been the case for years.

Target and Wal-Mart have elected to pursue their customers mainly using glitzy television campaigns,[17] which makes sense since 98 percent of American households have a television.[28] But why would Kmart stick with a marketing approach that reaches a little more than 63 percent of the same households on Sunday?[29] The Newspaper Association of America (NAA) has been tracking newspaper readership through the years and, sadly, reports that readership has been steadily dropping. Additionally, newspaper readership has been positively correlated with income and educational levels,[29] suggesting that Kmart's low- to middle-income customers are more likely to be seeing Wal-Mart's ads than Kmart's circular.

Kmart's advertising medium is only one part of the equation, its tag line is another. From its claim to be "The Savings Place" years ago to the BlueLight comeback of 2001 to its current efforts to sell "The Stuff of Life," Kmart's advertising has drifted a bit off course. But its trend toward including its brand names in its advertising, such as Martha Stewart and JOE BOXER, scores points for making the most of what Kmart has—exclusive brands.

In 2002 Kmart unveiled a new $25 million TV and radio advertising campaign designed to speak directly to its largest customer group—minority consumers, specifically Hispanic and African-American shoppers. Created by Don Coleman Advertising, the ads feature Chaka Kahn, gospel singer BeBe Winans, and music legend Jose Feliciano in Spanish-language ads.[30] Incorporating cultural icons into the company's marketing message may catch the attention of its target customers, but does it give enough reason for consumers to visit Kmart for their shopping needs? The jury is out on that one. And while using celebrities who are African-American and Hispanic will appeal to those audiences, what about the other 60 percent of Kmart's customer base that is not multicultural? What does the company have for them?

Another marketing for Kmart issue is that "The Stuff of Life" tag line is underwhelming. It's not a reason to visit Kmart, as "Everyday low prices" is a reason to stop at Wal-Mart. Nor does it describe who the company is speaking to. Sears' "The Good Life at a Great Price" is a strong positioning statement, which is essentially where Kmart is trying to go—great brands at great prices. The same holds true for Target's "Expect More. Pay Less" mantra. Kohl's' "That's More Like It" is the foundation that other seasonal ad campaigns are built on, such as the Holiday 2002 "More" campaign, and JCPenney's "It's all inside," gives a reason for customers to come to Penney's. Where Kmart hopes to take "The Stuff of Life" is unclear.

A tag line or theme line used in conjunction with advertising helps to communicate a company's "theme thought," says Dennis Altman in an online column.[31] A theme thought is an overarching subject or thesis that helps to reinforce a company's or a brand's identity and leverage its strengths. For example, he asks, does it describe a brand's superiority, as "It's not TV. It's HBO" does? Or does it solve a consumer problem, such as "Met Pays"? And does it inspire grand thoughts about the brand, such as Microsoft's "Where do you want to go today?"

Altman derides companies with useless tag lines that add nothing to the image of the brands they support. Examples include Winn-Dixie's "America's Supermarket," and United Air Lines' "Rising." In addition to being mindless, they destroy credibility and waste time, says Altman. Is Kmart's "The Stuff of Life" in the same category? Essentially, yes. According to Altman, "'The stuff of life' is an attempt to describe what consumers can find at Kmart. The fact that it [is not] clear marks its weakness. The line lacks any description of that the store stands for in terms of prices, quality level or consumer focus. It's trying to be all things to all shoppers. Compare that to Wal-Mart's 'Always the low price.'"

Apparently, Kmart wasn't wedded to its tag line, as it plans to start a new 2003 advertising campaign with the theme "You have to have it." The new slogan, of sorts, is supposed to emphasize the new freedom store managers have to stock what their local customers want.[32] However, this tag still does nothing to explain why Kmart is the place to turn to for what you have to have. "You have to have it" could refer to just about anything from just about any company, from Breyers and its ice cream, to Mercedes-Benz and its cars, to caffeinated soda of any brand.

Fan Sites

There are plenty of fan sites on the Web—sites set up by loyal groupies dedicated to the latest news about everything from bands, TV shows, celebrities, or products—but when an organization feels the need to set up its own fan site to generate support for its failing stores, it has the opposite of the intended effect. Instead of feeding the flames of pride and loyalty, Kmart's fan site at www.kmartforever.com evokes more pity than pride, more cynicism than loyalty. As one *Wall Street Journal* reporter described it, "sometimes big companies do silly things."[33] The fan sites set up by director of corporate communications Dave Karraker with $20,000, "shamelessly begs its employees and customers to give it compliments."[33]

Perhaps the first site of its kind, Kmartforever.com is a noble attempt to demonstrate to employees, management, and consumers that Kmart remains important to a segment of the population. But few observers believe it will have any significant impact. One such posting at F****dcompany.com questions its sincerity: "Maybe 50–100 years ago you could launch this kind of stupid PR campaign and actually influence people."[33] Of course, a parody site was quick to appear. Kmartsucks.net was developed to mimic the look and feel of Kmartforever.com but was later shut down by its hosting company, BizLand Inc., after BizLand was threatened by Kmart's attorneys.[34]

Whether the site actually serves to boost morale or not, people are visiting it. Shortly after its debut in the fall of 2002, Karraker reported that approximately 67,500 people had already visited the site and 1,500 of them had signed up to receive the Kmartforever.com newsletter.[33] Not a bad turnout.

Playing Catch-Up

Although Kmart's bottom line financials haven't looked rosy in years, things may be starting to look up. December 2002's sales netted a profit—the first since filing for bankruptcy in January 2002. Kmart reported net income of $349 million on net sales of $4.7 billion, which were still 5.7 percent lower than the previous year, but at least the company is improving its earnings.[35] However, even back in mid-2001, Kmart was making headway in reducing the pricing advantage its competitors held. Reported Burt Flickinger III of Reach Marketing, in 1999 Kmart's prices were 6 to 8 percent higher than its discount competitors on 1,000 top-selling products. By 2001, the difference was just 2 percent. Of course, the difference was probably showing up on its profit and loss statement—as a loss.

By early 2003, Kmart had reported that sales at stores open at least a year had fallen a total of 10 percent, presumably in part due to the company's bankrupt status. But the good news was that the company had positive cash flow through March 26, 2003. While certainly not providing assurance that losses were in the past, the up-tick was a "hopeful sign."[36]

The Store of the Neighborhood

In its bankruptcy reorganization plan filed exactly one year and two days after its bankruptcy petition, CEO Julian Day stated Kmart's intent to become "the store of the neighborhood." Although it is already a neighborhood store for many shoppers in urban locations, to be neighborhood-focused means a new way of doing business for the company. But Kmart intends to leverage its urban strength to the hilt. Says a Kmart spokes-person, "Kmart is the store of the neighborhood. We were in the urban markets first, and we're still in urban markets,"[37] suggest-ing that future store closures would not target its urban strong-holds. But will this position work for Kmart?

"Positioning themselves as the store of the neighborhood is probably a good idea," says George Whalin of California-based Retail Management Consultants, "but there are some chal-lenges. With stores located in both urban neighborhoods and on busy suburban streets, the concept of being the neighbor-hood store may not work everywhere." It may also be impossible for Kmart to adequately tailor each individual store's inventory to the local customer base. "It's easy for Kmart to say that they are the neighborhood store, but it will be much tougher to accomplish," says Whalin.

Almost by definition, being the store of the neighborhood requires that a retailer stock products that residents of the neighborhood want. So in late 2002, Kmart announced a new policy that gave store managers the authority to tailor their inventory orders to local tastes.[38] "It's a paradigm shift in terms of how you run the company in really putting the responsibility and accountability where it truly belongs, which is with the store manager," said former CEO Adamson at a press event at its new prototype store. "As we go forward, we will tailor the merchan-dise and categories of each individual store to address that neighborhood's needs."[39]

Ohio State University marketing professor Roger Blackwell suggests that Kmart study Aldi's food markets for tips on making a go at the store of the neighborhood concept. Aldi's 578 stores[40] carry far fewer items than major grocers—700 versus 25,000—and generally stocks less expensive private-label goods only in the most popular sizes. What makes Aldi's so successful, says Black-well, is that "they only carry the units that people need the most, and they sell as close to cost as possible."[6] The company claims that shoppers can find 70 percent of the items on their grocery list at the store. Aldi's formula, which Kmart would be wise to fol-low, says Blackwell, involves keeping the number of products it stocks low so that the inventory the store does have turns over faster, generating cash quickly despite the low margins.

Kmart also is pushing community-based initiatives to demonstrate the company's commitment to the local areas in which it does business, including health fairs, warm-coat drives, and charity fund-raisers to drive traffic and build loyalty.[37] In doing so, Kmart hopes to refocus consumer attention on its local stores and away from its corporate-level difficulties.

For its holiday 2002 advertising campaign, Kmart started driving home the notion of the company's neighborhood status by featuring local store managers in its national commercials. "The focus of the store manager piece [ad] is to build an emotional bond with consumers by demonstrating that this is a neighborhood store, a local store," said Kmart's Dave Karraker.[37]

The Authority for Moms

How Kmart's strategy to be "the store of the neighborhood" complements its aim to be "the authority for moms" is unclear. Certainly, women are the primary family shoppers, but are they more likely to shop at a store that carries products her family likes, or at a store that stocks products designed just for her?

At the moment, Kmart seems more likely to have products her family wants, such as grocery brands or kids apparel, than clothing just for mom. Except for Martha, few of Kmart's private brands appeal to its supposed core customer—young moms. Disney and Sesame Street clothes are presumably purchased by mothers for their children, but there are no high-profile apparel lines that target young women. Jaclyn Smith and Kathy Ireland are more for older women and JOE BOXER is juniors-focused. The company's new agreement with Thalia presumably will involve a clothing line, but her celebrity is strongest with Hispanic consumers rather than young mothers in general.

Marketing consultant Rob Gelphman believes Kmart's two positions—"the store of the neighborhood" and "the authority for moms"—can coexist, "but execution is everything," he says. Will Kmart go for a neighborhood store more like a convenience store or a high-end bodega? Or will the company simply try and offer many of the same products but change its operating methods to provide more neighborhood-friendly service? It's not exactly clear. "I like the effort. I like the thinking. I like the positioning. Will it work? Time will tell. Unfortunately, it may be too late. The company loses relevance by the day," states Gelphman.

Notes

1. "Commentary: Kmart's shopping list for survival," by Joann Muller, *BusinessWeek*, March 25, 2002.
2. "Q&A: Chief says Kmart needs patience, focus," *Detroit Free Press*, March 12, 2002.
3. "Walmart, Kmart, and the brand that lost its way," by Wally O'Brien, iaaglobal.org, May 1, 2002.
4. "Extending the brand," by Scott Davis and Cathy Halligan, Prophet.com, from *Target Marketing Magazine*, June 2001.
5. "Branding and positioning: There is a difference," by Rob Gelphman, *PRWeek*, February 25, 2002.
6. "Kmart must find niche to compete," by Becky Yerak, *The Detroit News*, January 23, 2002.
7. "Kmart must cut stores, carve niche," by Andrea Lillo, *Home Textiles Today*, January 28, 2002.
8. Kmart web site "corporate timeline" at Kmart.com, www.kmartcorp. com.
9. "Can Martha deliver merry?" by Amy Merrick, *The Wall Street Journal*, October 8, 2002.
10. "The Martha miracle takes root in L&G and blossoms in baby," by Mike Duff, *Discount Store News*, March 22, 1999.
11. "Kmart struggles to find effective marketing strategy," by Alice Cuneo, *Ad Age*, July 29, 2002.
12. "The rise and fall (and rise again) of JOE BOXER," by Paul Keegan, *Business 2.0*, December 2002.
13. "Kmart launches JOE BOXER line," by Mike Duff, *DSN Retailing Today*, August 12, 2002.
14. "Will Sears be more like Target than Kmart?" by Cathy Halligan, MarketingProfs.com, July 9, 2002.
15. "The future of Kmart (online interview)," with Eric Beder at Washingtonpostonline.com, January 25, 2002.
16. "Inside look at the bluelight battle plan," by Alice Cuneo, *Ad Age*, April 9, 2001.
17. "Kmart faces image issues," by John Chartier, CNNMoney, February 23, 2002.
18. "Home furnishings and housewares," by Julie Krippel, Hoovers Online, www.hoovers.com, May 6, 2003.

19. Home Improvement Research Institute report, "Home Improvement Market expected to reach record high level in 2002," www.hiri.org/currentresearch.htm, May 6, 2003.

20. Martha Stewart Living Omnimedia 10-Q report filed with the SEC September 30, 2002.

21. "Kmart: Martha Stewart still selling well," Reuters, November 18, 2002.

22. "Kmart's new ads are not bluelight specials," by Bob Garfield, *Ad Age*, March 4, 2002.

23. E-mail correspondence with Dennis Altman, associate professor of advertising, University of Kentucky, January 28, 2003.

24. "Kmart's 20-year identity crisis," Knowledge@Wharton, www.wharton.upenn.edu, January 30, 2002.

25. "The buzz must go on," by John Gaffney, *Business 2.0*, February 2002.

26. "Kmart: will continue newspaper ads," Associated Press, January 31, 2002.

27. Wal-Mart claims to have 100 million weekly shoppers per its "Wal-Mart Stores at a Glance" page at its web site, www.walmart.com, May 6, 2003.

28. Remarks by FCC Chairman William E. Kennard, Museum of Television and Radio, New York, New York, October 10, 2000.

29. "Facts About Newspapers 2002," Newspaper Association of America, www.naa.org/info/facts02/4_facts2002.html.

30. "The Ad Campaign to save Kmart," by John Gaffney, *Business 2.0*, April 2, 2002.

31. "Creating an impact," by Dennis Altman, Kentucky Business Online, www.kybiz.com, March 2000.

32. "Kmart execs upbeat," by Jim Higgins, *The Detroit News*, September 26, 2002.

33. "How one struggling firm hopes to improve morale," by Suein Hwang, *The Wall Street Journal*, October 31, 2002.

34. "Host suspends spoof site after company complaint," by Suein Hwang, *The Wall Street Journal*, November 13, 2002.

35. "Kmart logs first profit since bankruptcy," by Joan Villa, *Video Store Magazine*, January 14, 2003.

36. "Kmart debtholder pushed quick exit from Chapter 11," by Mitchell Pacelle and Amy Merrick, *Wall Street Journal*, May 6, 2003.

37. "Kmart's holiday appeal," by Jennifer Dixon, *Detroit Free Press*, October 15, 2002.

38. "Kmart seeks 'neighborhood market' tag, *Gourmet News*, November 2002.

39. "Kmart testing image with new layout, decor," by Debbie Howell, *DSN Retailing Today*, October 28, 2002.

40. Aldi web site, www.aldifoods.com.

Not Knowing Its Customers

"**K**mart thought their customer was anybody and every-body," says Tony Camilletti of JGA, a brand strategy and design firm, which has worked with Kmart. Un-fortunately, although shoppers at their stores may reflect a diverse group of consumers, they are not anybody and every-body. Exactly who they are, however, seems muddied.

Says Professor Don B. Bradley III of the University of Central Arkansas, "I think [Kmart was] using the shotgun approach that 'everyone is my customer,' when Wal-Mart knew darn well and Target knew darn well that 'everybody' wasn't their customer." But knowing your customer is one thing and being willing to structure your company to meet the customer's needs better than the competition is quite another.

"Kmart doesn't have customer focus, a deficiency arising from the company not knowing what it is or should be," reports a *Retail Merchandiser* article, which contrasts Kmart with Kohl's, the up-and-coming retailer. Unlike Kohl's, which goes squarely after the middle-income consumer, Kmart has essentially tar-geted everyone within a certain radius of its stores. The evidence is the millions of newspaper advertising circulars distributed each week to households nationwide. Instead of focusing its efforts on particular neighborhoods, income levels, educational backgrounds, gender, or home ownership status, for example, the company has simply gone after warm bodies who can read.

Its colorful advertising flyers promote its sale items in the hopes of driving customers into its stores, but the company's reliance on such circulars is dangerous. By training customers to shop based on the sale items promoted in the weekly store flyer, Kmart is setting itself up for failure when it cannot fulfill its promises. And that's exactly what happened in 2001 when Chuck Conaway suddenly discontinued its circulars. As *Ratoff Consulting* reported in its April 2002 issue, "Loyal Kmart customers preferred promotional shopping over 'consistent value.' That's why they shopped at Kmart in the first place. When promotional sales stopped, many of these same customers probably looked elsewhere for sale items. It was not surprising that many of its long-time customers did not show up at their stores."

Its geographically diverse locations also suggest very different target audiences. James Harris, President and CEO of Seneca financial, states, "If you look at your store locations as the way you define your customer, then Kmart has a very blurred image, in my opinion." Kmart doesn't think that customers in lower-income, urban neighborhoods are the same demographically as suburbanite middle-income families, does it? But when you look at a map of its store locations, you certainly get that impression. Kmart stores are located in inner city neighborhoods, upscale suburbs, and just about everything in between. But the customers who shop there are not all the same.

The Importance of Customer Identification

Points out retail and consumer products consultant Retail Forward's Sandra Skrovan, getting a grip on its customer base "is not only a matter of who is shopping the stores now, but also who is not shopping the stores and why." But identifying the highest-growth, highest-opportunity customer is even more important to a retailer's survival and growth, says Prophet's Cathy Halligan.

If a retailer is consistently increasing its sales and customer base, does it really matter whether it knows who is shopping there? Of course, the answer is yes. Only by knowing its customers can a store hope to sell more to its shopping public. Kmart is not in this situation. Its sales are slumping and its customer base, though loyal, is spending less each year with the company. By studying its shoppers and dedicating itself to meeting their needs, Kmart can adjust its inventory, introduce new products of great interest to its customers, ensure that in-demand merchandise is always in stock, and improve its financial results.

The good news for Kmart is that less than 10 years ago, the company was doing business with 70 to 75 percent of U.S. households, says George Rosenbaum of market research company Leo J. Shapiro & Associates. Even today, Kmart still counts approximately 65 percent of U.S. households as customers.

The economic slowdown could be partially to blame for the lowered consumer spending, but discounters usually benefit from economic downturns, say the experts. Just look at Target and Wal-Mart. This suggests that Kmart's woes run deeper than external factors such as economic growth. Kmart has to realize that it has a need for more information about its customers. So far, there has been resistance to the idea that the company might not have a handle on who's buying from them. Observers suggest the company needs to wake up.

Investment strategist Mark Scheinbaum relates a story about how Kmart turned its parking lot into a "road rally" so that customers could see NASCAR (National Association for Stock Car Auto Racing) racing cars, get kids involved in motor sports, and buy NASCAR memorabilia. It was an expensive and well-publicized event to draw in customers that fell flat. The problem was that most of the store's customers were single male migrant workers who walked or rode a bike to the store to see the road rally. Few had cars. The upshot, says Scheinbaum, is that "Kmart seemed to be clueless about its audience,"[1] despite its claims to the contrary.

Customer Research

Kmart certainly had research to rely on in figuring out who its customers were and what types of products they had bought in the past. And management was supremely sure of the accuracy and value of the information it collected; never mind that the data suggested strategies that ended up as total flops.

Robert Pasikoff, founder and president of New York–based Brand Keys, a brand loyalty consulting and research company, relates the story of a senior marketing researcher, at Kmart on a conference call in late 2001, who said quite confidently, "We maintain a database of 8 million transactions a month. Our K-trends tell us everything we need to know about our customers and how to better serve them."[2] Passikoff mused that normally he would have considered those remarks wishful thinking given Kmart's increasingly dire situation, but this individual was so confident of the statement that Passikoff had to brand it arrogance—foolish arrogance at that.

Most companies facing difficulties admit that they don't have all the answers, but not Kmart. Unfortunately, the company's falling stock and bankruptcy filing did nothing to quell that arrogance—the certainty that Kmart was all-knowing when it came to its customers. Passikoff commented, "Marketplace realities evidently didn't matter much to these folks. After all, what is a mere marketplace compared to billions of bits of research data? Kmart was comforted—maybe 'lulled' is a better word—by its trend data."[2]

Although Kmart had reams of data on which to base its plans and strategies, sadly, it didn't use the information well. It appears that the questions it asked were of little relevance to its customers. Or, as Passikoff puts it, "Clearly the data they based their decision-making upon did not reflect the way customers were going to behave in the near future." He cites the BlueLight Special flop as evidence that Kmart was out of touch with its customers, unable to make meaningful conclusions based on its K-trends analysis. The reason Kmart's data doesn't result in forward-looking observations and strategies is that it only looks back, rather than extrapolating to determine what customers' future purchasing decisions are going to look like, observes Passikoff. "Old-style research doesn't take into account how fast customer values are moving. It doesn't provide an early warning system to guide planning. It doesn't reveal what people really think, or more importantly how they are going to behave."[2]

Are Kmart's latest consumer research efforts accurate enough to get the company back on track? Mark Scheinbaum praises

Target's research program and suggests that Kmart's is behind the times: "Target was using the latest Census abstracts and demographic reports; tracking buying habits by zip codes, hiring marketing consultants to detect age and lifestyle trends. Kmart was deciding how to turn ugly bi-level stores into ugly single level stores."[1]

Professor Lars Perner of the University of California at Riverside suggests a number of research tools Kmart could be, and should be, using to learn more about its customers' needs and buying patterns. "The U.S. Census provides relatively detailed information about neighborhoods, such as what the demographics are in a particular neighborhood," he confirms, "but if you want to find out about people coming in you might offer people a small gift for filling out a survey." Focus groups, while often overused, are another technique Perner would suggest using, developing 10 store profiles—inner city versus suburbs versus rural versus high-income, etc.—and holding focus groups at each to determine commonalities and differences across the 10 profiles to help Kmart better tailor its stores beyond inventory selection. Mystery shoppers (consumers paid to pose as customers to test customer service levels) are another helpful tool, says Perner, "because often there's a really big disconnect between national headquarters and local management." Unfortunately, Kmart seems to be basing many of its brand and marketing strategy decisions on "outmoded research," as Robert Passikoff calls it, when what the company truly needs is "research that paints a realistic picture of your target audience's values. You need to understand what they are prepared to believe about your brand, and how they are prepared to act upon those beliefs.[2]

What-if analysis seems more appropriate for the company's situation, given that Kmart has been looking for marketing and branding strategies that will reverse the trend of customer defections. If the company is only looking at historical figures, soon it will have little to look at as losses mount. What-if scenarios allow marketers to add or subtract factors to determine what scenarios are most advantageous for the company. For example, what would happen if customer traffic increased 5 percent? Or if customer satisfaction rose 10 percent? What impact would that have on sales? These types of analyses can yield useful guidance regarding what tactics will do the most good.

Sales increases are not all the company should be studying. Given its poor brand equity, Kmart needs to revamp its whole brand identity to present a positive, attractive image that customers will respond to. The company needs to determine what that image is. To accomplish that, Kmart should analyze what impact store upgrades will have on the brand versus the cost of more employees, inventory adjustments, or fewer merchandise rainchecks. Hopefully, that's the type of process it undertook—to the nth degree—to decide to position itself as "the store of the neighborhood." If it used customer research wisely and well, customer interest in a large neighborhood store might ring out loud and clear from its data and helped nail down its brand strategy. But if it only looked back, and not forward, Kmart may be done. Its track record when it comes to marketing and brand strategy has been extremely weak, a casualty of its old-fashioned customer research process. "Studying the trends of those 'eight million transactions a month' clearly didn't help Kmart," says Passikoff.

Kmart's Past Customers

Drawing on its history as a five-and-dime operation, Kmart's early customer was the low- to middle-income consumer, says Rob Gelphman of marketing communications firm, Gelphman Associates. However, "Those customers have been seduced by Target and Wal-Mart and will never go back. The customer who once shopped at Kmart does not trust them anymore; there is no reason to give them a second chance. And people who never shopped at Kmart are not going to start now," he says.

As Kmart moved upmarket to target the middle-income market segment, so did Target and Wal-Mart. Says Gelphman, "Target and Wal-Mart took the middle class customer and have made inroads among the high end customer (millionaires shop at Target and Wal-Mart—how do you think they stay millionaires?). This leaves the low-end customer to Kmart, whom Target and Wal-Mart also appeal to. Target and Wal-Mart appeal to the entire spectrum of customers in terms of demographics. 'High quality at a discount' never goes out of style. Kmart is low quality at the same price. Where would you rather shop?"

One of the reasons that Kmart's customer base has changed, mainly through defections to the competition, is that the company refuses to invest in customer service. If Kmart had invested in employee training, retention, or labor in general, its past customers would still be around.

The Wrong Demographic

Even back in 1983, retail analysts were chastising the company for focusing on the wrong customer segment. In a *Financial World* article that year, the observation was made: "To retailing analysts, the most attractive customer group in the near future will be the fast growing population of 25- to 44-year-old college graduates living in suburbia and making $20,000 to $35,000 a year from professional and managerial jobs." The typical Kmart customer, says Lehman's Fred Wintzer Jr., is a blue-collar high school graduate in the $15,000 to $25,000 income bracket. Kmart needed to move upmarket to where the baby boomers were to reap the biggest rewards, but it didn't. "Kmart was in the wrong place at the wrong time," observed Thomas Schlesinger of St. Louis–based A.G. Edwards & Co.

By 1987, Kmart CEO Bernard Fauber described his target customer as "families who earn between $15,000 and $60,000 a year." This middle market, he says, is united by a single characteristic: a desire for top value at the lowest price. "That was the cornerstone of Kresge's success decades ago. It's the key to Kmart's prosperity today," he said in a *Fortune* article.[3] But the type of customer making $15,000 a year is certainly different from one making $60,000, and the fact that Fauber would lump them together indicates a weak understanding of the nuances of market segmentation. Interestingly, the target Kmart customer of CEO Floyd Hall's reign, following Fauber's, was women with children, despite the fact that the company's actual customer base was over 55 and making less than $20,000. A strategy to sell more to your target customer is very different when you currently don't sell to that market, but Kmart apparently didn't want to admit that it wasn't adequately reaching families with kids. Its target market was actually its *potential* market.

Unwilling to give up customers who are the biggest spenders—young families—Kmart continued stating its intent to be the store of choice for young families, without ever changing its business to appeal to that segment of the market. It should have either defined and targeted a more specific market niche where it has a service advantage, such as the more than 36 million senior citizens[4] who have a need for the in-store services Kmart already offers, especially the pharmacy, or reengineered Kmart to appeal to its desired customers. But it did neither.

Changing Times, Changing Customers

One of Kmart's problems, says Kurt Barnard, publisher of *Barnard's Retail Trend Report*, is that "Kmart's target customer changed over the years." He explains, in the 1960s and 1970s, "Kmart pursued customers with very modest incomes and very modest expectations." But that changed, and Kmart may not have been ready, says Barnard. What changed was that the low-income shopper became more sophisticated around the early 1980s. With the availability of wares from other discounters that were springing up everywhere, consumers became attuned to getting better-quality items at cheaper and cheaper prices. "They had more options," says Barnard.

Kmart didn't notice this, however, because they were too busy opening new stores. "The company's sole objective through the 1960s and 1970s," explains Barnard, "was store expansion." By opening hundreds of new stores a year, Kmart was becoming the "behemoth" it was striving to be. "The majority of retail discounters had 60, 70, maybe 80 stores in total," says Barnard, who has monitored the industry for decades and founded the International Mass Retail Association. Kmart was head and shoulders above the rest of its competition in its early days in terms of number of stores, but getting further behind in knowing its customer. By focusing so intently on new store locations, "Kmart completely lost sight of its customer," claims Barnard. It developed a "culture of expansion, where expansion was the goal, not serving the customer." And as its number of stores climbed, its familiarity with its shoppers plummeted.

Only years later did Kmart tear itself away from its expansion strategy when it looked up and noticed its customers shopping at its competition. "The company began to falter in terms of performance," says Barnard, which began the revolving CEO door. New leaders came and went for the next two decades as each one tried to develop a strategy, a plan to get Kmart back on track. Understanding what its customers wanted, and who they were, was the one job strategy they needed.

Futile Format Changes

Although former CEO Floyd Hall made a lot of smart decisions during his time at the helm, the rationale behind the introduction of the Pantry section into Kmart stores nationwide suggests a disconnect with the Kmart customer of the day. Believing that its "average customer is over 55 and makes less than $20,000 a year,"[5] according to the consultants at McKinsey,[6] Hall proposed a new Kmart format—the Pantry, containing lower-margin food and drug items located at the front of the store. His goal was to lure shoppers into Kmart for everyday items in the hopes that they would pick up higher-priced items on their way to the checkout counter. (Keep in mind that the distance from the front of the store to the checkout counter is barely a few feet, providing few opportunities for add-on sales.)

However, given that "the customer [it wants] to attract is the female shopper with kids at home," according to a Kmart spokesperson back then, putting lower-margin grocery items up front seems at odds with a program to encourage shoppers to buy more than everyday items. Most retailers might place grocery items in the center of the store, thereby encouraging mom to check out general merchandise on display as she walks to the Pantry section. Shoppers most likely to buy staples like cereal, snacks, and soap are lower-income consumers who don't spend a lot.[6] The net income Kmart generates from these customers is hardly worth its time.

The customers Kmart wanted to attract were younger and richer, yet the Pantry seemed designed to bring in customers much like the ones Kmart already had. Even Hall's executive vice president for strategic planning, Marv Rich, admitted at the time that the Pantry "can increase our sales. Not our profits."[6] That is, customers may buy more grocery items from Kmart, but were not expected to pick up higher-margin goods along the way.

Despite this, Kmart now is considering moving ahead with a push into more grocery items, essentially expanding its old Pantry section. Not because its customers are asking for more groceries, and not because it will differentiate Kmart from the competition—it won't. It appears that Kmart will stock more groceries as a way to get more business from its urban customers, who may have fewer options when it comes to food shopping. But customers at its suburban stores may not need the increased selection, especially when it means reducing its higher-margin inventory in other departments to make way for the food.

What Today's Consumers Want

To understand today's discount retail customers—their expectations and preferences—we can turn to a study conducted by *Chain Store Age* and Cap Gemini Ernst & Young in early 2002 by Leo J. Shapiro & Associates. Presumably, by learning what discount shoppers want today, retailers can do a better job of meeting those needs. However, says the study, "It's clear that a chasm exists between what consumers want and what retailers offer."[7]

On issues of pricing, consumers prefer "prices that don't fluctuate day-to-day" to the absolute lowest price. Shoppers also want "consistently good merchandise quality" and don't expect top quality. Where service is concerned, customers could care less about value-added services but care more about "hassle-free returns policies" and want to be treated courteously and respectfully by employees while in the store. Interestingly, a convenient store location is less important to customers than the interior environment; "clean, well-maintained stores, visible prices, and easy-to-navigate layouts" matter more.

Not surprisingly, Kmart did not fare well on these aspects, although the study demonstrated that the company certainly has a loyal shopper base—customers who are willing to continue shopping with the company despite its flaws. On the positive side, the study does provide Kmart with a game plan that can help improve performance and customer satisfaction, if it is willing to make some significant changes. Pulling back from its sale routine each week, improving its interior environments, and boosting the number of employees it has on the sale floor could do wonders for Kmart's bottom line, according to those surveyed.

However, its reorganization plan will address only one of the above-mentioned areas: store appearance. Even then, store upgrades will occur on a rolling basis, little by little, as Kmart determines which elements of its prototype stores it wants to incorporate into its older ones. Has Kmart even asked its customers what they want?

Kmart's Present Customers

According to a 2002 *USA Today*/CNN/Gallup poll studying Kmart, Wal-Mart, and Target, shoppers that prefer Kmart to Wal-Mart or Target are the less educated urban and rural dwellers (rather than suburbanites) and those with less than $20,000 in annual household income.[8] Consumers in the Northeast are also partial to Kmart, where Wal-Mart has less of an influence, but there also are pockets of heavy Kmart loyalty scattered around the country. "The least likely Kmart shoppers are the most affluent," says the poll. "Among households earning $75,000 or more annually, only 5 percent say they choose Kmart" over Wal-Mart or Target. The study found that customers with higher incomes generally prefer Target.

A *New York Times* article breaks down the differing customer bases more clearly, comparing the typical customers at Kmart, Wal-Mart, and Target.[9] Of the three chains, Kmart's customer has the lowest median income: $35,000 versus $37,000 for Wal-Mart's customer and $45,000 for Target's. It also has the fewest college graduates: 30 percent of its customers have a college degree versus 31 percent for Wal-Mart and 40 percent for Target.

The majority of its customers fall right in the 25- to 44-year-old age range, 51 percent, with 48 percent of Wal-Mart's falling in the same range and 56 percent of Target's. What is most interesting is that Kmart also has the lowest percentage of households with children under age 18: 38 percent versus 39 percent at Wal-Mart and 44 percent for Target. Given these figures, Kmart's focus on families with children seems odd. Why target a demographic segment where you do not have an advantage?

Microsegmentation

Despite Kmart's apparently outdated market research processes, in its reorganization plan the company states its intent to be the "store of the neighborhood." Essentially what that means is that Kmart is handing over inventory purchasing decisions to its store managers, rather than relying on corporate-level buyers to make buying decisions for each store. To better match each store's inventory to its local market, store managers will have the authority to tweak its orders.

Of course, Wal-Mart and Target have been doing this for years, points out Professor Lars Perner. Called microsegmentation, "It's a seemingly very simple concept that deals with tailoring each retail store to the local community." Wal-Mart, for example, takes into account hunting seasons for a variety of animals, little league season start and end dates, local sports standards, such as softball sizes, and the proximity of different types of outdoor recreational facilities to a store.[10] Target uses past zip code buying patterns to know which store needs more in-line skates and which need more Ben-Gay, for instance, says Mark Scheinbaum.

Whereas marketing segmentation is a technique that uses customer information, such as demographic data, purchasing history, and geographic data, for instance, to group similar shoppers, microsegmentation takes that process one step further, defining groups even more specifically so as to better identify purchase preferences and variables. Perner gives the example of a store in a resort community that could use microsegmentation to sell more vacation-related products by adapting its inventory to meet the demands of its many segments of shoppers. Using microsegmentation, the retailer might identify several segments of tourists: those who come in for a range of products, those who only need sunscreen, or others who only buy snacks. Product placement and selection might be decided based on the size of each of the store's microsegments.

Likewise, stores where customers typically walk to do their shopping might find several segments of shoppers that don't exist in suburban locations. But knowing which segments shop at Kmart, for example, could assist managers in making inventory selections and determining appropriate quantities. "Wal-Mart and Target have been very good at analyzing the actual sales patterns to stock up on the merchandise that is optimal for any given store location," says Professor Perner. Apparently, Kmart is the newcomer to this technique.

Identity Problems

Kmart's customer definition problems are directly related to the company's inability to carve out its own niche. As one executive stated in a *Home Textiles Today* article, "I think in some ways Kmart lost touch with who its customer is. It is lost between trying to be a discount store and a mass merchant."[11] Figuring out which market position it is aiming for could help Kmart zero in on its best customers.

What do you do when you're being squeezed between the low-cost supplier, Wal-Mart, and cheap chic retailer, Target? Kmart's answer seems to have been to try and cover all the bases. It hasn't worked. Wal-Mart and Target, however, know right where they stand. Wal-Mart was and is the low-price leader. "Target knows who it is—and who it isn't," states a *Visual Store* article. While Kmart tried to compete with Wal-Mart on price, Target has stayed out of the fray, preferring to position itself as "contemporary fashion at low prices."[12] Target also doesn't expect to benefit much from Kmart's troubles and anticipates that most former Kmart customers will take their business to Wal-Mart.[12] Identifying Kmart's strengths may help the company determine which customers it should go after.

Hiring Strategy

Instead of focusing on the customer base it had already developed through the years, Kmart's board of directors seemed intent on focusing on the customers the company didn't have. Why else would they have repeatedly hired CEOs from outside the company? Faced with the choice of hiring from within and building on the familiarity its senior managers presumably had with the company's customers, Kmart elected to turn to people with senior management experience, but without any Kmart know-how. They were more interested in bringing in someone who could attract new customers than in someone who might encourage their existing customers to buy more from Kmart.

"That's why [Kmart] brings the new people in," explains Al Ries of Ries & Ries branding strategy experts. "[Management] says, 'Our Kmart management only understands Kmart customers,'" so Kmart needs someone without Kmart experience in order to effectively attract new customers. Unfortunately, that creates a twofold problem, says Professor Don B. Bradley III. "[Kmart] doesn't have the people that they need to lead them out of [bankruptcy] and they don't have the expertise from the past to help them either." Interestingly, when Kmart found that hiring outside CEOs didn't bring them the CEO the company needed, the board turned around and did it again, as in the case with Chuck Conaway, James Adamson, and Julian Day. Adamson seemed to make some real strides at turning the company around, but had an initial learning curve to tackle that an insider wouldn't have had.

A company focused on doing more business with its existing customer base might have made different choices, however, drawing on the Kmart experience of a senior manager rather than turning to leaders who have only had experience elsewhere. Hiring from within fosters more incremental improvements than huge attempted leaps, that so far haven't worked. Managers already within a company know its culture, its strengths, weaknesses, and history and can use that knowledge to move the company methodically in a particular direction, rather than starting from scratch each time a new CEO takes over.

The "Primary Shopper"

Although young mothers have always been a target audience for Kmart, the company is redoubling its efforts to reach out to the "primary shopper," in part as a reaction to the success of several of its brands, namely, Sesame Street, Jaclyn Smith, and Martha Stewart.[13] Strong sales from those lines reinforced the idea that Kmart should pursue moms.

Unfortunately, those efforts may be too little, too late. Kmart's CFO Al Koch reported in a *Retail Merchandiser* article in the fall of 2002, "One customer group we do understand we've had a loss on is mothers with young children." Despite the admission that mothers are a key demographic for the company, Kmart didn't do enough to keep them shopping at Kmart. Following the company's bankruptcy filing, some of its core vendors stopped shipments of inventory of great interest to this group—diapers and baby wipes.[14] After finding such items out of stock, these shoppers may be among the most difficult to win back, indicated Koch. This especially is true when the likes of Wal-Mart and Target are pursuing young moms with a vengeance, too.

According to outside observers, Kmart still isn't doing enough to meet the needs of this group. "Kmart even now still hasn't invented a compelling enough concept for moms with kids," says Cynthia Cohen, president of strategy consulting firm Strategic Mindshare, in a *Women's Wear Daily* article.[15] Others wonder if Kmart knows what it is doing in targeting moms. Analyst Shelly Hale of Banc of America questions Kmart's assertion to be "the authority for moms" when the company has never proven that claim. According to Hale, "It may be wishful thinking on their part, though the reality may be different. [Kmart's] core customer may be the entire family, or perhaps not in the suburbs but the inner cities. But [the company] should base this decision on data,"[16] rather than wishful thinking. Other analysts believe the strategy "still lacks clarity."[17]

Although many of its product offerings are slated primarily for moms and families, its decision to sell guns and ammunition certainly cooled the interest of some antigun individuals. Said Eric Beder, formerly of investment bank Ladenburg Thalmann,

"The company was focusing on being the source for mom. . . . I am not sure how carrying ammo would lead to more sales to mothers."[18] Similarly, its partnership with Penske to operate in-store automotive centers didn't speak to its mom audience, and yet for years the company devoted valuable space to that endeavor. That doesn't mean that having an automotive service center doesn't make sense, if your target customer is men with cars that they like to work on themselves. And since Kmart has said it wants to do a better job of serving moms, shutting down its Penske joint venture following its bankruptcy filing fits its new target demographic.

Some analysts question Kmart's reliance on moms as its core customer base. Retail analyst Mike Porter of Morningstar, the investment research firm, says that "Targeting mothers is not a great strategy for Kmart. The problem is that Wal-Mart is already the store for mothers, fathers, grandmothers, etc." Kmart may not have the brand strength to position itself as the store for moms.

Another potential downside of this segment is the declining amount of time spent on shopping. As women become more burdened with family, work, spiritual, and community responsibilities, there is less time left for shopping. Much less. "The routine shopping trip is no longer the great escape," says Paco Underhill, author of *Why We Buy*. "It's now something that must be crammed into the tight spaces between job and commute and home life and sleep." Consequently, women spend less time in stores. According to Underhill, "The less time women spend in stores, the less they buy there, plain and simple."[19]

The upshot is that harried young moms may not be the sales cure-all that Kmart was hoping for long term unless, of course, it wants to develop services that moms need, such as grocery delivery, a shuttle service to the store, or in-store babysitting. Category killer Babies R Us, which goes squarely after moms in need of baby clothing, furniture, and equipment, provides special parking spots for mothers-to-be, an in-store changing room, and a lounge for nursing moms, not to mention large shopping carts with infant seats. But so far Kmart hasn't attempted any of these inexpensive tactics to demonstrate its commitment to moms.

If it has lost out with the young mother market segment, what other segments can Kmart target? One segment is its existing ethnic shoppers.

Ethnic Marketing

Not surprisingly, the company has recently begun paying a lot of attention to its strong multicultural customer base. Despite the fact that 40 percent of Kmart's sales are reportedly derived from ethnic minority shoppers,[20] the company has, until now, essentially ignored that customer base. Only recently has Kmart paid much attention to its loyal Hispanic, immigrant, and African-American customers. Multicultural shoppers account for 39 percent of the company's weekly shoppers, with African-Americans and Hispanics alone representing 32 percent of the company's customer base.[13]

Because of its urban locations, Kmart is also convenient for many Hispanic shoppers, 91 percent of whom live and work near major cities. A Kmart spokesperson also has stated that 55 percent of Hispanics live within 15 minutes of a Kmart,[21] while only 17 percent live near a Wal-Mart and 13 percent near a Target,[22] giving Kmart a clear advantage in wooing this consumer segment. Also, urban areas are one area Wal-Mart has stayed out of, notes Morningstar's Porter.

Another indication that Kmart's strategy may work is that Hispanics are now the largest minority group in the United States, according to the latest Census Bureau data.[23] As of July 2001, the Hispanic population in the United States surpassed the African-American population for the first time. Hispanics now number 37 million and represent 13 percent of the population. Non-Hispanic African-Americans total 36.1 million, or 12.7%. Also, the purchasing power of minority consumers is growing seven times faster than that of white consumers. African-Americans spent $469 billion consumer goods while Hispanics spent $348 billion in 2001.[24]

Starting in March of 2002, Kmart invested $25 million in a broadcast advertising campaign aimed at selling more to its 10 million-strong Hispanic and African-American customer base. These shoppers are clustered around Kmart's 300 urban locations and tend to spend more per trip than other customers: 87.5 percent more for African-Americans and 40.6 percent more for Hispanics.[25] The advertising campaign is in addition to the new four-page weekly Spanish-language magazine titled *La Vida,* which is distributed now along with weekly Spanish ad circulars to the hundreds of thousands of Hispanic homes.[26]

Within its stores, Kmart is allowing its store managers more control over inventory management, permitting products of interest to local shoppers to be stocked. And it is introducing a new line of clothing and costume jewelry, named Estilo, aimed at teens and young women. Only 364 stores were stocking the merchandise as of the summer of 2002, but Kmart was already considering broadening the brand to include men's and boys' sportswear.[27] Finally, a deal was inked with Latin pop sensation Thalia to lend her name to a line of clothing, shoes, and cosmetics available only at Kmart.[28] Clearly, the retailer is working hard to meet the needs of its multicultural customers.

Is ethnic segmentation a smart move? Some retail experts question its financial soundness. Although Hispanic and African-American customers may be a large, growing market segment, they may not be the most profitable for Kmart to serve. The median household income level nationwide was $40,816 in 1999, as reported in the 2000 census, but Hispanic households had an average income of $30,735 and African-Americans $27,910. "If you just look at market size when deciding what segment to target, you've got one eye closed," says Prophet's Cathy Halligan. Growth and profitability are two other important factors to consider, and multicultural consumers may not be as lucrative as Kmart seems to think they will be.

Although Sandra Skrovan of Retail Forward sees that targeting the Hispanic market, for one, is a good tactic because it is a "growing, underserved market," she questions how it fits with Kmart's larger long-term customer strategy. "It's like hitting a single when they need to start hitting home runs," explains Skrovan. "It's great to say that you want to go after the Hispanic market, but it is questionable whether the Hispanic market alone (in terms of sheer numbers of shoppers) is going to keep a company in a long-term, financially viable position."

Likewise, James Harris of Seneca Financial, believes that ethnic retailing "is a flawed strategy. It's a bit of a trap. Ames tried to do it and it just doesn't work." The main reason? People don't like ethnic marketing, Harris says. Ethnic groups not being catered to may feel slighted by the lack of attention, or the chain may become associated with one particular group, alienating others. Instead, "I think you need to define your market in a socioeconomic way and not by ethnic standards. . . . [Kmart] needs to reach a mass audience and in the United States that mass audience is a mixture of many different cultures. So I don't think you can market a nationwide company that way," claims Harris.

With Kmart's underperforming stores in suburban areas being closed, ethnic shoppers are becoming an even bigger proportion of its customer base as Kmart's urban locations increase in relative importance to the chain's survival. The good news is that the proportion of multicultural consumers is increasing nationwide at a growth rate seven times faster than the general population. The segment also controls $1.2 trillion in joint-purchasing power.[13] Kmart can't afford to ignore those numbers.

Another advantage for Kmart is that retailers currently serving the Hispanic and African-American consumer are fragmented, says Moringstar's Porter, providing Kmart with the potential opportunity to become the dominant player. But is Kmart able to meet the needs of these consumers better than its competition? That's not clear. Other than already being nearby, which is not a strategy in and of itself, does Kmart have enough to keep them coming back?

A Bird in the Hand

There are three ways to grow a business: sell to new customers, sell a greater quantity to existing customers, and/or sell higher-value products and services to existing customers. Despite the obvious fact that it is much easier and more economical to sell more to existing customers than to try and attract and retain new customers, Kmart seems to have been fixated on the customers it doesn't have—either the ones that got away (to Target and Wal-Mart) or the ones it hasn't yet won over.

Fortunately, CEOs Adamson and Day seem to have turned attention back to the loyal customers Kmart already has, with Adamson indicating, "I believe we could fix this company by getting customers to come back to our store one more time (per month)." Suggesting that Kmart may not even need to focus on winning back shoppers who have defected, Adamson says, "You don't have to borrow customers from other retail operations. We just have to do a better job of satisfying our existing ones and then potentially adding new ones."[29] However, Kmart hasn't stopped to ask itself if the customers it has are the ones it wants or needs. Can the company sustain itself, or thrive, through sales from customers who have a below average household income?

Customers as Liabilities

Just as Kmart is weeding out its poor-performing stores, it should be assessing its customer assets to determine which market segments are worth its time and attention. Segmenting the market geographically, psychographically, or by shopping habits, rather than just demographically, can help Kmart zero in on its best prospects. The company can also find out who are its lowest-ROI (return on investment) customer segments so that it can avoid spending money to reach them.

Segments that are large, growing, and are profitable to serve are the highest-value, highest-opportunity segments that Kmart needs to identify and target, counsels Prophet's Halligan. Segments that don't meet all of those criteria will not generate enough revenue to keep the company on the path to profitability. Typically, higher-income customers are more profitable because of less price sensitivity, but low- and middle-income customers who are frequent purchasers also may be highly desirable, depending on their buying behavior. To distinguish between the range of customers Kmart has, identifying high-value and low-value customers, the company needs to conduct sophisticated segmentation analysis—an analysis it doesn't appear the company has undertaken.

Kmart's Future Customer

"Kmart needs to determine who its customer base is not only today, but who it wants it to be in the future," says Sandra Skrovan. "A key question becomes: Is the customer in its stores today the customer it wants for the long term?" That's hard to say, but with customers defecting left and right, Kmart may be forced to work with the customer base it has today in order to stay afloat, whether those customers are the most lucrative or not. And according to the *Chain Store Age*/Cap Gemini Ernst & Young survey, Kmart has approximately one-sixth the base of loyal shoppers that Wal-Mart has; those are the shoppers who listed Kmart as the discount store in which they shop most often.

The bad news, according to Paco Underhill, author of *Why We Buy*, is that "there are no new customers—the population isn't booming, and we already have more stores than we need." As a result, the answer to improving sales isn't to try and attract new customers—there are no undiscovered segments—it is to sell more to existing customers. "The usual figure is that 80 percent of a store's sales will come from 20 percent of its clientele. So if stores are to grow, it will be by figuring out how to get more out of existing customers—more visits, more time in the store, more and bigger purchases."[30]

With the middle- and high-income customer served by Wal-Mart and Target, Kmart is left with the low-end customer, who has much the same expectations as the other segments. "Low-income customers crave quality and availability just as much as middle- and high-income customers," states Rob Gelphman. Unfortunately, "There is no new customer segment to appeal to. As a mass merchandiser, Kmart essentially targets everyone," according to Gelphman.

The solution? Kmart needs to focus on its "future-defining" customers, as Adrian Slywotsky calls them. Slywotsky, author of *Pattern Thinking*, explains in a presentation that "'future-defining' customers may account for only 2–3 percent of your total, but represent a window on the future."[31]

Kmart's future may rest with a microsegment of customers it hasn't yet identified, but which hold the key to its ultimate success.

Notes

1. "What about the Kmart scandal?" by Mark Scheinbaum, *Albion Monitor*, February 4, 2002.

2. "The arrogance of 'blue light' research," by Robert Passikoff, *Brandweek*, February 2, 2002.

3. "Nickels and dimes no more," by Jack Seamonds, *Fortune*, June 29, 1987.

4. "Older worker facts and figures," Seniorjobbank.org claims 65+ comprise 12.7 percent of population, May 6, 2003.

5. "Kmart pays a steep price: the discounter faces a crucial holiday season after a long slide," by Dan McGraw, *U.S. News & World Report*, November 13, 1995.

6. "Kmart is down for the count . . . and Floyd Hall doesn't look like the man to get it back on its feet," by Patricia Sellers, *Fortune*, January 15, 1996.

7. "How stores measure up in delivering the shopping experience," Cap Gemini Ernst & Young 2002 consumer awards, p. 5a, 2002.

8. "Shoppers pick Wal-Mart, Target over Kmart," by Lorrie Grant, *USA Today*, January 30, 2002.

9. "Built on the working class, Wal-Mart eyes the BMW crowd," by Constance Hays, *New York Times*, February 24, 2002.

10. "Smarter, faster, more profitable," *Intelligent Enterprise*, October 4, 2001.

11. "Q&A: If you were the CEO of Kmart . . . ," *Home Textiles Today*, October 11, 2002.

12. "Food fight," by Steve Kaufman, Visualstore.com/people/kaufman/foodfight.html, May 6, 2003.

13. "Population paradigm shift mandates new marketing," by Mike Duff, *DSN Retailing Today*, May 20, 2002.

14. "Kmart copes with loss of customers," *Retail Merchandiser*, August 29, 2002.

15. "Coming around again: Kmart's new ideas bear a familiar ring," by Vicki Young, *Women's Wear Daily* October 28, 2002.

16. "Kmart must cut stores, carve niche," by Andrea Lillo, *Home Textiles Today*, January 28, 2002.

17. "Kmart mired in identity crisis," by Anne D'Innocenzio, Associated Press, January 23, 2002.

18. "The future of Kmart (online interview)," with Eric Beder, Washingtonpostonline.com, January 25, 2003 (online transcript).

19. *Why We Buy: The Science of Shopping*, by Paco Underhill. New York: Simon & Schuster, 1999, p. 115.

20. "Kohl's succeeds while Kmart fails, says report," *Retail Merchandiser,* March 29, 2002.

21. "Kmart seeks 'neighborhood market' tag," *Gourmet News,* November 2002.

22. "It's a good thing," by William Plasencia, *Hispanic Magazine,* July/ August 2002.

23. "Hispanics now outnumber blacks in U.S.," by Genaro Armas, Associated Press, January 21, 2003.

24. "The ad campaign to save Kmart," by John Gaffney, *Business 2.0,* April 2, 2002.

25. "Kmart's new ads pin hopes on minority customers," by Theresa Howard, *USA Today,* March 24, 2002.

26. Kmart press release dated August 28, 2002.

27. "It's a good thing," by William Plasencia, *Hispanic Magazine,* July/ August 2002.

28. "Kmart con salsa: Will it be enough?" *Business Week,* August 30, 2002.

29. "Kmart's new CEO: 'Who is Kmart?'" BusinessWeek Online, March 15, 2002.

30. *Why We Buy: The Science of Shopping,* p. 201.

31. "The Profit Zone," by Adrian Slywotsky, www.mastersforum.com, September 12, 2000.

3

Underestimating Wal-Mart

"**I**f it weren't for Wal-Mart and Target, Kmart would be the most successful retail chain in the country, in my opinion," says Al Ries of Ries and Ries and author of *Positioning: The Battle for Your Mind.* And perhaps Kmart envisioned a world where that was actually the case. But in reality, Wal-Mart had been gaining on Kmart since its inception and Kmart didn't notice until it was too late. What Kmart failed to see was Wal-Mart wasn't just out to do things better than Kmart, it was out to dominate the discount retail arena.[1] One of the ways it managed to do that was through consistent competitive intelligence and maneuvering. All the while Kmart looked the other way.

"From the time anybody first noticed Sam [Walton], it was obvious he had adopted almost all of the original Kmart ideas. I always had great admiration for the way he implemented—and later enlarged on—those ideas. Much later on, when I was retired but still a Kmart board member, I tried to advise the company's management of just what a serious threat I thought he was. But it wasn't until fairly recently that they took him seriously," states Harry Cunningham, Kmart's first CEO, in Sam Walton's biography.[2]

However, Kmart didn't worry about the competition, much less recognize them. The company had a culture of conceit that was bound to catch up with them someday, says Tony Camilletti, senior vice president of brand strategy and design firm JGA, which has consulted with Kmart in the past. "Kmart had an over-confident culture. They didn't worry about competitors nipping at their heels." Apparently, Kmart never considered itself to be a competitor; in its own eyes, Kmart was the leader, bar none. When asked when that changed, Camilletti responded: "Since they filed for bankruptcy."[3] "Someday" was January 22, 2002.

See No Evil

For decades, Kmart chose to pretend that Wal-Mart wasn't a competitor or a threat. Perhaps by not acknowledging the pace at which Wal-Mart was gaining on Kmart, the company could pretend to retain its leadership position. It could stick to the same strategies it had always used, since Kmart had always been the dominant player. "Why change a formula that works?" was probably the thinking, whereas Wal-Mart was always on the look-out for an idea that was better than what they already had. Innovation, creativity, and role modeling were the hallmarks of Wal-Mart's philosophy, which had the same roots as Kmart's but morphed into something completely different.

According to Steve Greenberg, president of The Greenberg Group, a real estate consulting firm, "If anything, [Kmart] never stepped up to the plate to meet the challenge of Wal-Mart. Wal-Mart rolled right past them and they never stepped up to meet the challenge. Their fault, number one, was not recognizing that the competition was eating their lunch every single day and they refused to do anything about it. Obstinance and a lack of competitive spirit on their part."

"You always need to get a look at your competition," says Greenberg. "When your competition is doing something great, you need to respect it and respond to it and they didn't." Even in 1990, when Wal-Mart surpassed Kmart in sales and market share,[4] to become the largest retailer, Kmart did nothing radical to respond. Apparently, it didn't think it needed to.

Striving for Excellence

What Wal-Mart had going for it was a thirst for learning, and a drive for continuous improvement at a time when continuous improvement was not yet in vogue. Says Wal-Mart CIO Kevin Turner, "Sam Walton never had a goal of being the largest company in the world, nor did David Glass or Lee Scott [the previous and current CEO, respectively]. What we do talk about is being the best company in the world. And having something called the divine discontent, which says that you'll never be satisfied with where you're at or where you're going, and that you can always improve."[5]

Kmart prefers to try and take huge leaps forward, rather than the incremental progress Wal-Mart aims for, which may be why, when some of Kmart's initiatives fall flat, it falls further behind. Like the tortoise and the hare, Kmart had the lead and let it slip because of slow and steady progress on the part of its competitor.

Competing for Customers

Although Kmart may not have perceived itself as a competitor, it was certainly competing with Wal-Mart for customers. According to Sandra J. Skrovan, vice president of Retail Forward, Inc., a retail consulting firm, "As part of Retail Forward's annual U.S. Shopper Survey, we profile what the frequent shopper base looks like for Wal-Mart versus Kmart versus Target—what consumers who shop these retailers on a monthly basis look like in terms of life stage and income segments." The research shows that Wal-Mart and Target have two fairly distinct frequent shopper bases. "The profiles are largely mutually exclusive of each other in terms of the income levels that they attract, although there is some overlap in the mid-market segment. Wal-Mart's frequent shopper profile is primarily mid- to down-market, cutting across the family life stages, whereas Target predominantly draws the mid-to-upscale consumer."

"When we look at the frequent Kmart shopper profile, it is virtually identical to Wal-Mart. The two players are competing for basically the same base of customers, but for Kmart, it's largely an uphill battle because there are very few retailers today that can compete with Wal-Mart on price," says Skrovan. This could explain why, when Kmart filed for bankruptcy protection, Wal-Mart saw a jump in market share. Analysts linked the increase to Kmart's situation, with Rick Church, a retail analyst at Salomon Smith Barney commenting in a research note that "Wal-Mart sales increases mostly reflect increases in traffic which may be partially a result of Kmart's problems."[6] Until Kmart determines a strategy that makes it distinctive in some way when compared with Wal-Mart, it will continue to lose shoppers to Wal-Mart.

Technology's Role

It is common knowledge that Wal-Mart's true difference is its strategic use of technology. Virtually from day 1, Wal-Mart determined that information systems were the key to becoming—and remaining—the lowest cost discount retailer. Since it didn't have the resources, the number of stores, and the customer base that Kmart's predecessor S.S. Kresge, did 40 years ago, Wal-Mart decided that its advantage would be operational efficiency.

Today, Wal-Mart has three basic philosophies that guide its use of information systems. First, the company uses a centralized information system run from Arkansas, Wal-Mart's headquarters, rather than a decentralized system. Second, it uses common systems and common platforms, avoiding incompatibility issues and reducing training requirements. Third, Wal-Mart is a merchant first and technologist second, not the other way around.[5] Technology is treated as a tool that supports Wal-Mart's mission to be the best discount retailer around.

Kmart, in contrast, has a centralized system that it developed mainly to disseminate information rather than to gather it, but that is changing. However, it does not have common systems and platforms; many of the company's IT problems have cropped up over the years because it had parallel computing systems that were not compatible. The reason for that may go back to Kmart's proclivity for outsourcing pieces of its work. And although Kmart has never sought to be a technologist, at times its vision of itself has become murky. How technology could play a role in its success still is being sorted out.

Singleness of Purpose

Above all else, Wal-Mart's biggest advantage has been its unwavering commitment to Sam Walton's vision for a chain of discount retail stores that provides low-cost, name-brand merchandise. Although Wal-Mart and Kmart started down the same path at the same time, Wal-Mart has traveled much further because of its stick-to-itivness. Kmart valued change more than it valued vision, believing that no matter what it did, Kmart would always be the leader. This is probably why it didn't start taking note of Wal-Mart until the company had opened stores in its neighborhoods.

Wal-Mart's dedication to Sam Walton's concept has proved more valuable, and more lasting, than anything Kmart has done. Perhaps because Walton remained a visible figure within the company for most of Wal-Mart's corporate history, his influence continues to be felt. Because of Wal-Mart's low management turnover, the majority of current executives probably knew Walton personally. That is significant because knowing him and his priorities reduces the chances that the company will stray too far from his goals.

In contrast, Kmart layoffs, terminations, and regular employee turnover—which is reportedly as high as 150 percent at the store level—make it very likely that no senior manager ever knew Harry Cunningham, Kmart's architect, or even the CEOs who followed Cunningham—Dewar or Fauber. The lack of a personal connection to former leaders makes it much easier to shift course, take risks, and jeopardize the company's future. Kmart has never been able to stick with a business strategy much beyond a year or two, which is probably why it never recognized the value of consistency and persistence that Wal-Mart has demonstrated.

The Food Edge

Cynthia Cohen, president of strategy consulting firm Strategic Mindshare, brings up Kmart's struggle with groceries in its stores. "During Antonini's reign, the discounter was ahead of Wal-Mart when it put food in their Super K's. However, he wasn't able to evolve Kmart into a meaningful concept to its target market: moms with kids."[7] He also didn't recognize the power of Target, says Cohen. So when Wal-Mart entered the food side of the business, Kmart was being attacked from above and below—upscale Target and low-price Wal-Mart. Although Kmart has stated its intention to remain in the $300 billion supermarket business[8] by offering groceries, its recent closing of 60 Super K stores suggests the company is waffling.

The Research Edge

Many of the strategies and tactics that Sam Walton implemented at Wal-Mart were thanks to his study of Kmart. Walton was constantly in search of good ideas, and his competitors' stores were fertile territory for useful information. Kmart store managers may have thought nothing of Walton's rigorous study of their sites. As a result the company routinely gave away many of its secrets. In fact, it's safe to say that Kmart was one of Sam Walton's best sources of information. Using a variety of techniques, from the ridiculously simple to the more involved, Walton, and later some of his employees, would scout stores for business management tactics.

First and foremost, Walton was a diehard competitive intelligence gatherer. Wherever he went, whether on a business trip or vacation, Walton made the time to visit retail stores and study the shop's operations. New approaches, innovative solutions, and handy tips were all harvested through simple observation. It seems that rarely was he met with resistance, as if ideas and processes were not worth much to the stores he shopped. But to Walton they were worth plenty, and he gathered as much information about competing businesses as he could.

In addition to his powers of observation, which he used to monitor how busy a store was, what kinds of customers were there, how clean the store was, and how stocked the shelves were, Walton had no problem approaching employees, suppliers, and customers directly to inquire about the store he was visiting. These conversations often yielded useful information about the popularity of certain products and the most effective selling techniques. Taking a casual, nonthreatening approach, Walton was frequently able to learn a lot about a store simply by talking to workers about their jobs. He also engaged shoppers in friendly discussions about how prices compared to other retailers, what they typically bought, and how often they shopped there to better understand the local market and competitive positions of the players. Even today, Wal-Mart managers are expected to regularly shop local competitors to monitor prices and ensure that Wal-Mart remains the lowest-price retailer.

He also turned to the experts for advice before making a major investment or change to the business. What we now call "benchmarking," Walton probably considered a smart business practice. Before investing in checkout lanes situated at the front of the store, Walton traveled from Arkansas to Minnesota to see firsthand how two similar stores were faring with them in place. After witnessing the concept in action, Walton decided to have them installed in his stores as well.

Likewise, Walton visited the experts at NCR in the 1960s to attend a seminar in Dayton, Ohio when computing applications were just being developed. Not long afterward, he made a sizable investment in computing power, followed by other investments in satellite technology and inventory management systems that other retailers still have not matched. Wal-Mart's ability to combine sales and inventory data from its real-time network with public information sources like census reports and zip code profiling, plus good old-fashioned research, is a strength no other retailer can match at this point.

Of course, although Walton expected other retailers to allow him to scrutinize every aspect of their operations, he wanted to prevent anyone else from copying Wal-Mart's moves. To discourage such analysis, Walton instructed store managers to have anyone with a notepad or camera removed from the store, lest they be involved in competitive research.

This combination of information gathering and careful guarding of its own internal operations has moved Wal-Mart to the top of the industry, and Kmart never seemed to notice it was giving away its lead.

Involving Employees

Although Kmart often paid an hourly wage that was higher than Wal-Mart's, Wal-Mart involved its employees in its mission to be the best retailer in the world. Through stock options, profit-sharing, and plain old appreciation, Wal-Mart has always stressed to its employees the importance of satisfying the customer and their role in making the company successful. Making employees part of the process of satisfying customers—and communicating how essential they are to the company—results in an atmosphere and camaraderie that Kmart can't touch.

From the group cheer that Sam Walton used to lead during store visits to information sharing across the board to stock options and profit-sharing, Wal-Mart employees seem to get caught up in the upbeat attitude and prospects the company has to offer. All other things being equal, Kmart's store employees haven't had an upbeat attitude for years, and its bankruptcy status didn't help.

RetailLink

In the late 1980s, Wal-Mart debuted a dial-up system, later dubbed RetailLink, to provide suppliers with online access to Wal-Mart sales data and projections. Using electronic data interchange (EDI), on a closed system, suppliers could check on payment status and sales levels, while Kmart could issue purchase orders and communicate efficiently with its supply chain.[9] But RetailLink had started as a continuous replenishment system developed with Procter & Gamble. In a meeting in 1987, Sam Walton gave the marching orders for the system, saying, "The way we do things is way too complicated. You [Procter & Gamble] should automatically send me [Wal-Mart] Pampers, and I should send you a check once a month. We ought to get rid of all this negotiation and invoicing."[10] And that was the beginning of the work on a system that would enable Wal-Mart to communicate directly with suppliers, starting with P&G.

By sharing information with vendors through an online system, Wal-Mart's more than 10,000 suppliers could better manage their own businesses, as well as improve service to Wal-Mart. RetailLink processes more than 10 million transactions a day, providing suppliers with up-to-date data regarding sales of their products in the company's stores.[11] Wal-Mart later transferred the system to the Internet to streamline usage and improve performance.

Seeing inventory and sales data in real time, suppliers could project how much product needed to be shipped, to which stores, and when, essentially helping Wal-Mart with its own projections. Allowing suppliers to play an active role in managing Wal-Mart's own inventory gave the company an advantage that Kmart would never have thought of, had its own suppliers not pushed the company to develop a system similar to Wal-Mart's. That system would later be called the Kmart Information Network, and won a *Computerworld*/Smithsonian Award for its innovation.

Online Aspirations

Wal-Mart was one of the first retailers online, but quickly realized that it needed to overhaul its strategy. So it shut the site down and relaunched it in 2000, following several months of changes.[12] Despite Wal-Mart's industry stature, "Wal-Mart and Target are giants offline, but online they're shadows of themselves," reported Carrie Johnson, an analyst with Forrester Research. Wal-Mart's online sales in 2000 were just 1 percent of its total.[13]

One of Wal-Mart's moves was to eliminate sales of apparel online because they are low-margin items with high shipping fees. In place of clothing, Wal-Mart has moved upmarket to promote higher-ticket items that shoppers are used to buying online, such as DVD players and digital cameras, but which aren't allocated as much shelf space offline due to their size.

Another smart Wal-Mart decision was to pump up sales of popular gift items, such as movies, books, flowers, and jewelry.[13] "We want to offer customers enhanced services online and sell them products they might not buy in our stores," says Walmart.com COO John Fleming. Online shoppers can now rely on Walmart.com to gift wrap and ship presents, too.

Continuous Improvement

That Wal-Mart was an information technology pioneer in the retailing industry is no surprise because the company has been hailed as a leader and role model for companies looking to improve operational efficiency. But what makes Wal-Mart an even bigger standout is its continued commitment to staying ahead of the game. Whether through regular investments in the latest information technology, the acquisition of companies with capabilities or services the company needed and didn't want to develop in-house, or relationships with employees, Wal-Mart strives to be and have the best. In some cases, that having means the best managers; in others, the best cameras. Always, however, the emphasis is on securing the best possible pricing from suppliers so that the company could turn around and pass the savings along to its customers. Kmart was not able to incrementally improve, which is how Wal-Mart was able to surpass Kmart in virtually every way possible.

Fewer Decision Makers

One of Kmart's disadvantages, which it may have actually perceived as an advantage at some point, is its bureaucracy. The well-heeled organization that helped S.S. Kresge evolve into Kmart made fast expansion possible early on, but it became a liability somewhere along the line, especially with respect to Wal-Mart.

At Wal-Mart for many years, the only approval managers need to get for purchases or initiatives was Sam Walton's. There was no board of directors until the company went public, nor were there endless committees or gatekeepers to get by in order to receive a decision. There was just Sam. Keeping the approval process simple, by having just one person to turn to for an okay, surely sped the decision-making process. It also helped eliminate duplicate efforts, politics (to some degree), and cost, all of which were consistent with Walton's aim to be a lean, mean, merchandising machine.

Challenging the Leader

For whatever reason, former Kmart CEO Chuck Conaway decided to try and beat Wal-Mart at its own game in 2000. Feeling overconfident it seems, Conaway announced price cuts on 10,000 products that would bring Kmart's prices below Wal-

Mart's. Shortly thereafter, price cuts were extended to 20,000 items. At the same time, Conaway brought in $850 million in extra merchandise to meet expected demand. Unfortunately, the result of the new promotional program was surely nothing like what Conaway had envisioned.

Mike Porter, retail analyst with investment research firm Morningstar, believes Kmart's attack on Wal-Mart may have been an issue of pride. "Kmart used to be 'it' and management was obsessed with trying to get that back, rather than realizing that Wal-Mart had passed them by." In fact, hearing Kmart's challenge to beat its "everyday low prices," Wal-Mart simply turned to its suppliers, put pressure on them to lower their manufacturer's prices, and was able to meet or beat Kmart on its marked-down prices without hurting its own profitability.

Instead of boosting sales and attracting hoards of new customers, Kmart ended up with millions of dollars in inventory that didn't sell and had to be written off when sales didn't materialize. Kmart totally underestimated the clout that Wal-Mart had and the speed with which it could respond. How could that have happened? Why wasn't Kmart fully informed regarding Wal-Mart's capabilities, cost structure, and buying power? What information did Kmart have that would suggest that it could out-maneuver a well-oiled machine like Wal-Mart?

From the outside, it looks simply like poor decision making at the top. Suggests Porter, "Retailers have to come up with ways to coexist with Wal-Mart rather than trying to beat them . . . [Kmart] should have asked, 'What other fronts can we fight on?'" Instead, the company launched a frontal attack that was bound to be a losing battle.

Negotiating Prowess

Kmart's futile attempt in 2001 to become the lowest-price retailer by dropping prices on tens of thousands of its products proved the extent to which the company underestimated Wal-Mart's negotiating abilities and power. When Kmart decided to lower its prices, it did so without even consulting its suppliers to get their feedback on its grand scheme or to ask for support.

Although Kmart is certainly no match for Wal-Mart in terms of dollar volume of purchasing, it is still the number 3 retailer in the country. Suppliers hoping to continue selling to Kmart would presumably be willing to budge somewhat on their manufacturer prices if a higher volume of sales were involved or if the business were at risk—if they had been asked. But Kmart didn't bother asking for their help.

Wal-Mart, in contrast, surely approached its suppliers immediately after hearing of Kmart's plan in order to ask for reduced manufacturer pricing and to negotiate agreements that would allow the company to lower prices without significantly impacting its own profitability. Its "800-pound gorilla" status gives the company tremendous power with suppliers—power that Kmart had apparently discounted. So when Kmart's pricing challenge began, Wal-Mart was able to beat Kmart time and again, lowering its prices so that it could remain the low-price leader. In the end, Wal-Mart probably didn't lose much money, consumers certainly won with increased savings, and Kmart was the loser— losing money and customers through its antics.

Economies of Scale

One area where Kmart has never measured up to Wal-Mart is in economies of scale. At Kmart, it is missing. At Wal-Mart, it is leveraged to the hilt to take advantage of every possible cost savings. Financial analyst Ulysses Yannas of Buckman, Buckman & Reid, investment advisors, explains that where Wal-Mart's expansion was methodical and systematic, Kmart's was short-term-oriented—"opening a store without thinking of lasting,"—and without much concern for location. The result is a more expensive cost structure because costs cannot be split across multiple stores in a single area. Explains Yannas, if you have one store or twelve stores, it costs the same amount to advertise in the local papers or on TV, except that the costs can be allocated evenly across several stores when a market is sufficiently saturated. Clustering stores also provides economies of scale with respect to distribution, he says. "Clustering stores significantly reduces the distribution cost and helps alleviate out of stocks." Since Kmart did not sufficiently saturate a market, the cost per store to advertise was huge and in some cases could not be offset by local sales. Wal-Mart, however, planned its store locations strategically to take every advantage of multiple stores in one area.

Complacency

Instead of changing in reaction to Wal-Mart's rising influence, Kmart chose to stay put. But that decision was not made consciously, strategically, or even carefully and ultimately allowed Wal-Mart to surpass Kmart in market share, brand strength, and growth. Claims Professor Don B. Bradley III of the University of Central Arkansas, "I don't think there was one thing that caused [Kmart's] demise. . . . It was a lack of vision, a lack of reinventing yourself, a lack of forward thinking. [Kmart management] got too comfortable and didn't bother to change when everybody else was changing."

The Wal-Mart Way

Although a lot of things have changed about Kmart over the years—leadership, employees, store locations, and strategies, among others—Wal-Mart has aimed to hold fast to its mission, strategies, and employees. Where Kmart may have tried to be flexible, Wal-Mart preferred to be steadfast, sometimes unconventional. As Sam Walton states in his autobiography, "We started out swimming upstream, and it's made us strong and lean and alert." But just because he saw fish swimming the other way didn't necessarily make him want to follow. There was the common way and the Wal-Mart way of getting things done, as Walton saw it. "We at Wal-Mart have our own way of doing things. It may be different, and it may take some folks a while to adjust to it at first. . . . And whether or not other folks want to accommodate us, we pretty much stick to what we believe in because it's proven to be very, very successful."[14]

Savings to Customers

Another major difference between Kmart and Wal-Mart has been Wal-Mart's dedication to keeping costs low for its customers. As John Tschohl of the Service Quality Institute states,

"[Sam Walton] believed that a dollar saved is a dollar passed on to the customer."[15] Kmart, in contrast, has done what it could to keep costs low and pass any savings back to the company, mainly to benefit its executives, it seems. The only time that customers really benefited significantly from Kmart's prices was during its BlueLight Always campaign, which drove prices down, and Kmart into debt.

Long-Term Prognosis

Professor Stephen Hoch of the Wharton School outlines four factors that spell success or failure for retailers: location, price, assortment, and service.[16] Putting aside all other factors, when it comes down to just four, Wal-Mart still wins hands down:

1. Its locations appear to be newer, brighter, and cleaner than Kmart's.
2. Its prices are the lowest because Wal-Mart designed its entire operation around the lowest-price position—every aspect of the company supports that one focus.
3. Both Wal-Mart and Kmart have decent assortments of products, but Kmart has suffered from out-of-stock inventory where Wal-Mart has not.
4. Wal-Mart's service wins by a wide margin over Kmart.

Using Wal-Mart as a benchmark rather than role model, Kmart needs to assess its strengths and weaknesses, compare them to Wal-Mart's, and determine which of its strengths it should focus on exploiting. Wal-Mart may be one of the best retailers around, but it is not without its faults or weaknesses. By taking a tip from Wal-Mart's competitive intelligence tactics, Kmart can significantly improve its understanding of Wal-Mart and its own operations.

Notes

1. "Watch out for competitor roadblocks," published in *CI Magazine*, January 30, 2002, at cipher-sys.com.

2. *Sam Walton: Made in America,* by Sam Walton with John Huey, New York: Doubleday, 1992, p. 191.

3. Telephone interview with Tony Camilletti, January 10, 2003.

4. "Kmart Corp.-History," Gale Group Business and Company Resource Center, online file, January 21, 2002.

5. "Inside the world's biggest company," by Abbie Lundberg, *CIO Magazine,* July 1, 2002.

6. "Wal-Mart, Target prosper from Kmart woes," by Anna Driver, Reuters, February 7, 2002.

7. "Coming around again: Kmart's new ideas bear a familiar ring," by Vicki Young, *Women's Wear Daily,* October 28, 2002.

8. *Wal-Mart: A History of Sam Walton's Retail Phenomenon,* by Sandra Stringer Vance and Roy Scott, New York: Twayne Publishers, 1994, p. 166.

9. "How Kmart fell behind," *Baseline Magazine,* December 10, 2001.

10. "It all began with Drayer," by Christopher Koch, *CIO Magazine,* August 1, 2002.

11. "Kmart missed the opportunity Wal-Mart found in technology," by Mike Wendland, *Detroit Free Press,* January 26, 2002.

12. "Orbitz launch among best in e-commerce history," by Michael Pastore, Jupiter Research, July 10, 2001.

13. "Retailers discover leap to Web's a doozy," by Jon Swartz, *USA Today,* December 18, 2001.

14. *Sam Walton: Made in America,* p. 66.

15. "Kmart's failure," Service Quality Institute web site, www.customer-service.com, January 30, 2002.

16. "Kmart's 20-year identity crisis," Knowledge@Wharton, www.knowledge.wharton.upenn.edu, January 30, 2002.

4

Lousy Locations

mart made poor choices with respect to its real estate. Not just one time, not just a few times, but repeatedly. Why? Some experts remark that the company simply did not foresee the shift in residential neighborhoods that would ultimately draw its customer base away from its shopping centers. Others chastise the company for the city-focused strategy that limited the market area Kmart could draw from. But the fact that the director of shopping center development and marketing at Kmart in the 1990s was jailed for accepting bribes and kickbacks for steering contracts to a particular developer[1] may be even more telling.

Ultimately, however, the company's ability to auction off only 57 of the 283 locations it had up for bid during the spring of 2002 underscores the sense that its properties are not nearly as valuable as the company may have believed.[2] Whether Kmart overpaid for them is unclear, but the fact that no one wanted them surely is. In the end, says Sandra Skrovan, vice president of Retail Forward, Inc., Kmart "finds itself today with a lot of old, undesirable types of locations."

Interestingly, good or bad, the company apparently wasn't keeping close tabs on where all of those locations were. "Neither Kmart's general counsel nor its real estate department knew how much property the company owned because too many people made decisions without supervision," reported the company's lead bankruptcy counsel Jack Butler in a *Detroit News* article.[3]

A Collection of Stores

Kmart's problems started years ago, as it rushed to roll out its discount retailing model in the 1960s. From its origins as the S.S. Kresge five-and-dime chain, Kmart stuck with the company's urban-focused strategy, later expanding into the outskirts of cities and still later, the suburbs. By opening storefronts or converting existing Kresge stores to the Kmart format, the company planned to dominate metropolitan areas, where most consumers were then clustered, says Skrovan. But whether its urban/suburban strategy paid off is in dispute.

Calling Kmart's location strategy "schizophrenic," Jim Harris, president and CEO of Seneca Financial Group and an adjunct professor of business at Columbia Business School, explains, "[Kmart] opened many stores in the inner city areas for a number of years and then branched out into suburban areas and the suburban strip mall. But it did not expand particularly well, because as it grew it did not always grow profits. Obviously Kmart made some mistakes along the way in where it opened stores." But the cities and suburbs were where most consumers were clustered in those days, and that's where Kmart wanted to be.

During the 1970s, Kmart's sales growth was fueled by new storefronts. More locations and higher sales were the goals. New outlets at any cost seemed to be the mission, resulting in "a hodgepodge" of locations, says Britt Beemer, chairman of Charleston-based America's Research Group and author of *Predatory Marketing*. According to Beemer, Kmart opened stores wherever it could get land, regardless of location. Instead of a systematic approach, Kmart seemed to be opportunistic, jumping at most opportunities that presented themselves. Little attention was paid to whether new Kmart stores were cannibalizing existing stores or how a new store would affect inventory management and merchandise delivery. Even then, during its heyday, Kmart's strategy was seriously flawed, and no one recognized it.

Unfortunately, Kmart didn't study the competitive landscape very carefully. As a result, it left some geographic markets open to competition. Rather than developing a chain of stores, "where each marketplace you enter is covered thoroughly," says Beemer, "Kmart had a collection of stores. A collection of stores is a store here, here, and here, kind of like trophies." But by the time the company realized its predicament, it was already battling Wal-Mart.

Wal-Mart flew under Kmart's radar for years, climbing its way to the top through shrewd negotiation, methodical site selection, and a cost-cutting mentality. For its part, Kmart reveled in its leadership position for too long. Seemingly believing that it could do no wrong, the company selected store locations willy-nilly, simply in order to increase its number of outlets.

Wal-Mart, to its credit, moved much more slowly to expand than Kmart—in 1962 it had but one store to Kmart's 18. By 1966, Kmart had opened 162 stores and Wal-Mart had nearly 24. Instead of heading for the high-end, high-rent sites, upstart competitor Wal-Mart aimed for the less expensive rural areas. Started the same year as Kmart, Wal-Mart's origins are in Arkansas. Says Harris, "Wal-Mart pursued a different strategy in terms of opening stores in less populated areas and used its stores as a magnet to attract people from great distances to shop."

Land in the country was cheaper and Wal-Mart preferred to build its own stores from the ground up, thereby controlling its costs and layout. Says Seneca Financial's Harris, "[Wal-Mart] went out of its way from day 1 to make sure it was getting the best possible price on every single product that went through the store. It leveraged its buying power very effectively with real estate operators, developers, and suppliers." Wal-Mart also judiciously followed the construction of new stores with the addition of distribution centers that could serve stores within a day's drive, to ensure that its low-cost pricing strategy would not be interrupted.[4] That meant building stores where large parking lots could be constructed to maximize the number of shoppers, and making it easier for delivery trucks to get in and out of the facility as quickly as possible.

Scaling Back

By the 1980s, Kmart had recognized that opening more stores would not help its stagnant sales growth—at that point Kmart scaled back its new store openings. During the 1990s, as the company began promoting its new Big Kmart—and later its Super Kmart—format, new stores were opened and existing stores retrofitted, but rarely were old stores shuttered. By the 2000s, some had become a liability.

Part of the problem, says Harris, was management's attitude about store closings. Corporate executives are often empire builders, he says. That is, "Most businessmen, when given a choice between having a small profitable operation and a large marginally profitable operation, would much rather have the large marginally profitable operation because they will feel more important." Consequently, when companies run into difficulties, management will figure out ways in which they can preserve as big an organization as possible rather than shrinking it to a more financially responsible size (one that generates a positive return on investment rather than a negative). Says Harris, "They will subsidize marginally performing operations to maintain a large organization."

At Kmart, that means that a percentage of its existing stores are not pulling their weight. Of its stores remaining after the first round of closures, "I would say that less than 20 percent are really, really good locations," notes Harris. Of the rest, "There's probably another 60 percent that are okay and then another 20 percent that probably need to be closed or are very marginal and probably won't survive."

By the end of 2002, Kmart was down to 1,715 discount stores and 117 Supercenters[5] following its shuttering of 283 locations. Then-president Julian Day indicated that Kmart would be closing more stores, although which ones management hadn't decided. "Kmart likely will end up closing some more stores, only because having been in retail for a considerable amount of time, you always end up with some stores you wish you didn't have," stated Day.[6] For its part, Wal-Mart continued to grow at an ever-quickening pace, especially since Kmart's geographic expansion was now backtracking.

Rumors were rampant in late 2002 that Kmart would close an additional 500-plus stores nationwide. However, January 2003 brought the announcement of just 316 more store closings, due to occur by March 2003, a large number, certainly, but some observers were expecting nearly double that.

The Fallout

Because of its real estate strategy, Kmart's impressive sales figures climbed ever higher each year during the 1970s. But it wasn't until the 1980s that CEO Robert Dewar saw in hindsight that the latest new store openings had added nothing to Kmart's bottom line. "Their old stores couldn't keep the same-store sales growing," says Stephen Hoch, professor of marketing at the University of Pennsylvania's Wharton School. That is, overall sales increased, but only because there were new stores added continually, not because existing stores became more profitable.

Between 1976 and 1980, Kmart had averaged 238 new stores each year but hadn't improved the company's profitability one iota. Its sales had grown from $6.8 billion in 1976 to $14.3 billion in 1980, but Kmart's net profit margin on those sales had fallen, from 3.1 percent to 1.3 percent.[7] Dewar, Kmart's second CEO, had initiated the company's growth-through-store-expansion strategy. In 1980, when it had become obvious that new stores weren't improving Kmart's bottom line, he was replaced. New CEO Bernard Fauber cut the annual number of new stores to 50 in 1980, but didn't have a new growth strategy to replace the former one.

At some point Kmart started having more difficulty finding new locations, says Professor Hoch, so it started opening smaller stores, which turned out to be less profitable. The difficulty may have been that they carried less inventory and were located in lower-potential areas, suggests Hoch. The assumption appeared to be that smaller neighborhoods could get by with smaller storefronts, which was later proven incorrect as customers became dissatisfied with the limited selection.

Second-Mover Advantage

Although most companies aim for "first-mover advantage," which frequently provides a wide-open market opportunity and little competition, Wal-Mart had a second-mover advantage, says

Professor Hoch. By allowing Kmart to take the lead and stake out locations in metro areas, Wal-Mart strategically stayed away from them. In the end, by not having to maneuver around existing structures and nearby competitors, as Kmart did in the more urbanized areas, Wal-Mart may have ended up with better locations and fewer restrictions.

Dr. Bart Weitz, professor of marketing at the Warrington College of Business at the University of Florida, would agree. "Kmart is at a disadvantage because it is an older discount store . . . its locations are poor because the market migrated." By moving into some markets much later than Kmart, Wal-Mart had an advantage, he says. "It's a lot easier when you're the new kid on the block" and can go straight to shopping centers in development, rather than being locked in to older sites, as Kmart may have been.

Thomas Baird, associate chairman of the marketing department at Ball State University, explains that, "Wal-Mart came in later and located where [the population] was growing, where there was easy access." In contrast, "Kmart hasn't been much of a draw to shopping centers," states Hank Gordon, president of Laurich Properties, in a *Las Vegas Review-Journal* article.[8] Or, put another way, "Kmart suffered from its early success in opening a lot of stores in urban settings. It's an example of what you could call first-mover disadvantage," according to Professor Hoch. Consequently, many Kmart stores are older and located in less attractive urban areas, he adds.[9]

"Wal-Mart and Target are less likely to open locations in the middle of a large city, where there is less land to build parking lots and stores. Instead, Wal-Mart and Target follow the same patterns as suburban sprawl," says Steve Roorda, an analyst with American Express.[10] For its part, Kmart started in the cities and has maintained its stores there, despite the disadvantages. Since space is at a premium in urban settings, storefronts and interior layouts seem more congested and less appealing. Delivering merchandise is also more of a challenge, which makes it difficult to achieve economies of scale. "The only reason you would go to a Kmart over a Wal-Mart is that the Kmart is significantly closer to you than the Wal-Mart," says Hoch, summarizing what many retail experts have said. Kmart claims that most Americans are closer to a Kmart than a Wal-Mart, which fails to explain why Kmart's sales are sliding and Wal-Mart's continue to rise.

Population Shifts

The key to selecting good locations is understanding who your customers are, which some argue Kmart never has, as well as their shopping patterns. However, selecting a great site today doesn't mean that the site will continue to perform forever. In fact, eventually it will be necessary to relocate the store in order to take advantage of new traffic and shopping patterns—essentially, to go where the shoppers are. As Professor Hoch points out, Kmart had a solid percentage of locations in areas where population declines were the norm, such as in the Rust Belt and the Northeast, rather than in the Southeast and the Southwest, where the population was increasing. "So Kmart ended up sitting on a whole bunch of lousy locations, most of which are in the upper Midwest and the Northeast," he says.

On a more micro scale, Kmart ended up with long-term leases on locations in communities from which the population had migrated. Kmart established stores in spots that had high traffic 20 or 30 years ago—"in the nation's older strip malls and suburbs"[11]—but today are left behind. Kmart operates primarily in leased facilities, typically with 25-year terms and multiple five-year renewal options that give the retailer the right to stay put for up to 50 years beyond the initial noncancelable term. Only 133 of Kmart's stores are owned by the chain.[12]

According to Retail Forward's Skrovan, "Kmart was busy plunking stores in somewhat older urban areas, which were then the population centers. [But ultimately] people migrated to the suburbs and even further beyond the suburbs to tertiary, [less important] areas within big metropolitan areas," she says. But Kmart remained in the plazas a mile or two down the road from where the real action is—where the regional shopping centers are, or the newer malls and plazas. And they apparently have no plans to shift operations to where the action is.

A case in point is Conway, Arkansas, says Professor Don B. Bradley III of the Small Business Advancement National Center at the University of Central Arkansas. When Wal-Mart opened its first store in Conway, there were 20,000 to 25,000 people. They continued moving to better locations and now the town has 45,000 people and five two supercenters, and Kmart has the same number of stores, in the Little Rock area. "Even in a town that small, [Wal-Mart] recognized that people were moving out [to the suburbs], that traffic patterns were changing," says Bradley. So what did Wal-Mart do? It relocated its stores to follow its customers, despite the fact that they were all profitable. "Kmart just stayed in the same old areas," he explains. On a larger scale, continues Bradley, "As people moved to the suburbs and as traffic patterns changed in large cities . . . [Kmart] didn't open as many new stores, plus they kept a lot of their old ones . . . they didn't follow their customers. They took the attitude that 'customers are going to come to us because we've got a good price.' And so I see that one of their biggest problems was location."

An unexpected consequence of its urban strategy has been that Kmart is now frequently located in lower-income neighborhoods. Unfortunately, lower-income neighborhoods often don't produce the revenue the company needs, and yet Kmart has been resistant to leave.[13] Lars Perner, visiting assistant professor at the Anderson Graduate School of the University of California at Riverside, points out another problem with locations in poorer areas: "If you are in lower-income areas, you're also very vulnerable to people who defect if they can find something even cheaper elsewhere, such as at the 99-cent stores that are creeping up with increasing frequency."

No Relocation

As Americans moved out of the cities and into the suburbs, Kmart began to suffer. If it had chosen to relocate it stores to follow its customers, the repercussions might not have been as great. But it didn't. It held firm, confident in the ability of its existing stores to continue to attract customers, even when the trends and sales reports were indicating otherwise. Relocation, apparently, was not a strategy that was discussed, although it should have been.

"The most common reasons for relocation are an adjustment to shifting demographics to best serve a target customer base;

overall upgrading of real estate (visibility, access, signage, etc.); economics (a better deal); and changes in format (size, free-standing vs. in-line vs. mall, etc.)," stated Michael Wiener and Howard Makler in a 1999 issue of *Shopping Center World*.[14] Although all these reasons make perfect sense, Kmart did not make a regular practice of relocating its stores to better sites. Whether due to the cost, inconvenience, or a lack of foresight, Kmart often elected to stay at its existing locations. In contrast, other retailers make a regular habit of picking up and moving. Most major drug stores have been moving their in-line strip center locations to freestanding units with drive-throughs, for example. Grocery stores often expand their older stores, making room for new products and services and rejuvenating sales at the same time. But like many movie theaters that are more than five years old, many Kmart stores would be considered obsolete.[14]

Although the 283 leases Kmart tried to unload in June 2002 at auction were just a small portion of its real estate portfolio, those locations were the only ones the company was jettisoning at the time. No other leases or properties were on the market then. In contrast, in December 2002, Wal-Mart had 391 locations on the market. Whether because they are underperforming, are in older plazas, are too small, or have been replaced by newer sites, these storefronts were available. Assuming a 75,000-square-foot average footprint leased at approximately $6.00 per square foot, that's $180 million worth of real estate up for grabs, points out Biff Ruttenberg, CTP (certified turnaround professional) of Atlas Partners in Chicago. By selling these sites, Wal-Mart will recoup some of the funds it needs to relocate stores regularly, which is a routine part of its business strategy. Turning locations over frequently ensures that sites are new and are situated in a high-traffic shopping plaza, and that the company remains nimble enough to take advantage of new opportunities as they arise. A by-product of Wal-Mart's relocation strategy is that the company frequently has access to the newest locations when it wants them.

Explains Will Ander, senior partner of consulting firm McMillan/Doolittle, successful retailers build into their budget a regular line item for relocations and renovations. By antici-pating the need for a shift to where the area's population is migrating, a retailer can continue to grow its sales. Apparently, Kmart didn't do that. It seemed more concerned about locking in a noncancelable lease term that could stretch as long as 75 years. Using an in-house real estate staff that only the largest organizations can afford,[15] Kmart should have had access to sophisticated site selection strategies, including demographic analyses, competitor evaluations, benchmarking, zip code analysis, and cannibalism reports. Armed with this information, Kmart should have been able to predict which areas were going to shrink and which were going to grow, which shopping centers were going to draw the kinds of customers it wanted, and where it was likely to succeed. But the company's lack of success at sustaining same-store sales over time and repeated efforts to overhaul its store interiors through the years suggest the lack of any kind of relocation plan. It may have had the capability to plan for relocations; it just chose not to.

Letting Formats Get Stale

As the discount retail pioneer in its early days, Kmart appeared willing to experiment and to take risks as new marketing approaches were tried. The former S.S. Kresge company realized that "that kind of store wasn't going to make it anymore, so they moved to Kmart," a new store format and marketing approach, says Professor Bradley of Central Arkansas. Later the company would introduce the Big Kmart store format and the Super Kmart, which sold food items in addition to its standard merchandise. Kmart also tried internal layout changes, such as the addition of the Pantry, for grocery items, but such modifications were atypical. Over the course of its 40-plus-year history, format changes were rare.

At the same time, its nemesis Wal-Mart was constantly reinventing itself to stay current with its customers' needs and preferences. "Wal-Mart is always on the move," says Bradley. "They're selling gas and moving international. They're experimenting with specialty stores. They're always trying something. They don't leave it alone; even the Supercenters they're building today are smaller than they used to build. And it's constantly what I call reinventing yourself or evaluating what you're doing." But as the discount retail market shifted again in the 1980s, Kmart missed the signs that another strategic adjustment on its part was necessary. "There was another big shift," reports Bradley, "and they didn't realize it. They didn't react."

The shift was that Wal-Mart recognized an opportunity in metro markets—Kmart's markets. "That's when Wal-Mart altered its location strategy from a predominantly rural small-market strategy into tackling some of the metro markets," says Sandra Skrovan of Retail Forward. Wal-Mart was able to build stores in newer, high-growth areas in the suburbs where Kmart's established stores had already been bypassed by the migrating population. Kmart's neighborhoods consisted more of older and lower-income consumers. Says Skrovan, "They were stuck with a lot of old real estate and didn't really move to locate new stores where the population was moving until it was somewhat too late in the game." More recently, Wal-Mart has indicated its intention to move into the final frontier—cities, Kmart's stronghold. Although Kmart currently has the edge, unless it cleans up its act and renovates its existing locations, Wal-Mart will have no trouble moving in and scooping up its customers.

Ignoring Financial Realities

"Kmart made the classic retailing mistake," says Seneca Financial's James Harris in an article carried on Microsoft's bCentral.com web site. "They invested in stores that weren't working." Instead of closing down stores that weren't offering a solid return on their investment, like many other companies Kmart chose to keep them open. "In effect, you're subsidizing a poor performer," he explains.

"What tends to happen when retailers close stores," he says, "is they look at the ones where they're losing money at the store level, so the store itself is not making any money." The decision to close those stores should be easy. But the next tier of stores is more tricky, says Harris. "Then you'll find another group that make money at the store level, but don't really contribute much to overhead. And those stores should be killed, but never are." The argument frequently is that they're not costing the company money in terms of needed cash infusions from corporate, but in fact, they *are* costing the company money because other stores have to make up the financial shortfall. And they certainly aren't a big boost to the bottom line.

Claims Harris in the bCentral.com article, Kmart's troubles began around 1994, when the company's financial results started trending downward: "Over a 10-year period, margins declined, return on capital declined, yet the company continued to put money into new stores with no real return." Instead of focusing on its return on assets or equity, which would have indicated a poor investment, the company forged ahead with new store openings.

The importance of weeding out unprofitable stores is addressed in an article in *Shopping Center World* in 1999. Authors Michael Wiener and Howard Makler say, "Unprofitable stores are a drain. By closing an unprofitable store, an astute retailer will reduce negative energy and improve its bottom line. Customarily, we may be talking about a small percentage of a retailer's stores, perhaps 5 percent or 10 percent of the total store count." Although closing 5 to 10 percent of a store's locations may not necessarily mean the difference between success and failure, the savings can certainly add up. And, considering that in most cases savings can instantly go to the bottom line, putting underperforming stores—"surplus real estate"—up for sale is often a smart move. "This is one of the reasons many retailers have a continuous flow of new surplus stores."[14] Many retailers, perhaps, but not Kmart, which has been reluctant to let any store go, if its real estate history is any indication. The same *Shopping Center World* article points out that companies focused on new store openings are often too busy to devote the needed time to disposing of surplus real estate. Kmart certainly falls into this category. Its whole history has been devoted exclusively to new store openings—more so than any other business strategy.

Interestingly, back in the mid-1990s, Kmart did invest time and energy in trying to boost revenue by selling or leasing sections of its parking lots. More than 500 locations where the company had long-term leases on the properties were being pitched as potential sites for restaurants, automotive shops, or other retailers. Kmart hoped to generate much-needed cash through the subleases to stave off the potential for bankruptcy even then.

John Austin, head of the parking lot leasing initiative for CB Commercial Realty in Roseville, California, was quoted as saying the property sales would be a "significant seven-figure sum," while leases would be a "much larger number" over the course of 20 years.[16]

Landlords would receive 20 to 50 percent of the rental income generated from a new tenant in the parking lots, which would be somewhere between $50,000 and $125,000 per store per year.

Said Don Spindel, retail analyst at St. Louis–based A.G. Edwards & Sons Co., Inc., in the *Baltimore Business Journal* article, "Certainly, in theory, it's an ideal way to better utilize the space." What actually happened, however, is that many landlords let the parking lots languish, only adding to the impression that Kmart's properties were not well maintained. Instead of revitalizing its real estate, Kmart's assets became run-down. Whether the landlords' decision not to invest in maintaining the parking lots was because the sites were not worth it, or because Kmart simply did not push the issue, is unclear. The result is the same, however—poorly maintained properties.

Another issue, states America's Research Group's Britt Beemer, is that Kmart never fully saturated its supercenter markets. Its "collection of Super K stores" didn't provide adequate economies of scale, ultimately costing the company money. "[Kmart] never opened up enough stores in any of the markets they went into to be able to advertise the marketplace sufficiently." Instead of moving methodically across the United States, Kmart jumped from city to city, he says, never getting back to open up more than a few supercenter stores in major markets. Consequently, Kmart was never able to amortize its advertising costs efficiently in these major markets, causing a financial drain on the few stores it had in each market. It was a fractured location strategy that ultimately impacted its long-term financial viability.

Payoffs and Bribes

"There were always rumors going around about the effectiveness of Kmart's real estate operation," says Jim Harris. "There were allegations made that some of the real estate decisions were made for monetary reasons"—that kickbacks were received by Kmart real estate personnel from developers for going into second- and third-rate locations at higher rates than would have ordinarily been attainable. Those allegations proved true.

In 1996, the former director of shopping center development and marketing at Kmart, Michael Dowdle, "pleaded guilty to conspiracy to defraud the retailer by accepting bribes and kickbacks in return for steering contractors to a Milwaukee developer" involved in Kmart real estate deals, reported *Women's Wear Daily*. Dowdle was charged with accepting $750,000 in return for approving $170 million in business deals involving the sale and lease of 43 Kmart properties between 1988 and 1993. Dowdle later pleaded guilty to conspiracy to accept bribes and kickbacks totaling $500,000.[17] A Michigan real estate broker also pleaded guilty to paying bribes to Dowdle, and an attorney who served as outside legal counsel to Kmart for the real estate transactions was charged with failure to disclose knowledge of the kickbacks. In addition, a Kansas City banker and two Milwaukee lawyers were convicted. Michael Skiles, the former senior vice president of corporate facilities for Kmart resigned that year after charges were filed against Dowdle. Six longtime employees in the real estate department were also fired, although Kmart claimed the firings were unrelated to the convictions.[18] It apparently took the opportunity to clean house.

Shortly after this incident, Kmart revised and expanded its ethics manual to include specific terminology regarding kickbacks and bribes.[19] Ostensibly to prevent a recurrence of the real estate scheme, Kmart outlined in detail what behavior was not acceptable in that regard. This new "integrity pledge," which its 65,000 managers and 30,000 vendors were required to sign, suggests that Kmart suspected such activity was more widespread than a single individual. At the same time, as more stringent ethical guidelines were put into place, the company also set up telephone hotlines through which anonymous tipsters could report abuse. In signing the code of ethics, Kmart employees were also agreeing to turn in anyone whose conduct violated the code.[19]

Despite the code's goal of encouraging witnesses to step forward and point out unethical behavior inside the company, even as recently as 2002 and 2003 employees felt it necessary to resort to anonymous letters to authorities to report improprieties. Repeatedly, letters were sent to media and government officials citing vague examples of improper behavior on behalf of executives still employed by Kmart. If Kmart's code was clear and well enforced, employees should have had no worries about coming forth to report fraud, accounting irregularities, or looting. The fact that they continue to remain anonymous suggests that they fear repercussions by coming forward.

In the late 1990s, in its efforts to ferret out wrongdoing, Kmart also felt it necessary to further investigate relations between staff and suppliers, hiring a New York–based private investigation firm to do the dirty work. Kroll Associates Inc. was retained to delve into similar business dealings. Kmart reported shortly after hiring the firm that a civil suit had been filed in Texas against a Houston real estate broker who had apparently represented both sides of a store lease in Webster, Texas, resulting in a lease that was unfair to Kmart.[18] By representing both sides of a real estate transaction, the broker may have caused Kmart to pay more than was fair for the location in question.

Are such activities still going on at Kmart? It sure sounds like it. The anonymous letters sent to Detroit-area media outlets and government agencies in early 2003 contain allegations about Kmart's real estate practices, suggesting that the company may not have cleaned house well enough. One letter in particular, which arrived the day after Kmart announced its second round of store closings, implied that Kmart's internal investigation did not go far enough and will result in only "token" punishments for individuals who caused Kmart's financial collapse. The letter also alleges that Kmart closed several Michigan locations "because of the corrupt actions and unethical real estate transactions made by many past and some current Kmart executives."[20]

No Takers

If there was any doubt about the quality of Kmart's locations, a bankruptcy auction in June 2002 that brought no buyers for a slew of company leases should end the debate. Two hundred eighty-three leases were put on the auction block, ranging from 40,300 to 182,714 square feet in size and situated in freestanding, strip, and mall locations in 40 states. Kmart retained DJM Asset Management and its marketing partner, ChainLinks Retail Advisors, to assist in disposing of the leases.

Although John Foster, Kmart's senior vice president for real estate management was quoted as saying, "We have been advised by DJM and ChainLinks to expect a great deal of interest for both retail and non-retail uses,"[21] there were few buyers. Very few. In the end, the nation's largest shopping center company,[22] Kimco Realty Corporation, purchased 54 sites for $43 million, leaving the majority of available locations for other buyers.[2] Unfortunately, even at fire-sale prices, buyers were rare.

What's interesting is that Kimco is Kmart's landlord at 75 of its locations, with those sites accounting for 12 percent of Kimco's base rents from its entire portfolio. Of the 75 Kmart locations Kimco already owns, 13 were closed Kmart stores slated for the chopping block.[23] At the time, Kimco also expected Kmart to close 10 more stores it owned and which it did not expect to be able to lease again by the end of 2002. The fact that Kimco did not see the need to bid for more of its own locations, electing to simply allow Kmart to give the closed stores back, suggests that Kimco recognized the low value of the stores. If the locations were actually desirable, wouldn't more bidders have appeared? "Yes," says Seneca Financial's Harris. That none did "suggests that the leases were all above market rents or that the properties were just not viable to begin with."

In addition to Kimco's purchases, other successful bidders included The Vons Companies, which bought one site in California for $2.2 million; Spencer Management, which bought one in Michigan for $1.1 million; and Woodmont Real Estate, which bought one in Louisiana for $350,000. Otherwise, 10 sites were withdrawn from the auction, and two were terminated by landlords Inland Real Estate Corporation and Hanover Mall Realty Associates. The remaining 214 had no successful bidders. Perhaps the auction's reserve price (the minimum price Kmart was willing to accept) was too high. Perhaps the sites need more work than buyers were willing to undertake. Or perhaps the locations were just worthless. The lack of buyers suggest that at a minimum, they were worth less than Kmart estimated. (Several months after the auction, three retailers were given permission by the bankruptcy court to assume 11 of Kmart's leases for sites in various U.S. cities. Bids from Burlington Coat Factory, Kohl's, and Home Depot were accepted.[24])

Kmart is certainly not the only retailer to be plagued by poor locations—even top performer Wal-Mart has some. As the *Los Angeles Times* reported, "Even the healthiest of chains are not hesitant about closing poorly performing or outdated stores." But where Wal-Mart has been proactive, Kmart has been slow to jettison its underachievers. Of its 3,500 stores in December 2002, Wal-Mart had 391 underperforming stores up for sale or lease[25]—the equivalent of approximately 11 percent of its portfolio. That figure includes 98 stores that had been added to the list just in the last six months.

In January 2002, the same month Kmart declared bankruptcy, the company had 2,114 total stores in its portfolio and, through its auction, would later brand 13 percent of those locations as worthy of sale.[26] That's in line with what Britt Beemer of America's Research Group expected. About 10 to 15 percent of most chains consist of underperforming stores, says Beemer, with Kmart probably falling closer to the 15 percent end and needing to close about 300 stores.[27] But is that enough? "They've gotten the dogs out of the system," claimed Neil Stern of McMillan/Doolittle in a *USA Today* article.[28]

In its second round of closings, announced in January 2003, an additional 316 stores were slated to close by March 2003; 326 were initially announced, but the company reached agreements with landlords at 10 stores to restructure the leases.[29] With the final round of closures, Kmart's real estate portfolio now contains just 1,509 stores, a little less than 75 percent of its prebankruptcy holdings. However, until those stores were identified, Kmart had no property on the market, whereas Wal-Mart has made more than 10 percent of its holdings available to new tenants. That's the true difference between the companies—instead of being complacent, Wal-Mart actively seeks out new and better sites for its stores, selling off its surplus real estate. Kmart, in contrast, waits until a store's sales hit rock bottom before deciding to close it or put it up for sale.

Following Kmart's final round of store closing announcements, *Detroit Free Press* columnist Tom Walsh declared, "The blood-sucking stores are gone. One-third of Kmart stores were losers, sucking money and life from the rest of the company."[30] And turnaround specialist Jay Alix, founder of AlixPartners, which is helping Kmart in its turnaround bid, claims that "Kmart is left with a great cluster of stores, in the right locations."[30]

The Importance of Real Estate

Of course, Kmart's real estate was the major reason the company filed for bankruptcy in the first place. By filing for bankruptcy, Kmart was effectively relieved of its obligation to meet the terms of the long-term, noncancelable leases it had signed for its stores. That means it could renegotiate the rate and term to better serve its needs, or just walk away, if it so chose, without any legal repercussions.

After the first round of closures, the *Los Angeles Times* reported, "Kmart said that by declaring bankruptcy, it no longer will be obligated to pay leases . . . on 350 stores that previously were closed or are being subleased to others." Revenue generated from store closings, combined with cost savings, were expected to add approximately $550 million in cash savings in 2002, with $45 million saved annually thereafter, and improve the company's earnings before interest, taxes, depreciation, and amortization (EBITDA) by approximately $31 million annually.[31]

To survive, however, analysts and Kmart execs knew that more stores would have to be closed. A December 2002 United Press International article stated that Kmart expected to close between 200 and 300 more stores in January 2003, ending up with approximately 1,500 stores by the summer of 2003 as it attempts to exit bankruptcy.[32] However, later in December, after weak holiday sales results starting pouring in, store closing estimates had risen to 300 to 500 stores for Kmart.[33] The actual number was 316 stores nationwide, including one distribution center.

Burt Flickinger, managing director of New York–based Strategic Resource Group, believes that Kmart's across-the-board closures was the wrong way to go. Kmart should have "completely exited the Southwest and Southeast and made its last stand in the Northeast, upper Midwest, and the West," he says in an *Arizona Republic* article.[34] But Kmart elected to make its store closing decisions more on financials than anything else, evaluating the performance of its stores today as an indicator of how they will continue to do in the future. Other industry observers suggest that Kmart should have looked at how the stores could perform in the future, once armed with new renovations, merchandise, and focus. Instead, Kmart elected to use the past as its guide to the future.

Closing more stores to shore up its financial position may help make the company attractive to a potential buyer, but its poor real estate condition may hamper a sale. "A buyer looking at a chain of stores that is losing money would be hard-pressed to bid more than the underlying real estate for it," confirms Seneca Financial's Harris. And since only a portion of Kmart's portfolio consists of desirable sites, Harris doubts a U.S. company would be interested. But a foreign company might, such as French retailer Carrefour, the world's second-largest retailer. Despite denials by Carrefour, which runs supermarkets and discount retailers, rumors persist that the company is considering the purchase of Kmart.

The Opposing View

Not everyone agrees that Kmart's locations are dogs. In fact, several experts laud Kmart for their site selection. The fact that few sold during its real estate auction does not suggest poor locations, but simply reflects the retail downsizing and tough economic times we are in, says Leo J. Shapiro & Associates' George Rosenbaum. The fact that its retail operations are situated in 324 of the 331 Metropolitan Statistical Areas (MSA's) in the

United States is evidence that the company has actually dominated the urban markets.[35] According to Rosenbaum, that gives
Kmart 86 percent coverage of the U.S. market, meaning that 86
percent of all households are in close proximity to a Kmart,
another sign that the store locations are well planned, he says.

"I actually think that Kmart has done a fairly good job when
it came to real estate," says Steve Greenberg, president of the
Greenberg Group, a real estate consulting firm. "They, for the
most part, are where they should be. . . . They control either
through ownership or through a long-term lease space, some wonderful real estate where in most cases they were probably saving $2,
$3, $4 a foot, and the market vendor today could have been charging $18 a foot, depending on how you divide that space."

Whether Kmart did a good job or bad job at selecting its
retail locations, everyone seems to agree that real estate was one
of the main reasons the company sought bankruptcy protection.

The Real Estate–Bankruptcy Connection

"It is a wonderful thing to declare bankruptcy in today's market
because either way you are going to walk away from 100 percent
of the locations you didn't want," says Steven Greenberg. "You
would like to walk away with some money, but at worst you just
walk away."

Greenberg says, "Bankruptcy has become a vehicle that businesses use today to get out of trouble. When your debt reaches
a certain point—greater than your assets—you start thinking
about declaring bankruptcy in the form of Chapter 11 [for reor-
ganization]." Then it becomes the bankruptcy court's responsibility to raise as much money as possible for the company's
creditors. The court aims to sell the leases, sell the properties,
whatever they can, to raise money. But whether buyers appear
or not, Kmart is free of the leases it doesn't want. Its 15-year or
25-year obligation no longer exists. The company walks away
from it, explains Greenberg.

A *USA Today* article in early 2002 estimated that Kmart would
save $1 million to $2 million per store per year by closing under-
performers.[36] But with a bankruptcy filing, Kmart's savings go

even higher. "It's a very powerful tool used today in retailing to shed hundreds of stores, which is exactly what they've done," says Greenberg.

Notes

1. "Dowdle pleads guilty to Kmart defraud plan," *Women's Wear Daily*, May 13, 1996.
2. "Notice of auction results" posted by DJM Asset Management on its web site for the June 18, 2002, auction of Kmart leases, www.djmasset. com.
3. "CEO aims to boost Kmart image," by Karen Dybis, *The Detroit News*, May 5, 2003.
4. *Wal-Mart: A History of Sam Walton's Retail Phenomenon*, by Sandra S. Vance and Roy Scott, New York: Twayne Publishers, 1994, p. 110.
5. "Kmart plan to sell more food shelved," by Jennifer Dixon, *Detroit Free Press*, October 23, 2002.
6. "Coming around again: Kmart's new ideas bear a familiar ring," by Vicki Young, *Women's Wear Daily*, October 28, 2002.
7. "Can Kmart come back again?" by Stephen Taub, *Financial World*, March 31, 1983.
8. "Las Vegas Kmarts benefit from fast growth, low rent," by Hubble Smith, *Las Vegas Review-Journal*, March 9, 2002.
9. "Kmart's 20-year identity crisis," Knowledge@Wharton, www.knowledge. wharton.upenn.edu, January 30, 2002.
10. "Analysts Predict Kmart closures," *Associated Press*, January 23, 2002.
11. "Kmart, the Big Box, and the role of planning in American cities," by Samuel Staley, PhD., Reason, Public Policy Institute, www.rppi.org.
12. Kmart's 2001 annual report, p. 8, 46.
13. "Kmart hopes to see green in White Lake," by Debby Garbato Stankevich, *Retail Merchandiser*, December 1, 2002.
14. "Surplus real estate: Causes, solutions," by Michael Wiener and Howard Makler, *Shopping Center World*, May 1, 1999.
15. "Site selection: How to play the game," by Michael Meltzer and Brian Smith, *Canadian Retailer*, at the publication's web site at www.retailcouncil.org/cdnretailer/cr2000i5_siteselec.asp.
16. All information about leasing of parking lots from "For sales or lease: Kmart parking," by Karen Lundegaard, *Baltimore Business Journal*, November 8, 1996.
17. "Exec sentenced to six months in prison, ordered to pay $500,000," *Beloit Daily News*, July 30, 1996.

18. "Kmart shows integrity," by Matt Roush, *Crain's Detroit Business*, April 22, 1996.

19. "Retailers toughen ethics codes to curb employee abuses," by Read Hayes, *Stores,* July 1996.

20. "Corruption helps sink Kmart, say employees," by Karen Dybis, *The Detroit News,* January 16, 2003.

21. "Kmart reorganization won't be cheap," Visualstore.com, April 5, 2002.

22. "Surprise lenders," by Donald Ratajczak, *Atlanta Journal-Constitution,* January 27, 2002.

23. "Kmart files for Chapter 11," *SNL Real Estate Securities Weekly* at www.snl.com, January 28, 2002.

24. "Court OKs takeover of Kmart leases," *Retail Merchandiser,* September 25, 2002.

25. "Surprise lenders," by Donald Ratajczak, *Atlanta Journal-Constitution,* January 27, 2002; this article's content was reported on by Jesus Sanchez, *Los Angeles Times,* January 29, 2002.

26. Financial press release dated January 2002 on the Kmart.com web site showing 2,114 total stores on January 2, 2002.

27. "Kmart must cut stores, carve niche," by Andrea Lillo, *Home Textiles Today,* January 28, 2002.

28. "Kmart takes aim at 284 underperforming stores," by Lorrie Grant, *USA Today,* March 10, 2002.

29. "Kmart sees store closings costing $300 million," Reuters, January 28, 2003.

30. "Emergency surgery may help save ailing retailer, by Tom Walsh, *Detroit Free Press,* January 15, 2003.

31. "Kmart to close 284 stores," *Retail Merchandiser,* March 8, 2002.

32. "Kmart faces more store closings," United Press International, December 11, 2002.

33. "Kmart eyes 300 store closings," United Press International, December 24, 2002.

34. "Kmart to lay off 37,000 more," by Glen Creno, *Arizona Republic,* January 15, 2003.

35. Kmart 2001 annual report, operations section on p. 6 of online document.

36. "Troubles continue at Kmart, top management out," by Lorrie Grant, *USA Today,* January 18, 2002.

5

Ignoring Store Appearance

What one area of Kmart's operations is in greatest need of attention? The cleanliness of its stores. "Disorganized," "dingy," and "tired" are all terms that have been used to describe the current state of affairs inside most Kmart retail outlets. In some respects, the state of the stores may reflect management's thought process—muddled, stuck, or just plain overwhelmed by Kmart's situation. Most important, the stores' appearance is a big reason shoppers are spending less with the company.

Kmart's reliance on store openings as its means of generating new revenue and sales growth during the 1970s had a major impact on its existing stores—they were left behind. Or, as Buckman, Buckman & Reid financial analyst Ulysses Yannas puts it bluntly, "They looked like pigsties."

Unfortunately, Kmart's stores are an important aspect of its brand asset, explains Rob Gelphman, president of the marketing communications firm Gelphman Associates. "By letting the inside of the stores decline in appearance, they let one of their key assets deteriorate . . . uncleanliness will have a lasting and hard-to-remove impact on customers." Ignoring the appearance of its stores has cost Kmart customers and profits, and has damaged its reputation.

The Basics of Retailing

"Retailing 101 starts with the notion that a store has three distinct aspects: design (meaning the premises), merchandising (whatever you put in them), and operations (whatever employees do)," states Paco Underhill in his book *Why We Buy: The Science of Shopping*. "These Big Three, while seemingly separate, are in fact completely and totally intertwined, interrelated and interdependent, meaning that when somebody makes a decision regarding one, a decision has been made about the other two as well."[1]

Further, he says, the strength or weakness of any of the Big Three can either relieve or stress the pressure to perform that the other two elements face. In Kmart's case, the dirty, disorganized appearance of its stores puts more pressure on merchandising and operations to make up for the neglect. And yet, most consultants and analysts report that products are frequently cluttered and out of stock and that employees are nowhere to be found, which means that Kmart's Big Three are all ineffective and failing.

A Culture of Suffering

Kmart's current store environment is a by-product of its origins as a five-and-dime, explains George Rosenbaum, chairman of market research firm Leo J. Shapiro & Associates, which has studied Kmart for years. Founder Sebastian Kresge's vision for Kmart was to increase the footprint of his variety store 10- to 15-fold and sell more products at prices less than what area department stores were charging. His vision became a reality in the 1960s as Kmart took the lead in discount retailing. In exchange for prices that were discounted approximately 20 percent from other retailers, customers were expected to shop virtually unassisted, in a plain store with few shopping amenities. Customers did all the work and were rewarded with significantly lower prices on everyday goods. The company's tag line at the time was "The Savings Place."

In addition to expecting customers to serve themselves, wait in long checkout lines, and put up with a poorly lit interior,

Kmart didn't feel any urgency to have products in stock at all times. Says George Rosenbaum, "Kmart used to be out of stock on about 20 percent of its inventory, which they seemed to feel was acceptable. They'd do their best to have it on hand, but they also believed it might not be a bad thing to be out of stock on products sometimes, too. It would show customers what a good value they were getting." Consequently, customers were often inconvenienced when the item they were looking for was unavailable. According to Rosenbaum, this concept that the customer had to suffer in return for paying lower prices permeated the entire Kmart culture, ultimately impacting every aspect of the company. "The tragedy is that Kmart never got past the idea that if you give the customer something, you have to take something away," such as comfort, service, or convenience, says Rosenbaum.

Kmart's competitors did get past it, however. Regional discounters such as Venture, Ames, Hills, Zayre, and Bradlees proliferated during the 1970s, differentiating themselves by designing more user-friendly stores, reports Rosenbaum. Going head-to-head against Kmart in some markets, the competition made sure merchandise was in stock, priced products clearly, installed better lighting, hired more employees, kept checkout lines moving swiftly, placed signage throughout the store for easy movement, set up in-store product displays, pushed service with a smile, and generally made the stores more visually attractive. Customers were not expected to suffer in order to earn savings, making it an entirely different shopping experience. Although most other discounters have adopted this attitude toward store ambiance and service, Kmart seems to hold on to its "medieval thinking," as Rosenbaum puts it. Unfortunately, this explains why so many Kmart stores are in a sad state. Customers are still suffering.

Why Appearance Matters

Store appearance reinforces a company's brand image. How designers treat such elements as lighting, flooring, shelving, displays, and signage impacts how a company as a whole is perceived. "It's not simply design," explains Steve Kaufman, editor of *VM+SD*, a visual merchandising and store design publication. "It's environment and mood creation and branding."[2]

Similarly, store appearance can influence purchasing decisions, claims Paco Underhill. "Many purchasing decisions are made, or can be heavily influenced, on the floor of the store itself. Shoppers are susceptible to impressions and information they acquire in stores."[3] This could be bad news for Kmart, where the impression of late has not been a good one. A store's appearance also can define who shops there. "To some extent, the appearance of a store is an expression of the identity of the people who shop there," says George Rosenbaum, which explains why as a store becomes less attractive on the outside, fewer people want to go inside. Who wants to perceive themselves as a run-down, unsightly box?

Although a store's exterior attractiveness does impact who shops there, the interior atmosphere is even more important. For instance, a trendy, bright store blaring loud pop music (think Old Navy, for example) is more likely to attract teenagers than a plush, wood-trimmed store softly playing jazz (such as Ann Taylor), which aims to cater to the 30- to 40-something set. Store appearance can determine who your shopper is, as well as how much he or she purchases.

Once inside the front door, consumers spend less time shopping in an unattractive store than in a more pleasing environment. The shopping experience as a whole can significantly impact a store's performance—the more enjoyable a store environment, the longer a consumer may stay. Says Paco Underhill, "The amount of time a shopper spends in a store depends on how comfortable and enjoyable the experience is." For instance, booksellers like Barnes & Noble and Borders have added coffee bars in recent years to heighten the enjoyment of the shopping experience in their stores. Within Kmart stores, however, shoppers frequently find dirty floors, disheveled displays, and crowded aisles, all of which discourage consumers from remaining in the building.

That's important because "the longer a shopper remains in a store, the more he or she will buy."[4] As Kmart shoppers have become less comfortable in their surroundings, they're spending less. Where Kmart shoppers used to spend $200 to $250 per year with the company in the 1970s, they're now spending more in the $100 to $150 range, says George Rosenbaum (which is worse than it looks since those figures are not adjusted for inflation). Making its stores visually attractive, easy to navigate, and clean could go a long way to bringing Kmart customers back. The company just needs to make the investment.

Kmart's Growth Mode

Kmart's focus during its early years in the 1960s and 1970s was on opening 100 new stores a year, boosting earnings by 20 percent, and becoming a top-ranked long-term growth stock.[5] Most of Kmart's existing stores were built during the expansion push of the 1960s and 1970s, with just 10 percent of its sites being built during the 1980s.[6] "Build stores and they (customers) will come," was the mantra, says Kurt Barnard, president and chief economist of Barnard's Retail Consulting Group, and publisher of *Barnard's Retail Trend Report.* Although money was pumped into building bright new stores, existing stores quickly became a second priority. And they stayed there, for decades.

"Kmart was so busy opening new stores, it forgot about its existing ones. This attitude led to problems in the mid-1970s when consumers started switching from older to newer discount stores offering higher-quality merchandise at reasonable prices. . . . But instead of shifting with its customers, Kmart responded by stopping its discount store expansion," writes Stephen Taub in a 1983 *Financial World* article on the company. As competitors began operating in its markets, they began offering customers alternatives to the Kmart experience—alternatives that were bad news for behind-the-times Kmart.

During its new store push, which lasted more than 15 years and pushed Kmart into debt, Kmart's existing stores began to show "deplorable neglect," says Kurt Barnard. Kmart became known as the sloppy store, and no one wanted to shop in such a neglected environment. Essentially, "Customers began to dislike the stores they had come to love," he explains. When customers began to complain and Kmart saw its revenues shrinking, CEO after CEO promised to invest in store upgrades and major renovations. But its debt load prevented the company from jumping in with both feet. Finally, between 1990 and 1995 all the stores were finally overhauled under Joseph Antonini, reports Professor Paul Argenti of the Tuck School at Dartmouth, who was involved firsthand in the process. Only at the end of that massive period of renovation, more than five years had passed and it was time to overhaul the stores again, but the company was almost bankrupt. Never before or after 1995 did Kmart renovate or upgrade all of its stores as part of one unified program.

Between 1990 and 1994 "approximately 1,700 stores were refurbished and several hundred closed or relocated," claims a Kmart case study,[6] with impressive results. The amount spent per visit increased 30 percent with the average number of customer visits climbing 23 percent. Most telling was that "renewed stores were 35 percent more profitable than older stores."

So why has it been more than 10 years since Kmart has initiated such a rejuvenating program? "Kmart undertook the change process too slowly," says Professor Paul Argenti. "The store format changes took too long," putting the company at a significant disadvantage. But instead of securing needed financing to jump-start the process, Kmart let the stores languish.

Senior retail analyst Eric Beder, of Ladenburg Thalmann, summed up the situation in a January 2002 Washingtonpostonline. com discussion: "The store shopping experience, while improved, definitely still reflected 10-plus years of neglect under prior management."[7] The company has made improvements where possible, and where it didn't cost much, in an effort to put a Band-Aid on the stores' wear and tear.

Today Kmart still has cluttered, outdated store environments. And while Kmart sorts out its difficulties, Target and Wal-Mart are absorbing its customers. Instead of the 11 percent sales declines[8] that Kmart has been experiencing, Target same-store sales grew 10 percent in early 2002 and Wal-Mart's 11 percent.[9] Target has 1,148 locations[10] and Wal-Mart more than 3,200[11] in the United States alone. On the horizon, however, is a new Kmart store model. But can the company afford to convert all its locations in time to make a difference? Even after bankruptcy, the company will be restricted financially. Can it do enough to bring customers back?

The Upgrade Cycle

In 1981, nearly 20 years after Kmart's founding, Kmart CEO Bernard Fauber aimed to remodel the worst of Kmart's existing stores and upgrade the remainder. Fifty stores received a complete redo and 400 were partially renovated by improving the decor, enhancing merchandise displays, improving the lighting by adding fixtures, and bettering service by lengthening the checkout counters. All good starts, but even two years later, in 1983, more than 1,000 stores (more than half of all the Kmart stores in the chain) still required renovation. By then, what really would have helped Kmart get ahead of the discount retailer pack—upgrading its existing stores—had been put on the back burner. But soon after, Fauber returned to his initial plan of renovating more than 1,000 of the existing stores.

Unfortunately, by 1986, *all* the stores needed updating, so he increased his budget to $2.2 billion to overhaul all 2,180 locations. He would be replaced before he could carry out his renovation plan.

His successor, Joseph Antonini, tried to build on Fauber's renovation program with his own renewal program that, again, called for Kmart's stores to be upgraded. The only time in Kmart's history that the company "methodically undertook the renovation process" was during Antonini's tenure, says Paul Argenti. But by the late 1990s, when another round of changes should have begun, the modernization program had once again stalled. Given that unmodernized stores were losing 1 percent a year in 1992, while modernized stores were experiencing 7 percent sales increases and expanded stores were seeing 14 percent increases, with relocated stores seeing as high as 23 percent increases, one has to wonder why Antonini did not make such improvements a higher priority.

Floyd Hall began renovating stores shortly after he took over as CEO, in 1996, but never finished. The same goes for Conaway. Adamson, who probably realized his tenure would be short-lived, did initiate a new prototype store for the next CEO to roll out. But Julian Day indicates that a complete overhaul will not be forthcoming in the near future.

Few Format Changes

Although Kmart's lack of attention to its existing stores has caused a decline in sales and damage to its brand, the underlying issue is a lack of planning. As a general rule, retailers need to plan for the regular relocation of and change of format of their stores—and actually carry through on their plans. Stores that once generated significant revenues can quickly become unprofitable under-performers if left to stagnate. Shoppers want fresh, new interior designs on a regular basis. As a result, retailers are pushed to change their format, or interior layout and appearance, every few years. But did Kmart overhaul its format regularly? Hardly.

"In retailing, you'd better renovate your store every five years," says analyst Ulysses Yannas. "You can stretch it maybe to seven," at the outside and not lose customers. However, Kmart often stretched its renovation cycle well beyond five or even seven years, which is why the company has such a reputation for a down-at-the-heels appearance. "Unfortunately, they didn't modernize or put as much money into the remodeling of their stores as they should have," summarizes Professor Bart Weitz of the University of Florida, which is surprising given the long-term leases Kmart generally holds. The length of its leases is longer—25 years or more—than the typical format change that retailers routinely undergo to keep stores fresh. Which raises the question of why weren't expenses for format changes built into the budget.

Although many argue that some of Kmart's geographic loca-tions were undesirable, the stores' internal appearance was of equal concern. Some retail gurus would contend that the loca-tions were actually less of a liability than the stores' condition. Leo J. Shapiro & Associate's Rosenbaum points out that Kmart stores had approximately 86 percent coverage of U.S. house-holds, meaning that a Kmart store was within easy reach of 86 percent of the country's residences. But even with such great coverage, if the stores are unappealing, a convenient location won't bring in shoppers.

Although few retail consultants see Kmart's bankruptcy as good news for the industry, real estate commentators see a potential upside. Matthew Harding, president of the Levin Management Corporation, notes in a *New York Times* article in December 2002 that Kmart's situation may give landlords the opportunity to "take back" space and to update shopping centers.[12] "Renovations and upgrading are something any shopping center owner needs to address every 10 to 15 years," says Harding. "The demands of consumers change, and the requirements of retailers change." This provides an opportunity for commercial real estate owners to attract new tenants by breaking up large spaces to create new, smaller storefronts or simply by renovating existing space to make it current. Some of Kmart's store closings could yield economic rejuvenation at some malls, but don't count on it happening everywhere.

Bringing Back the BlueLight

For better or worse, one of the few things associated with Kmart is the BlueLight Special. Begun as a promotional gimmick in 1965 but stopped in 1991,[13] the BlueLight Special was a sudden sale on a particular item available only to those customers in the store at any one moment. The on-the-spot promotions were announced via the public address system, inviting customers to come to the particular department where the sale was occurring for a brief period of time. For example, the manager might announce a BlueLight Special on light bulbs in aisle 8: a four-pack for 50 cents, for the next 20 minutes. The location of the promotion within the store was indicated by a spinning blue light, hence its name.

Although Kmart was certainly known for this particular type of sale, BlueLight Specials also were considered lowbrow and cheap. So it is puzzling why Kmart would choose 10 years later, in 2001, to suddenly bring back the BlueLight Special as a marketing theme within its stores. The "reinvention of the Blue-Light" concept consisted of bright blue bands that were applied on the white walls inside Kmart stores, complemented by a large hanging display consisting of an illuminated circle of royal blue fabric 10 feet in circumference—a "larger-than-life blue light."[13] When the light was turned on, the new Kmart BlueLight special logo was projected onto the floor and moved in a circle. A new stick figure mascot designed to look like a walking, talking blue light was also introduced and incorporated into Kmart's marketing message.

The BlueLight Special as an in-store promotion, however, was apparently only sporadically reintroduced in 2001 within the stores—customers didn't start hearing regular BlueLight Specials announced—and beyond the blue rectangles and hanging visual display, it was never fully carried out as a theme that was meaningful. Part of the problem was understaffing; another was lack of employee enthusiasm for the program as a whole. Within the stores, overhead signs were not redesigned to coordinate (they are currently shades of easy-to-miss pastel), nor were racks and displays made part of the new look.

"They took a perfectly wonderful icon and just exploited it to the point it became meaningless. It became just another price promotion," said Tony Camilletti, senior vice president of Michigan-based JGA, a brand strategy and design firm, in a *DSN Retailing Today* article.[14] And customers didn't respond. Rather, the store interior looked even more fractured, disjointed, and cluttered. Not to mention confusing.

Today many stores have the big hanging blue light still set up, but not illuminated, and the blue bands running along back walls, but little else remains of the promotional campaign. Kmart needed a promotion that improved the appearance of its stores, rather than taxing its staff and cluttering its decor.

Store Autonomy

Explains JGA's Camilletti, "The real problem was accountability at the store level. [Kmart] corporate came up with a concept, but the stores wouldn't necessarily implement the program as planned, which weakened the concept. The stores were very autonomous." Unfortunately, a chain the size of Kmart "really needed consistency to drive the branding message home."

There are many other examples of the stores ignoring corporate's directives. For instance, to improve the customer's shopping experience, Conaway dictated that a new checkout lane should be opened whenever there are three customers in a line.[14] That rule certainly hasn't been enforced chain-wide. Either store managers don't see the need for quick response to lengthy customer waits, or they simply haven't been allocated the payroll dollars to afford enough cashiers to make that happen. (One former area manager admitted to making "phantom pages" overhead to appease customers standing in long lines. The manager knew that additional employees weren't available to reduce the long wait, but had no other way to reduce customer frustrations.)[15]

Conaway also instituted bonuses for all store employees tied to a store's customer satisfaction rating as a motivator to improve performance. So far, those bonuses have been few and far between. Instead of boosting morale and encouraging employees to be more friendly and helpful, the bonuses were only paid to 15 percent of Kmart's stores in 2000.[14] Again, either store management didn't communicate the bonus program fully to its associates, or there weren't enough employees on hand to make a difference on the customer satisfaction continuum.

A Poor Shopping Experience

The Second Annual Shopper Report, prepared in 2002 by Leo J. Shapiro & Associates for *Chain Store Age* and Cap Gemini Ernst & Young, evaluates how stores measure up in delivering the shopping experience. Not surprisingly, Kmart fares poorly. "Kmart does not win for pricing, product assortment, service, ease of shopping or an enjoyable shopping experience," the report finds. "These are the everyday issues of in-stock position, cleanliness and friendly sales help that Kmart has failed to improve year after year."

The Kmart management seems unconcerned about whether their customers enjoy shopping with them. An interview with Claes Fornell of the University of Michigan in the *New York Times* in December 2002 indicates that Kmart has always scored low in customer satisfaction, and unlike its competitors, it hasn't made up much ground. Fornell reports, "At the University of Michigan, we measure customer satisfaction in something called the American Customer Satisfaction Index. When we started in

1994, a high-service retailer, Nordstrom, for example, had very high customer satisfaction scores, whereas at the other end of the spectrum we probably had Kmart and Federated. Now everybody, including Wal-Mart, scores about the same in customer satisfaction. Even Nordstrom seems to have lost the edge. So it's more difficult to compete when everyone is offering the same level of service. Kmart is still below the others, and so is Federated, but not by a whole lot."

Although Kmart managers may not pay much attention to customer satisfaction scores, its falling ratings are affecting its income statement. The company reported a loss of $3.26 billion for fiscal 2002 on sales of $30.8 billion. Those figures represent a decline of 17.5 percent from 2001 sales of $36.2 billion, when Kmart reported a loss of $2.6 billion. The "massive sales decline" was blamed in part on the closing of nearly 600 stores and associated reorganization costs.[16]

Overwhelmed Employees

In addition to appearance, however, is the issue of service. "I think [Kmart's] issue is really about the store being very uninviting, a complete lack of service," says Steve Greenberg, president of The Greenberg Group. "You've got to stand in the aisles and scream for someone to help you and I don't know that someone will." Echoes analyst Ulysses Yannas, "Not having service in the store is always bad. You lose sales, besides alienating people."

Author Paco Underhill points out that "most firms are constantly looking to save money on labor. From the businessperson's point of view, this falls under the heading of operations. From the shopper's perspective, it means service. Retailers try to maintain service while cutting labor, which is usually impossible to do."[17] And that is what has happened at Kmart.

"As far as I can establish, 80 percent of the employees' time is spent behind the walls" at Kmart, says Yannas, back in the stock rooms. In fact, Yannas's 80 percent estimate is right on target. Then-CEO Chuck Conaway exclaimed in a 2000 *Business Week* article that he was "astonished" to learn that the average store clerk spends only

22 percent of his or her time interacting with customers. "That number should be 60 or 70 percent," said Conaway.

Underhill calls this the "interception rate," or the percentage of customers who have some contact with an employee. "All our research shows this direct relationship: The more shopper-employee contacts that take place, the greater the average sale." And when it comes to use of the dressing room, employee contact becomes even more crucial. Underhill reports that the shopper conversion rate, or the percentage of shoppers who actually buy something, increases by 50 percent when there is employee-initiated contact of some kind in the store. But that rate climbs by 100 percent when there is employee-initiated contact and use of the dressing room. As Underhill explains, "A shopper who talks to a salesperson and tries something on is twice as likely to buy as a shopper who does neither."[18] But at Kmart, most stores have no dedicated staff overseeing the dressing rooms beyond removing clothes that have been left behind. That's a major lost opportunity.

Although employees may, in fact, be inaccessible part of the time, another weakness at Kmart is the number of employees in the store at any one time. Finding employees for assistance is often hard not because they are working in the back, but because there simply aren't very many on the clock. Even before Kmart declared bankruptcy, employees complained about the lack of available human capital.[19] While Wal-Mart employed an average of 313 employees per store and Target 177, Kmart averaged just 120 associates per store. According to its 2002 annual report, Wal-Mart had a total of 1,383,000 employees and 4,414 stores worldwide. Target employed far fewer employees—approximately 220,000—but had just 1,242 stores as of December 2002.[20] Kmart had just as many employees as Target—about 220,000—but more stores, 1,831, earlier the same year.[21] This figure is significant because having fewer employees means fewer opportunities to serve Kmart customers, as well as to keep the store looking neat and clean. It's much easier to do all that is needed with 300 or more employees than with less than half that number.

Having too few employees means that customers are denied the assistance they need while shopping. Typically, says Ulysses

Yannas, "You walk in, you can't find somebody to ask a question." The problem is that employees are frequently the only people who can resolve purchasing-related issues regarding inventory, sizes, and pricing. And questions slow the entire buying process down. Questions "delay the checkout counter and create huge lines," he says, which then cause customers to reevaluate their planned purchases. The longer the lines, the longer the wait, the more customers who will desert their shopping carts.

Lines are one of the top six things shoppers hate most, reports Paco Underhill in his book, with asking questions being another[22] or, more specifically, having to ask dumb questions of employees because the answer is not readily available. But employees who are rude, slow, or uninformed are equally disliked, according to Underhill, and are a reason for shoppers to go elsewhere. The remaining three things shoppers hate most are too many mirrors, out-of-stock products, and hard-to-find price tags.

In addition to a dearth of customer service, Kmart is also being forced to short-change shoppers on the timely stocking of new inventory, as well as the routine straightening and cleaning of store displays and walkways. Which is exactly where it appears the company is stuck—unable to afford more employees, yet being pushed to improve its store appearance by shoppers who are increasingly defecting to cleaner, brighter Wal-Mart and Target stores. A former area manager complained about the shortage of employees to restock goods, saying, "Freight had to be off the floor by 10:00 A.M., but with minim[al] staffing, this rarely happened. Customers often complained and tripped on pallets and boxes. There were times when we had 100 pallets but only enough space for maybe 50. The remainder had to be stored unworked on the sales floor or in storage containers behind the store. This created a nightmare when trying to locate items for customers or to set an ad."[15]

In a *USA Today*/CNN/Gallup survey of 1,011 adults conducted in January 2002, shoppers ranked Kmart third, behind Wal-Mart and Target, as their preferred place to shop. One of the issues raised was lack of help. Said one shopper who was surveyed, "I was having trouble finding stuff at Kmart, and they didn't have as much help as Wal-Mart." For Kmart, it's a Catch-22. The company can't afford to hire more employees to better maintain its stores and serve its customers, and yet that's exactly what its customers are demanding.

It's Not a Good Thing

The one brand Kmart has done the most to promote has got to be Martha Stewart, the queen of good taste. Since establishing a relationship with Stewart in 1987, Kmart has pumped millions—if not billions—into associating the Martha Stewart Everyday brand name with Kmart stores. But was that a good move? Not if your stores look like Kmart's.

Bringing in the Martha Stewart brand as a way to "sway Kmart away from pure price competition and low prices" turned out to be a "failed positioning point," says Professor Lars Perner of the University of California at Riverside, mainly because of the huge disparity between the upscale, luxurious image of Martha Stewart and the downtrodden, unkempt reality of Kmart's store environments. "You come in and shop in many cases in run-down stores that don't have particularly high-quality merchandise and the physical condition of the stores are so poor," and yet you're trying to associate one with the other. It doesn't work, says Perner. Or at least it doesn't work as well as it could if the stores looked as chic as Martha's merchandise.

Dining in the Past

A sign that Kmart's identity is rooted in the past is its in-store food court, called a KCafé, which trumpets the availability of Little Caesar's Pizza. Although Kmart's goal in partnering with Little Caesar's as far back as 1990 was to align itself with a "branded food operator,"[23] Little Caesar's brand cachet has been damaged, which hurts Kmart's image even further.

The Kmart–Little Caesar's relationship is one of the oldest and largest agreements of its kind, claims Michael Scruggs, Little Caesar's senior vice president of global operations.[24] The two companies began to discuss and test the store-within-a-store concept in 1990 because of a friendship between the leaders of the two companies, Michael Ilitch of Little Caesar's and Joseph

Antonini, Kmart's former chairman. The pilot program was successful, so they signed a five-year agreement to install Little Caesar's Pizza Stations in Kmart stores. After the initial contract expired in 1995, Kmart took two years to research developing its own food concept but ended up coming back to Little Caesar's in 1997 for another five-year deal, which expired in 2002 and is being renegotiated.

Is it in Kmart's best interest to commit to another five years with Little Caesar's? Perhaps not. Explains Rob Gelphman of Gelphman Associates, "Little Caesar's' position is two pizzas for the price of one. Low cost is their stated value proposition—not quality, and certainly not taste. When everyone competes on price, it is almost impossible to move up and compete on quality, or performance, or functionality. You are stuck on price. Kmart is now looked at as the low-cost, low-quality leader. Having Little Caesar's as a partner does not help."

Considered one of the "Big Four" of the pizza industry, which also includes Pizza Hut, Papa John's, and Domino's Pizza, Little Caesar's has considerably downsized in recent years. According to a 2001 article in *Nation's Restaurant News*, Little Caesar's reported the closing of 1,086 stores between 1998 and 2001, representing a 40 percent decline in total units.[25] The company operates 411 units within Kmart stores,[26] which is approximately 10 percent of its 4,000-plus locations in total. At the end of 2000 Little Caesar's also had 1,086 KCafés selling its pizza. Through Kmart's closing of 283 stores in 2002, Little Caesar's lost nearly 100 more pizza outlets.[24] In 2002, Little Caesar's opened about 60 new units and closed more than 230, including 20 within Kmart stores.[26] The large volume of store closings suggests either a concept that isn't working any more, or franchisees that aren't being supported by the parent. Either way, industry reports verify declining pizza volumes overall and regular Little Caesar's franchise store closures.

Kmart's alliance with Little Caesar's underscores the perception that Kmart's stores are troubled. Also, there has been no national television advertising of Little Caesar's as of 2001,[26] which means that there is little promotional money behind the brand that can help Kmart—Little Caesar's isn't a strong draw that can bring customers into the store. Says Gelphman, "Building a brand through co-relationships and trying to leverage brands into an 'uber' brand is difficult and often disastrous if the other brand does not pull its own weight. It's a guilt by association challenge."

Little Caesar's also is protecting itself in reconsidering its alliance with Kmart. In addition to being paid $5 million it was owed at the time of Kmart's bankruptcy,[24] the company wants Kmart to update the look of its Little Caesar's franchises. "They're getting old, so it's time to update them," says Little Caesar's Michael Scruggs. But given Kmart's history of ignoring its own stores, its in-store Little Caesar's franchises may be facing an uphill battle for a makeover.

Back in 1997, Kmart reported that its in-store restaurants generated $350 million each year in its then 1,850-plus locations.[23] That's an average of nearly $190,000 per store. Just think how well the company could do with Starbucks or Krispy Kreme running its food operations.

Missed the Boat

Although Kmart can be faulted for not staying current with its store updates, an even bigger misstep occurred in the early 1980s, as the superstore format was gaining momentum, says George Rosenbaum of Leo J. Shapiro. At the time, both Kmart and Wal-Mart were building supercenters—combined grocery and general merchandise operations under one roof—at a fairly even pace. Kmart had its Super K stores, and Wal-Mart had Wal-Mart Superstores. In fact, Leo J. Shapiro & Associates studied the supercenter concept at that time and found an overwhelmingly positive response from consumers.

From the retailers' perspective, the supercenter concept boosted revenues through cross-shopping. "Women loved the idea of combining one out of every three trips to buy groceries with shopping for general merchandise items," reports Rosenbaum. The supercenter format increased revenues by encouraging grocery shoppers to buy more general merchandise items while shopping, and by enticing general merchandise shoppers to pick up food items at the same time. And Kmart had the advantage. A big advantage. Although Wal-Mart was a strong competitor, at the time Kmart had much better food offerings. By using food wholesalers to supply its stores with fresh groceries, rather than building its own warehouses for food storage, as Wal-Mart did, Kmart could "pick off the best locations in the United States for its supercenters because it was not constrained by the location of its distribution centers, as Wal-Mart was," says Rosenbaum.

However, before it could leverage its advantage, "Kmart conceded the supercenter business to Wal-Mart," states Rosenbaum. Just as today, its stores were run-down, disorganized, and in desperate need of an overhaul. And it had gotten to the point that it was time to fix them or risk a major sales downturn. So instead of pushing ahead with its supercenter strategy, Kmart decided to back off and invest in existing store renovations. That hesitation allowed Wal-Mart to gain the upper hand. If management had developed a plan for continuously maintaining and upgrading its stores, Kmart would never have had to take its eye off the supercenter prize. Having to do so was a major misstep on Kmart's part.

The Store of the Future

Once again, Kmart sees the need for a major merchandising overhaul and is taking a fresh look at how its stores should appear, feel, and operate. But is it too late? Under the leadership of turnaround specialist Peter Arnell of the Arnell Group, part of the Omnicom Group Inc., Kmart has developed a prototype store to guide its next round of upgrades and renovations. Although the stores are being hailed as the new Kmart shopping experience, in effect they are a sign of what has been wrong with Kmart. The fixes are an admission that the stores have been in drastic need of renovation, inside and out. The good news is that the changes make sense and are a drastic improvement.

"I was very impressed with what they did," says Tony Camilletti of JGA. "What impressed me most is evidence that the company was able to ignore its past habits. They were able to be objective about what they needed to do." Breaking from the traditional store layout, Kmart has introduced a new way to shop that it hopes will bring customers back. In addition to its White Lake, Michigan, prototype store, four stores in the Peoria, Illinois, market are also being converted as test sites. On the exterior of its White Lake store, customers find the traditional Kmart red logo has been replaced with a jazzy lime green and a muted gray. "Green symbolizes growth and nature," explains Peter Arnell in a *Wall Street Journal* article. "Red is a common color that is too often used for other brands like Target."[27]

What Tony Camilletti liked most about the exterior changes was the addition of the name of the city underneath the Kmart sign out front. "Only fire stations and post offices do that," he comments. "Subtly, Kmart is saying that it's part of the community. It's a small thing, but small things like that resonate with people." Inside the difference is "unbelievable," remarks analyst Ulysses Yannas. "Wider aisles, better presentation of merchandise—which was, and is, a horror show at the older stores. Sections are lowered so you don't have to climb like a monkey to get something because you won't find anyone to get it for you, better lighting, better finish. The whole effect is different."

With comparable store sales growth falling since 1999 from a high of nearly 5 percent in 1999 to a low of 0 percent in 2002, Kmart needs a major facelift. The White Lake prototype—Kmart's "Store of the Future"—is based on feedback from customers and associates and a study of shopping patterns. How those suggestions were implemented is also a test to see if the company has heard its customers correctly.

Once inside the store, customers notice a main aisle, that was widened to 25 feet and features key Kmart brands, including JOE BOXER and Disney. "Brands such as Martha Stewart Everyday, JOE BOXER, Disney and Sesame Street have been moved toward the front and have their own sections, rather than being spread throughout the store. In the Martha Stewart section, there are signs showing the product being used and product tips that customers can take with them," reports *The Wall Street Journal.* Hanging from the ceiling are four signs that direct shoppers to each department using simple white icons on a green background. Conspicuously absent are the blue stripes across the back walls that were designed to pull in the BlueLight Special theme Kmart had just reintroduced in 2001 after a 10-year hiatus. Camilletti describes the atmosphere as "almost European-inspired, clean and simple, with elegant lines, a spacious feeling" and gives Kmart kudos for doing "just what they needed to."

According to Yannas, departments also have been reconfigured within the store to be adjacent to a more appropriate product mix. Departments were shifted to focus special attention on categories of interest to mothers with young children, the company's primary customer. All infant products were consolidated, for example, bringing together clothing, diapers, food, and accessories in a new Baby Gear section. A muted green and gray carpet was added in apparel, accessories, and home decor to provide a more comfortable shopping environment. Aisles were widened throughout the store and products are displayed out of the box to better engage the customer. But $1 million worth of merchandise was also removed in order to allow the aisles to be made wider and shorter.[8] And, most notable for its primary shoppers, Kmart introduced various amenities to make shopping easier and more pleasant for moms.

Although initial reactions to the prototype have been very positive, former CEO Adamson cautioned that the company currently can't afford to renovate every one of its stores, which would take five years to complete. But can it survive that long? And will it be ready to start the renovation cycle again after five years?

At an estimated $200,000 to $600,000 per store to remodel, Ulysses Yannas estimates that with 1,500-odd stores to make over into Stores of the Future, the total cost would be in the neighborhood of $640 million, assuming an average of $400,000 per store. Although that figure sounds beyond the financial reach of Kmart at the moment, Yannas points out that company is currently spending $250 million a year "to more or less maintain the stores—minor touchups." Given that, spending a little more for a fresh start seems to make sense.

Kmart has the money, he says. "The company last year charged $750 million on depreciation, a noncash item. With $250 million for store maintenance, the company is left with about $500 million a year to spend on store renovation, more than adequate to renovate its stores over a two- to three-year period." Proceeds from the sale of its real estate—or savings from lease terminations—could also be reallocated to fund store capital expenditures. Kmart's first lease sell-off netted $46.5 million, on top of first-year projected savings of up to $550 million, which could be applied to the needed store renovations.

For now, Kmart just plans to just study customer response to its new prototype, with the intent to apply what it learns to existing stores, rather than attempting a total re-do. *The Wall Street Journal* reports that the company will focus on changes that boost sales the most. Said Adamson, in the article, "If it's the wider aisles, say, that are really a home run, it's not difficult to take that out to 1,800 stores."[27] Although this approach makes sense, it also smacks of the typical half-hearted Kmart *modus operandi*. Instead of jumping in with both feet and making a commitment—right or wrong—to do something that can only be better than what the company has now (stores in desperate need of a makeover), management is dipping its toe in the water to gauge reaction. Camilletti agrees, commenting that "execution has been a problem, although the initiative has been there."

Kurt Barnard, publisher of *Barnard's Retail Trend Report*, seemed to express a popular opinion when he commented to the *Detroit Free Press*, "It's a good idea to broaden aisles and have better light, that is something that every retail store must be mindful of. Is it enough to bring customers into the stores? That I don't know."

Notes

1. *Why We Buy: The Science of Shopping*, by Paco Underhill, New York: Simon & Schuster, 1999, p. 184.
2. "Design war: Kmart stores often do not send a focused message," by Lorene Yue, *Detroit Free Press*, February 12, 2002.
3. *Why We Buy: The Science of Shopping*, by Paco Underhill, New York: Simon & Schuster, 1999, p.32.
4. *Why We Buy: The Science of Shopping*, p. 33.
5 "Mass appeal," by Barry Stavro, *Forbes*, May 5, 1986.
6. "Antonini's Long-Term Strategy Was Right for Kmart," case study featured on the web site of Joseph Antonini's consulting firm, JEA Enterprises, www.jeaenterprises.com/casestudy.htm.

7. "The future of Kmart (online interview)," with Eric Beder, Washing tonpostonline.com, January 25, 2002.

8. "A test in White Lake Township," by Lorene Yue, *Detroit Free Press,* October 18, 2002.

9. "Kmart takes aim at 284 underperforming stores," by Lorrie Grant, *USA Today,* March 10, 2002.

10. Target.com web site, December 29, 2002.

11. Walmart.com web site, December 29, 2002.

12. "New Jersey retail space; in the market for shopping centers, buyers line up," by Antoinette Martin, *New York Times,* November 8, 2002.

13. "Sights, sounds on the sales floor," by Nicole Stafford, *The Observer & Eccentric Newspaper,* July 15, 2001.

14. "Improve the in-store experience," by Debbie Howell, *DSN Retailing Today,* March 11, 2002.

15. "Phantom pages and false impressions," retailworker.com web site, www.retailworker.com/modules.php, January 28, 2002.

16. "Kmart loses $3.26 billion in year," by Karen Dybis, *The Detroit News,* March 25, 2003.

17. *Why We Buy: The Science of Shopping,* p. 186.

18. *Why We Buy: The Science of Shopping,* p. 171.

19. Comment made by Roger Valdez, former Kmart employee, during phone interview, October 18, 2002.

20. Target Fact Card as stated on its web site dated December 5, 2002.

21. Press release on Kmart web site dated January 22, 2002.

22. *Why We Buy: The Science of Shopping,* p. 159.

23. Kmart press release dated September 23, 1997.

24. "Kmart hustles to keep pizza," by Karen Dybis, *The Detroit News,* September 20, 2002.

25. "Ex-Pizza hut vps plan big Little Caesar's franchise," by Amy Zuber, *Nation's Restaurant News,* July 16, 2001.

26. "Pizza power 2002," *Pizza Marketing Quarterly,* www.pmq.com, January 5, 2003.

27. "Turning Red Ink to Green?" by Amy Merrick, *The Wall Street Journal,* October 15, 2002.

Technology Aversion

Kmart's information technology (IT) infrastructure has been called "archaic," "antiquated,"[1] and "outdated and inefficient,"[2] and has been cited as one of the main reasons the company has lost its competitive edge to the likes of Wal-Mart and Target. As a *DSN Retailing Today* article summarized, "The flow of information through the retailer's vast network of more than 2,000 stores was slow at best and created a web of problems that put the retailer behind the times."[2] Rather than improving the company's operations, its information system proved an impediment to progress. What Kmart needs most, say analysts, is a robust, unified IT backbone[3] to run everything from cash registers to inventory management to logistics planning. It seems the company is coming closer to that objective with each round of technology investment, but it is not quite there yet.

Kmart's IT problems, however, had nothing to do with the amount of money the company spent on technology. Through-out its history, several CEOs made multimillion dollar investments—even billion dollar expenditures—in information technology, which should have propelled the company forward. The problem was that Kmart never truly adopted the technology that was made available, deciding instead to rely on the judgment and instinct of its management. Kmart could have invested $100 billion in technology and management still would have made poor decisions.

Ultimately, "Without having certain systems in place, [Kmart] basically lacks the information necessary to manage the business effectively," says Sandra J. Skrovan, vice president of Retail Forward, Inc. Intuition and instinct can only go so far when trying to manage the operations of thousands of retail stores, as well as the back office merchandise management, human resource management, and accounting functions. Kmart needs technology, but it is unclear whether management understands how critical a unified information system is to the company's success.

Technology's Importance

Although Kmart has been investing in technology as a means of competing with Wal-Mart, it is doomed to fail until it recognizes that technology in and of itself is not a strategy—it is an enabler—as a Harvard Business School case pointed out years ago.[4] An analogy provided by *Minneapolis Star Tribune* columnist Isaac Cheifetz also hits home. In expressing the importance of "competence before technology," Cheifetz likens technology to a race car. "A skilled driver will go faster; a mediocre driver will hit the wall."[5] Kmart seems to be just now shifting into second or third gear.

A typical retailer has five key business processes that can be managed efficiently by technology: merchandise planning and management, manufacturing/sourcing, distribution/logistics, store operations, and central administrative functions.[6] How that system is designed however, is totally dependent on the mission and strategy of the company its supports. This requires that a company define its strategy clearly before proceeding to design an information system. The problem is that Kmart didn't have a clear vision of what the company was aiming to achieve. As former CEO Jim Adamson stated while the company sorted out its future during bankruptcy, "The issue is who is Kmart."[7] How can you decide how you want your company to function, what performance factors are critical, or how best to meet customer needs when you haven't solidified what you want the company to be?

That these questions have to be asked suggests that for at least two decades, Kmart may have been spinning its wheels, trying to shift into fourth gear without moving through the first three.

Whereas Wal-Mart sought to use technology to revolutionize how it did business, exploring the myriad ways computing systems could support its mission to provide "everyday low prices," Kmart limited its thinking, focusing mainly on using information systems to cut costs and reduce waste. Not surprisingly, its growth has also been limited. Said David Glass, Wal-Mart's chairman, in Sam Walton's biography, "In retail, you are either operations driven—where your main thrust is toward reducing expenses and improving efficiency—or you are merchandise driven. The ones that are truly merchandise driven can always work on improving operations. But the ones that are operations driven tend to level off and begin to deteriorate,"[8] which is an apt description of the predicament Kmart finds itself in. Instead of seeing technology as a means to an end, Kmart got sidetracked, perhaps by Wal-Mart's increasing fortunes, and began to see technology as the end itself. That's when its progress really slowed.

A Slow Start

As early as 1966, Wal-Mart made the strategic decision to invest heavily in computing power, enabling the retailer to be the first in its industry to automate much of its processes. Sam Walton attended an NCR seminar in the early 1960s and became hooked on the promise of more efficient operations on a large scale. He reflects, "One of the main reasons we've been able to roll this company out nationally was all the pressure put on by me . . . to invest so heavily in technology."[9] During the 1970s and 1980s, Wal-Mart adopted newer retail technology, including back-end computers for each store, electronic cash registers, and UPC scanners for nongrocery items. By 1973, nearly one-third of Wal-Mart's stores were equipped with computers. Kmart didn't make the same effort until 1978, more than 15 years after the Kmart store format had debuted.

Sam Walton remembers the early days in his biography: "During that period in the late 1970s when Kmart's management had such a strong resistance to any kind of change, that resistance included investment in systems. At the same time, our fellows were just absolutely convinced that computers were essential to managing growth and keeping down our cost structure. Today, of course, they've been proven so right that they look like geniuses."[10] And Kmart still hasn't caught on to the power of information.

It wasn't until Kmart CEO number 4, Bernard Fauber, took the helm that Kmart first considered investing in information technology—or at least the first time they actually did it. A technology investment may have been debated, but was not acted on fully until the 1980s. In the late 1980s, Kmart invested $3 billion in technology in order to become more cost competitive. Its investment enabled nearly 500 of its stores to be equipped with the latest and greatest in scanners, credit card processors linked by satellite, and the ability to monitor inventory and sales data. This was a good step forward for about 25 percent of its stores, but the other 75 percent were still in the dark ages.[11] In contrast, *all* of Wal-Mart's stores were able to collect and process real-time sales and inventory data and had been for years.

Former CIO Dave Carlson depicts Kmart's information system in 1985 as one that was cobbled together over time. He states in a *CIO* article, "When I was brought into Kmart [in 1985] they had five different point-of-sale (POS) environments. Within two years, we came up with an architecture that allowed all scanning stores in the United States and Canada to be implemented on exactly the same hardware platform. We saved about $40,000 per store with that architecture and saved $80 million to $100 million."[12]

In 1987, then Kmart CEO Antonini announced a $1 billion investment in technology adoption, the same year that Wal-Mart invested $20 million more in its own satellite communications system, which enabled the company's headquarters to communicate directly with each store without paying long-distance phone charges. Real-time data access became a clear advantage for the Wal-Mart, which was then able to distribute timely information regarding inventory, management updates, and pricing changes. During those same years, Wal-Mart introduced an electronic data interchange (EDI) system called RetailLink that made suppliers part of the inventory management process, allowing them to access sales data and projections and to propose new sales strategies for their products. Kmart, in contrast, had to be pulled into supply chain collaboration by its vendors, who talked about Wal-Mart's system. But by 1992, Kmart had caught up with Wal-Mart on that score, boasting 2,000 vendors in its own EDI network and winning a *Computerworld/* Smithsonian Award for its Kmart Information Network.

By 1999, during Floyd Hall's tenure as CEO, Kmart's investment in technology was beginning to pay off, enabling the company to track 2 billion transactions a year from more than 85 million households. By 2000, Kmart anticipated e-mailing promotional materials to households as well. Around 2000, the company was also shoring up its infrastructure, investing $328 million to install new scanners and point-of-sale registers at some stores in order to speed up the checkout process.

In 2000, a few months after he took over, CEO Chuck Conaway announced a $670 million investment in technology and logistics infrastructure, including a new inventory management system and new state-of-the-art scanners for all of the chain's stores; faster cash registers in the company's 300 highest-volume stores; to help speed up the checkout process, a new planning, forecasting, and replenishment system; and a new merchandise management system to assist buyers in better tracking the movement of product, as well as improvements to Kmart's existing distribution and logistics network. The $670 million investment was $135 million more than Floyd Hall's projected expenditures for 2000, which had been increasing before his departure.[13] Clearly, Kmart was picking up the pace of investment, but was it enough? "They're exactly the right things to do," said Brian Hume, a retail consultant with Atlanta-based Martec International Inc. "The secret now is all in the execution."[13]

Shortly before he stepped down as CEO in 2002, Conaway pledged $50+ million to build an entirely new supply chain and inventory management system, scrapping $130 million in outdated supply chain hardware and software that were now obsolete. Is Kmart's current CEO, Julian Day, willing to keep the technology ball rolling in the right direction for Kmart? That remains to be seen. Its reorganization plan mentioned little about technology investments.

"Wal-Mart is a large factor of why Kmart is in the position it is in," says Retail Forward's Sandra Skrovan. "Whereas Wal-Mart invested in the infrastructure—the systems technology and business processes—to really drive cost efficiencies in its business and drive prices down for consumers, Kmart just didn't make that same type of investment. So, for Kmart, I think a key issue is the lack of competitive infrastructure, systems technology, and supply chain management that would give it the ability to play on a level field with Wal-Mart."

Why did Kmart allow this to happen? That's what puzzles Professor Don B. Bradley III of the University of Central Arkansas. "[Kmart] couldn't see that Wal-Mart was building distribution centers? They couldn't see that they were going to satellite communication? They couldn't see that they were going to electronics, bar codes, and things like that? They had the opportunity to do all those things but they didn't take it to the same level that Wal-Mart did." Now, the best that Kmart can hope for is to become more competitive than it is today, but it can't expect to meet or beat Wal-Mart technology-wise. "Wal-Mart is just going to keep going and going," says Skrovan. "Even if Kmart revamps the infrastructure and puts better processes and technology in place today, it would likely still trail Wal-Mart."

"Early on, Kmart passed up the opportunity to computerize inventory and ordering into centralized systems because local managers balked about giving up control," reports Joanna Krotz of Microsoft's bCentral.com web site. "Wal-Mart, on the other hand, installed efficient electronic systems everywhere it could."

Professor Paul Argenti of the Tuck School at Dartmouth argues that Kmart had the opportunity to do what Wal-Mart did, but management thought and acted like a big company when it was facing competition from an upstart. "It's a whole lot easier to start from scratch, as Wal-Mart did," he says, than to play catch-up by replacing existing systems in one fell swoop. The idea probably wasn't even considered. Part of Kmart's overall problem has been its centralized structure, with "one-size-fits-all" type decisions being made from Kmart's headquarters in Troy, Michigan, says Professor Theo Addo, associate professor of information systems at San Diego State University. "Everything was mandated from the very top, which resulted in a lack of managerial flexibility at local sites."

By 2002, Kmart was ranked 43rd on the *InformationWeek* 500, a list of top IT companies, based on its staggering two-year $1.4 billion investment in rebuilding and refurbishing its operational infrastructure and its progress in implementing needed IT changes.[14] ("More money than Kmart has spent in the last decade on IT," said a Kmart spokeswoman).[15] Was that a one-time accomplishment based solely on the size of its investment the prior year, or will Kmart commit to remaining on this esteemed list?

The Link with Strategy

Information technology investments can be segmented into four tiers, explains a 2002 McKinsey Global Institute report. As retailers move from investments in the "basic cost of doing business" to the "extended cost of doing business" to "differentiating" to, finally, the "next frontier" of investments, information collected becomes more specific and enables companies to provide a richer, more satisfying shopping experience to their customers. Capabilities increase from simply moving products from suppliers to customers, to delivering the right product to the right place at the right price, to delivering the right product to the right customer at the right price with the right experience. Kmart has been stuck in the "extended cost of doing business" portion of the continuum for decades, while their competitors have moved on to more advanced tiers, racking up cost savings and sales improvements along the way.

"Kmart has always had a clash of what the IT guys knew they needed, and the spending of money in other parts of the business," says Wayne Hood, financial analyst with Prudential Securities, in a 2001 article in *Baseline Magazine* (incidentally, this may explain the company's high CIO turnover rate). And because money was invested elsewhere, rather than on IT,

Kmart's systems are old—not just obsolete, *really* old. According to Eric Beder, a financial analyst formerly with Ladenburg Thalmann, in some cases, "The cash registers were actually older than the people running them." Unfortunately, the aging system often would be brought to its knees by a single cash register. "If one cash register went down, the entire store would have to close because all the registers went down," says Beder of Kmart's circa 1960s checkout system.[16]

Although the company certainly has been funneling cash into its IT operations of late, is money enough to make a difference? Is the Kmart culture able to shift to see technology as a critical operational tool? It's doubtful, says Professor Addo. "Kmart has a reactionary, rather than proactive, IT strategy." Whereas most CEOs today see IT as an asset to be leveraged, involving the CIO in business strategy decisions as a valued contributor, companies like Kmart focus on IT as a means of generating cost savings and efficiencies, and little else.

Kmart's Seasonal Merchandise Management System

Kmart has made technological progress in fits and starts throughout its history. Back in 1992, the company developed a system in-house to help it optimize sales of seasonal merchandise, while reducing the chance of overstocks in some stores. At a cost of $2.5 million, Kmart's Seasonal Merchandise Management System (SMMS) was debuted and projected a total return of $240 million.[17] It was so well constructed that Kmart won an ESPRIT Award for its system, which was originally developed to help the company better manage its holiday goods, which were only a small portion of its total inventory. Seasonal merchandise is critical for retailers because of the short time frame in which to sell off the supply and reap the higher margins they can generate. In the first year of its implementation, in 1992, SMMS enabled Kmart to generate an incremental $28.9 million in profits just by improving seasonal merchandise sell-through rates.

The key was making information easily available to Kmart headquarters and its individual stores. Before SMMS, managers had to flip through hundreds of pages of computerized data to find out how merchandise was selling. But with the new system, overnight sales and inventory data from all stores is uploaded to the SMMS database, to be accessed the next morning by buyers and merchandise planners. By being able to see which stores have too much seasonal inventory and which have too little, inventory can be transferred to balance out supply. Stores with high demand can enjoy higher profits from increased sales, and stores with low demand can avoid costly overstocks.

With such a terrific system, the only real question is why Kmart isn't using it 365 days a year, for all of its lines? "What happens the rest of the year?" asks Professor Addo. Limiting the system's use to managing only Christmas or back-to-school merchandise is short-sighted, he says, taking a Band-Aid approach to demand-based forecasting. Why Kmart isn't capitalizing on the system's optimal potential is curious.

Ignoring Information

Unfortunately, the systems the company has developed were pushed aside or ignored by managers, rendering them useless. Former CIO Dave Carlson reports in a *Baseline Magazine* article that Kmart had deeper problems with merchandising management. "The company had fallen into the habit of expanding the variety of products it sold without paying enough attention to which items produced the most sales. IT could design the data warehouse and produce the analysis showing what products were gathering dust on the store shelves, but store managers had to decide what to do with that information. Ultimately, they chose to ignore it, he says."[18] Carlson "said that the retailer's top officials ignored many reports generated by the IT department that could have saved millions of dollars,"[19] including proof that store managers were ignoring inventory data. Carlson says that when he presented his evidence, he was told to stop producing the reports.

Unfortunately, management's mistrust of its information system continued long after Carlson's departure in 1995. Kmart ultimately expanded the storage capacity in its NCR system to 92 terabytes, which "will churn out all the information you need about what's selling and what's not," said Carlson. But the amount of information stored and reported is worthless unless management asks for it and takes action on the results.

Remember the 15,000 trucks of inventory that Chuck Conaway ended up writing off shortly after his arrival at Kmart? Those trucks filled with inventory existed because management didn't believe its own information system. Said Carlson, "They had trucks, and trucks, and trucks of inventory just sitting there,"[4] left over from Floyd Hall's efforts to boost sales through more circulars. Although Conaway ended up selling off the aging merchandise, the inherent system problems still had not been addressed completely so that out-of-stock reports continued during Conaway's tenure, ultimately pushing Kmart into bankruptcy a few months later.

Store Communications

Kmart's focus on finding ways to better push information out to its stores is in stark contrast to Wal-Mart's more collaborative approach. Whereas Kmart sought technology to enable corporate-to-store information sharing, Wal-Mart looked for a means to share information system-wide, from corporate to store, from store to store, and from store to corporate. Walton's research in the 1980s hit on satellite communications as a means of facilitating information sharing. In 1983 Wal-Mart contracted with Macom & Hughes Corporation to build a satellite, for $24 million. Despite its high price tag, the satellite system turned out to be Wal-Mart's saving grace. Reported Walton, "Once we had those scanners in the stores, we had all this data pouring into Bentonville over phone lines. Those lines have a limited capacity, so as we added more and more stores, we had a real logjam of stuff coming in from the field." The idea that useful information might come in from the field probably didn't cross Kmart's mind for years. It was too sure that headquarters had all the answers. As of 1992, Wal-Mart had spent almost $700 million on the computer and satellite system installed throughout the corporation. According to Walton, "it's the largest civilian data base of its kind in the world."[20] Only the Pentagon has more storage capacity.[21]

Said Walton, "It's only because of information technology that our store managers have a really clear sense of how they're doing most of the time. They get all kinds of information transmitted to them over the satellite on an amazingly timely basis: their monthly profit-and-loss statement, up-to-the-minute point-of-sale data that tells them what's selling in their own store, and a lot of other paper they probably wish we wouldn't send them."[22]

Whereas Wal-Mart has looked for ways to encourage communication and collaboration across stores, Kmart has held on tightly to its centralized model. As former Kmart employee and writer Rick Waingate observes, "Even as recent as six months ago, Kmart was pushing a culture whereby the home office knows best."[23] His advice, "Management must encourage ideas from the ground up, not from headquarters down," is right on target. Hopefully, new CEO Julian Day won't ignore this advice.

Weak Execution

Despite repeated attempts to automate many of its business processes, Kmart's all-or-nothing approach also has been a problem. Attempts to quickly upgrade its information technology infrastructure have been stymied by a chicken-and-egg quandary. As McKinsey reports, trying to implement technology across the board frequently doesn't work. "Successful retailers developed their IT architecture by developing capabilities in a logical order—they initially built out basic capabilities such as support functions, supply chain management, and POS systems, and then on top layered more sophisticated merchandising and revenue management capabilities. When retailers tried to deploy more sophisticated applications out of sequence, they were generally not successful," states the report. Although Kmart is not cited specifically here, it's obvious that the company would fall into the category of unsuccessful information technology implementation.

Similarly, Isaac Cheifetz reports in a 2002 newspaper column, "As far back as the late 1980s, Kmart was spending millions of dollars on state-of-the-art inventory management systems. But the systems were a technological Band-Aid on unhealed business wounds and did little to improve the customer experience, market share, or profitability."[5] Even as Chuck Conaway invested hundreds of millions of dollars to modernize the company's infrastructure and logistics network, analysts were skeptical that Kmart could make it work. "All the technology in the world is not going to work unless you have the proper training and processes in place in the stores, and I think that's going to be a real challenge for them," said Carol Ferrara, a Gartner Group analyst.[13]

Professor Theo Addo counsels, "Companies have to take a three-pronged approach to IT. For IT solutions to be effective, businesses have to have technology, effective business processes, and trained IT personnel." Underlying these three capabilities is corporate culture, with a "command-based culture not as strong as an innovative one." Unfortunately, Kmart's culture is clearly command-based, suggesting the company has a way to go before it can leverage its IT assets.

Failing to Leverage the Internet

With 1–2 percent of discount of shoppers increasingly checking retailers' merchandise online before heading to the store, says Leo J. Shapiro's George Rosenbaum, e-commerce is still growing as a marketing vehicle. In fact, online shopping accounts for just 1.3 percent of the total $3.16 trillion retail industry, according to the Department of Commerce, which indicates tremendous potential growth.[24]

One of Kmart's biggest failures, argues marketing communications consultant Rob Gelphman, is that it failed to properly take advantage of Internet technology. "Kmart totally misread what the Internet could do to bolster or evolve their brand," he says. Wal-Mart and Target "took Internet technology and used it to streamline operations, wring out costs, and improve efficiencies and productivity. They looked at it as a way to improve profitability. Their strategy was to focus on the bottom line. If top line revenues saw an impact, that was gravy. This was particularly prescient as at the time, the Internet as a profitable sales channel still had not been proven. Wal-Mart and Target realized this and looked at the Internet as a way to learn about this new medium and improve their business operations at the same time. They used the Internet to augment brand and position. They ultimately increased sales because they improved service, added goods available, and created ease of purchase-elements which all further contributed to an improvement in the brand name of the products."

Contrast this with Kmart's approach, says Gelphman, which looked at the top line and required creating another brand. "While the use of Bluelight.com could be considered leveraging the existing brand, it still did not offer a value proposition. The position was emulation, not creation or innovation. The Kmart brand by this time was already in trouble. They jumped in with both feet, not realizing the bottom was hard to find."

Basically Kmart said, "'We're going to use the Internet to increase sales.' But what they didn't realize was that people were not looking for another sales outlet. They were looking for easier access to more, cheaper, great goods," says Gelphman. With Bluelight.com Kmart's original web site, all that Kmart did was successfully "take people out of the store."

The problem with Kmart's web site, says Gelphman, is that it eliminated the possibility of those ancillary purchases that consumers never intend on making, but end up with because they come across them in the store. The bag of M&Ms, the potato chips, the copy of the *National Enquirer*—all are thrown in the offline shopping cart, but aren't even available online. That's where Kmart is missing out by limiting its online product selection.

Kmart was late to launch a web site, which it did in 1999 as a separate entity, financed through a number of sources, including Softbank Venture Capital, Softbank Capital, and Martha Stewart Omnimedia, as well as Kmart, mainly because of two previous failed attempts.[25] Explained Bluelight's then-CEO Mark Goldstein, "The standalone spinoff model is all about building great product in an unfettered environment where we don't have to deal with corporate bureaucracy."[26] Keeping the e-commerce entity separate was a smart move, but short-lived, unfortunately. Kmart ended up buying out its partners in 2002 as part of the bankruptcy process, turning Bluelight.com into a wholly-owned subsidiary and redirecting shoppers to Kmart.com.

The company also built in some operational complexities up front that other e-tailers haven't had to contend with. Bluelight.com often sold merchandise at prices lower than its retail stores, or sold products that the stores don't carry at all. But one of its big selling points was that shoppers could still return items to Kmart stores. "We tell online shoppers that they can return items at any Kmart store, so obviously, we have to keep that merchandise segregated," explained Ed Winter, Kmart's director of return logistics, in a *Retail Merchandiser* article.[27] Separating online versus offline purchases and identifying what the customer paid were glitches in the system. To help identify products that had been sold online, the company tags its merchandise with a code that tells an employee where the product was sold and for how much.

Initially, Bluelight.com was part of the big push to offer free Internet service to Kmart's customers. Starting in 2000, customers who made a minimum amount of purchases at the web site would receive totally free internet service through partnerships with Yahoo and Spinway, a wholesale Internet service provider (ISP). It was a genius move that quickly attracted more than 3 million subscribers in the first six months,[28] 40 percent of whom were new to the Internet.[25] That achievement was an important part of the company's efforts to make it easy for its existing customers to go online and make a purchase, an activity complicated by the fact that 57 percent of Kmart's 30 million customers did not yet have Internet access. Bluelight was one tool the company could offer to improve those numbers.[29] Kmart's partnership with LifeMinders, a direct marketing company with an opt-in subscriber list, also provided some benefits. Bluelight could offer its subscriber base online personalized e-mail offers, including BlueLight Specials, and provided product offers and information about Kmart to LifeMinders' 15 million subscribers.[25]

Kmart ended up buying Spinway but then discovered that its costs were rising faster than sales, and it switched to low-cost service, rather than totally free, as it had been. For $9.95 per month, customers can now get access to the Internet through the Bluelight.com ISP, which was bought in October 2002 by United Online for $8.4 million as part of Kmart's bankruptcy proceedings. Visitors to the Bluelight.com URL are currently redirected to Kmart.com, although United Online receives a commission for every customer click-through.[30]

Holding on to the Bluelight.com brand was important to Kmart, which found that Bluelight.com customers spent more than the typical web surfer. "We've found that Bluelight.com customers have bigger (online) baskets and generally spend more at Kmart.com (the new site where shoppers are directed)," said Kmart's Dave Karracker.[30] The retraction from Internet involvement was apparently due to the need for focus, says the Kmart spokesman. "It was more about us providing a valuable service and the fact [that] Kmart needs to focus on its core competencies."[30]

Another factor may have been Bluelight's falling number of users. The number of visitors to the site in October 2001 was off 25 percent from October 2000,[31] suggesting that Kmart's web strategy wasn't all that it was cracked up to be. The company then slashed jobs as a cost-cutting measure, reducing operating expenses by 75 percent, but still needed a minimum $10 margin on online sales to make it; higher-margin goods like pharmacy orders, jewelry, and high-end toys were emphasized to achieve that objective.[31] Or maybe there were behind-the-scenes issues that couldn't be resolved. Either way, Kmart elected to start over, once again, with its web site.

The decision was an economic one, because of Kmart's bankruptcy, but in the long run, will it become a strategic issue? Could an Internet presence have become a competitive advantage? Even before Bluelight's sale, a Jupiter analyst questioned the long-term viability of the site. "Bluelight has proven itself quite successful this year [in attracting subscribers], but that has not proven to be a profitable business model. The real question is whether the success [with subscribers] is sustainable,"[26] said Dylan Brooks.

Professor Pete Fader of the University of Pennsylvania's Wharton School, didn't necessarily agree with Kmart's decision to create a web site with a separate identity, saying "I think in general, beyond Kmart, companies that tried a different presence on and offline made a huge mistake." He cites JCPenney's approach as making more sense and suggests that "Kmart could have and should have mimicked what JCPenney did," which was using its web site to be another customer touchpoint, but integrating it with the rest of its operations. The JCPenney web site had the same merchandise, which could be shipped home or picked up at the store, giving customers another reason to come in and do some more shopping. Not only does an in-store pickup save shipping costs, he says, but you get them in the store again. Kmart decided to set up its site using a different brand name and offer a limited selection of products, many of which were not available in its stores. Different strategy, different results.

Lack of Commitment from the Top

If management had truly believed that information technology was the key to its future success, it certainly didn't show it. Kmart needed an IT champion at the top, and it never had one. Even during CIO Dave Carlson's tenure, from 1985 to 1995, he worked with a CEO who "prided himself on never having used an automated teller machine and used an assistant to print e-mail."[19] Such admissions clearly demonstrate that information technology was not a priority for the company. Up until about two years ago, e-mail and videoconferencing were nowhere to be found at Kmart.[23]

Without an IT champion, Kmart's chances of changing its corporate culture are slim to none. Management sets the tone for the company as a whole. Someone who doesn't know how to get his own e-mail communicates by his actions that technology is not critical to success. It's that kind of thinking that put Kmart at the disadvantage it has now. Says San Diego State's Professor Addo, "As the head goes, so does the body," meaning that the top executive defines the company's culture, including what kind of role IT will play in its success. So far, Kmart's head has been on other issues, with its managers and staffers following likewise.

The situation can be turned around, asserts Addo, but there needs to be a CEO who has a good understanding and vision of IT capabilities in the business world. Additionally, there must be a strong CIO who is willing to educate senior managers about the benefits of technology and to translate technical jargon into business terms that are easily understandable. "A strong CIO can thus help to inculcate a new culture," he says, but only if senior managers are flexible enough to consider new information and change as needed. The strongest CIO in the world will have no luck trying to change the corporate culture of a company in which management is content to keep things operating as they always have. Kmart doesn't appear to have the luxury of staying in place, so current CIO Karen Austin may have an opportunity to turn things around once and for all. Addo notes further that "virtually all of the successful organizational transformations involving IT have resulted from a good working relationship between the CEO and CIO."

The Revolving CIO Door

The challenge to overhaul its information technology system has been even greater at Kmart because of its revolving CIO door; the company has had six CIOs since 1994.[32] Few projects begun under one CIO were ever continued or completed under the next, requiring that work be stopped and restarted with each changing of the guard. And for nearly eight months, from late 2001 to early 2002, Kmart was totally without a CIO to set or guide its technology strategy,[21] until it hired from within and promoted Karen Austin to the top technology spot. Of course, the CIO changing of the guard mirrors turnover at the top, with Kmart having had three CEOs since the mid-1990s. The last CIO, Joseph Osbourn, was in his position only a few months until he was replaced by Chuck Conaway's choice for technology leader, Randy Allen. AMR Research Inc. retail analyst Janet Suleski surmises that Osbourn's ouster was more related to Conaway's preference for having "his own new team," rather than for any failings on Osbourn's part.[15]

Still, instead of shaking up the IT group yet again, Conaway could have chosen to keep Osbourn in place until the dust settled. Considering the massive technology initiatives underway, keeping IT staff in place would have aided the company's efforts to get ahead. But Conaway chose not to, setting the company back again. Granted, Kmart is well known as the industry laggard when it comes to information technology, but its history of hiring and firing CIOs in quick succession seems counterproductive. Part of the problem, however, lies in senior management's unrealistic expectations of information systems to "drive a company to prosperity," says *Computerworld* columnist Bill Laberis.[33] "This unrealistic belief was born in the 1980s when the concept of 'information as a competitive weapon' was nurtured. It's a competitive weapon, but almost never is it the defining competitive weapon."

Those unrealistic expectations of IT may have been behind Kmart's decision to let CIO Dave Carlson go in 1995, despite his many accomplishments during his tenure. Described as a "true CIO star and innovator" by *Computerworld*,[33] it is confusing why Kmart would elect to change course once times got tough. Later CIOs, however, may have left due to a lack of financial support from the company. Jim Dion, president of Chicago-based retail consulting firm Dionco Inc., suggests in a *Computerworld* article that past CIO departures may have been caused by budget constraints imposed by Kmart.[15] Or, stress may have played a role.

"A CIO's job is extremely stressful," says Professor Addo. The CIO is the person who has to understand both technology and the business well enough to effectively exploit IT. "The CIO is also the one person who has to be concerned about what all the other departments in the company want." For example, determining what kind of merchandise tracking reports buyers need has to be coordinated with the figures accounting wants. And information needs of the individual stores have to be taken into consideration, as well as those of everyone else in the company.

This is why the turnover rate for CIOs is normally very high, according to Addo. Kmart may not be that unusual with its revolving door, although it can't afford to keep starting over with the building of its IT infrastructure.

Self-Service Experience

If Kmart's aim is to improve the customer experience, it's interesting that the chain invested so heavily in self-service units that enable shoppers to get in and out of the store with as little employee interaction as possible. Especially since Paco Underhill has shown a direct relationship between employee interaction and sales. By discouraging employee contact, Kmart is, in effect, discouraging sales.

Named FastLane, the self-service units let shoppers scan, bag, and pay for their purchases without the help of a cashier, except when problems occur or authorization is required. In stores where the units have been installed, they are accounting for between 35 and 40 percent of all transactions. The original goal was eventually to have them installed in all of Kmart's stores; by January 2002, 1,300 were in place.[34]

A little more than a year later, however, in February 2003, Kmart went to court to void its contract for the self-service checkout aisles. With 790 self-checkout machines in place at that time, Kmart was spending $2.2 million a month in lease payments and expected to save $55.7 million over the next few years by having them removed.

Part of the issue was the problems the equipment was creating. "(Kmart) believes that there are intangible risks involved with the self-checkout program, including lost checkout aisle sales and shrink (the general term for losses from theft or miscounting)," stated the filing. But by suggesting that the company might try self-checkout equipment again in the future, it appears the problem may be less with the equipment and more with the company's cash flow.[35]

Current Activities

Kmart's current CIO, Karen Austin, has been concentrating on solidifying the company's IT infrastructure after combining its core hard-line and soft-line systems in early 2002. She believes that accomplishment will "eliminate overhead, shorten lead times, and simplify store and distribution center operations."[32]

Kmart has also rolled out several applications of technology designed to "enhance customer service."[36] In addition to self-service checkouts, which are in most, if not all, of Kmart's stores nationwide at this point, many stores also have BlueLightning systems that enable customers to have their shopping carts pre-scanned and bagged with the use of hand-held scanners. The customer then is given a BlueLightning card they can hand to the cashier that includes all the information on the items in their bags; then all the cashier needs to do is ring up the sale. The items have been bagged, and the processing time is much shorter. The idea is that when lines get too long, employees can be called into action with the scanners, speeding the checkout process and improving convenience.[36] Of course, this makes the dangerous assumption that there are actually employees available to be called into service during high-volume periods.

Another initiative in place, reportedly at some stores, is Blue Dot. Using the same hand-held scanning units as the Blue-Lightning service, employees can track down inventory. When a display shelf has been emptied of product, an employee can scan the shelf label to learn whether the merchandise is in the back storage area or on order. At the end of the day, a list of empty shelves can be generated and used to restock. Basic re-plenishment reports are also available through the system to identify consistent outages.[36]

Kmart's pharmacies also received a technological upgrade in 2001 that allows customers and doctors to leave messages when the pharmacy is closed. The interactive voice response system also has a Spanish-language option.

Getting Ahead of Itself

Although there are many examples of how far behind Kmart is technologically, the company is making strides to get ahead of the curve. In his book, *Why We Buy,* Paco Underhill offers an example of a great use of technology at Kmart that was simply misplaced within the store. In writing about the importance of transition zones in stores—the space immediately as you enter a store, where customers generally need to adjust to their new sur-roundings—Underhill describes an information kiosk Kmart had installed in "the zone" a few years ago. He says in the book, ". . . we tested an interactive computerized information fixture that had been designed for Kmart by a division of IBM. It had a touch screen and a keyboard, and you'd ask it where men's underwear was, for example, and it would give you a map of the store and maybe a coupon for T-shirts or socks. A terrific idea, executed well."

The problem was that these great kiosks weren't getting used by customers. The average number of times customers turned to the kiosk for help was 72 times a day. Given the number of shoppers to a typical Kmart store, that's a pittance. Underhill explains, "The problem was that no one admits, six steps into a store, that they don't know where they're going . . . . Placing the computers too close to the door had turned them into very expensive pieces of electronic sculpture. The store gave up on them right away."[37] But at least Kmart had tried something new.

In some cases, an organization is simply not ready for new technology, says Professor Addo. "If an organization is not ready, no amount of technology is going to be effective. It may work in the short run, but not the long run," he reports. Kiosks may have been a great tool if Kmart had understood its customers' needs more clearly.

IT Troubles as a Catch-All

It's a widely-held belief that Kmart has always had an outdated IT infrastructure. However, its antiquated information system is not the source of all of its troubles, and a state-of-the-art system isn't a cure-all. *Computerworld*'s Laberis wisely points out, "The belief persists in some quarters that IT somehow can overcome failings in marketing, sales, or other key strategic and operational areas," when in fact, it can't.[33] Kmart's IT system is a symptom of its problems, as well as the key to catching up to competitors that have passed it by.

Notes

1. "Kmart sings the blues," by Liz Simpson, www.lizsimpsonpress.com, October 4, 2002.

2. "Improve in-store technology . . ." by Doug Desjardins, *DSN Retailing Today,* March 11, 2002.

3. "Tough pro will run Kmart," by Jeff Bennett, *Detroit Free Press,* March 12, 2002.

4. "How Kmart fell behind," *Baseline Magazine,* December 10, 2001.

5. "When elephants learn to rock and roll," by Isaac Cheifetz, *Minneapolis Star Tribune* column, April 7, 2002, linked on www.opentechnologies.com/CC040704.htm.

6. "IT and productivity growth in the retail sector," McKinsey Global Institute, www.mckinsey.com.

7. "Kmart's shopping list for survival," by Joann Muller, *BusinessWeek,* March 25, 2002.

8. *Sam Walton: Made in America,* by Sam Walton with John Huey. New York: Doubleday, 1992, p. 62.

9. *Sam Walton: Made in America,* p. 206.

10. *Sam Walton: Made in America,* p. 207.

11. Kmart had 2,000+ stores as of 1981, per Kmart's web site "Corporate Timeline," www.kmartcorp.com, May 6, 2003.

12. "The benefits of hanging around smart people," by Emelie Rutherford, *CIO,* June 1, 2001.

13. "Kmart moves to catch up on IT," by Carol Sliwa, *Computerworld,* July 31, 2000.

14. "Despite economic slowdown, retailers press ahead with IT spending plans," by Susan Reda, *Stores,* July 2001.

15. "Kmart names new CIO," by Carol Sliwa, *Computerworld,* September 15, 2000.

16. "Kmart: Death of a retailing icon?" by David Schepp, BBC News, January 22, 2002.

17. "A seasoned performer," by Megan Santosus, *CIO Magazine,* January 15, 1995.

18. "Code blue," by David Carr and Edward Cone, *Baseline Magazine,* December 10, 2001.

19. "What ails Kmart," by Andrew Dietderich, *Crain's Detroit Business,* 2000 (www.digitaldetroit.org/web/main/feb02_news/feb02-04.html), January 3, 2003.

20. *Sam Walton: Made in America,* p. 213.

21. "Kmart missed the opportunity Wal-Mart found in technology," by Mike Wendland, *Detroit Free Press,* January 26, 2002.

22. *Sam Walton: Made in America,* p. 221.

23. "Target vs. Kmart—a store-level view," by Rick Wingate, *DSN Retailing Today,* May 6, 2002.

24. "Statistics reveal incremental online shopping growth," by Ephraim Schwartz, *InfoWorld,* December 30, 2002.

25. "Bluelight shaping up to succeed where Kmart's previous e-tail attempts failed," by Melody Vargas, About.com, January 26, 2003.

26. "Attention online shoppers," *CIO Magazine*, October 1, 2000.

27. "Home Depot, Kmart, Sears focus on logistics," by Pete Hisey, *Retail Merchandiser*, January 1, 2002.

28. "BlueLight's second-round financing gets green light," *Forbes*, August 14, 2000.

29. "Bricks-and-mortar retailers go online," by Jonathan Burton, Cisco Systems, January/February 2001, http://business.cisco.com.

30. "Bluelight.com sale goes before bankruptcy judge," by Jim Wagner, Internetnews.com, October 11, 2002.

31. "Retailers discover leap to Web's a doozy," by Jon Swartz, *USA Today*, December 18, 2001.

32. "Kmart looks within for CIO," compiled by Meredith Levinson, *CIO Magazine*, July 1, 2002.

33. "Why do good CIOs have to be the fall guys?" by Bill Laberis, *Computerworld*, August 7, 2000.

34. "Can self-service help Kmart beat bankruptcy blues?" by Lou Hirsch, CRMDaily.com, February 7, 2002.

35. "Kmart seeks to void contract," by Karen Dybis, *The Detroit News*, February 13, 2003.

36. "Kmart details ongoing technology deployment," Kioskcom.com, May 30, 2000.

37. *Why We Buy: The Science of Shopping*, by Paco Underhill. New York: Simon & Schuster, 1999, pp. 48–49.

7

Supply Chain Disconnect

Effective retailing technology allows companies to manage inventory by efficiently storing, shipping, and stocking items that its customers want. Inventory management is key to a company's success or failure, and Kmart seems to be the poster child of poor supply chain management. Since as far back as Joseph Antonini's leadership, Kmart has had logistics issues.[1] Another recent CEO, Chuck Conaway, went so far as to admit that supply chain management was "the Achilles Heel" of Kmart.[2]

"Supply chain management" is simply the latest buzzword—replacing "inventory management"—used to describe the information flow from cash register to store computers to an order-entry system that keeps product replenishment in sync with store needs. Supply chain efficiency, says Liz Simpson, a business commentator who writes regularly for a U.K. supplier magazine, is knowing what each store needs through an IT network that enables inventory to be supplied directly from the supplier, rather than through enormous warehouses. That's what Wal-Mart has been striving to do for years, and where Kmart should be headed. Sadly, Kmart hasn't made much headway of late.

Boasted Sam Walton in his biography, years ago, "I think it's fair to say that our distribution system today is the envy certainly of everyone in our industry, and in a lot of others as well. We now have 20 of these [distribution] centers placed strategically in our trade areas around the country—still mostly within a day's drive, or about 350 miles, of the stores they serve. Combined, they account for more than 18 million square feet of distribution space. We stock over 80,000 items in our stores, and our warehouses directly replenish almost 85 percent of their inventory, compared to only about 50 to 65 percent for our competition. As a result, the gap from the time our in-store merchants place their computer orders until they receive replenishment averages only about two days. That probably compares to five or more days for a lot of our competitors, which don't ship as much merchandise through their own network."[3]

Unfortunately, Kmart's supply chain has always been behind the times, as its regular out-of-stock notices on hot items indicate, while causing an overflow of less popular products. The lack of real-time data access results in higher inventory carrying costs, poor buying decisions, and increased markdowns when products don't sell as anticipated. Financially, it has resulted in lower sales and lower profit margins per square foot. Kmart earns $245 whereas Target earns $275 and Wal-Mart $440. Kmart's gross margins are 2.0 to 3.0 percent whereas Target's are 5.5 to 7.0 percent and Wal-Mart's are 5.5 to 6.5 percent.[4]

Although the company has invested billions to develop a state-of-the-art system, it's still light years behind its main competitor, Wal-Mart, with no recent mention of what steps it is taking to improve this critical system.

The Supply/Demand Disconnect

Poor supply chain management led to inefficient merchandise management at Kmart. Being able to query data regarding product sales would have allowed the company to order more of what customers were buying, less of what they were not, and to predict what merchandise mixes were going to be popular in the future. That is the epitome of an effective system. Or, as Anne Obarski, executive director of Merchandise Concepts, explains it, the five rights of merchandising: the right merchandise, the right time, the right quantity, the right price, and the right location.[5]

However, there is a time element involved, advises Liz Simpson. "Monitoring what sells quickly is key," she says. Finding out what customers want to buy is critical. "If you don't know what they need, then you aren't in the best position to meet that need." And being able to respond rapidly to shifts in product demand separates the retail winners from the losers. Despite Kmart's need for speed and flexibility in order to support its weekly promotional blitzes, the company continually fails to react quickly to shifts in demand. This makes its earlier Blue-Light Special campaign even more curious, given the obvious stress it placed on an already overworked system.

Behind Kmart's supply chain issues, however, is its lack of a clear understanding of its customers' needs. Without knowing its customers and their needs, Kmart is unable to effectively stock merchandise in a timely manner to meets those needs. "Kmart should have gotten to know its customers on a store-by-store basis," says Simpson. Collecting data for each individual store and using technology to capitalize on that data would have significantly improved its operations, she says. However, customer demand could not be adequately met using the existing technology in place at Kmart.

The Root of Kmart's Problems

Lack of a powerful information system at Kmart goes back as far as the company's founder, Sebastian Kresge. But it was Robert Dewar, CEO number 3, who became severely hampered by the lack of a means of monitoring and tracking product inflow and outflow as Kmart tried to grow exponentially. As the number of stores in its chain grew by hundreds each year, keeping pace with supplying each store with merchandise became ever more difficult.

Later, Bernard Fauber recognized the value of investing in information technology in order to lower the company's cost structure. In the late 1980s, Kmart invested $3 billion in technology in order to become more cost competitive. Its investment enabled nearly 500 of its stores to be equipped with the then latest and greatest in scanners, credit card processors linked by satellite, and the ability to monitor inventory and sales data.

Joseph Antonini continued the automation process the company desperately needed, addressing the outdated distribution system, which wasn't keeping pace with Kmart's inventory management needs. One sign that Kmart's distribution system needed overhauling was that it provided the slowest delivery of merchandise among its competitors. Wal-Mart made daily deliveries to its stores from its centrally located distribution centers scattered across the United States, and Target made deliveries every three to four days, while Kmart made deliveries every five days—just once a week. Kmart's delivery schedule was partly due to its decision to subcontract its entire trucking operation and another example of the company's shortsightedness. Without control of a fleet of delivery trucks, improving its delivery schedule and inventory management system is almost impossible. But building its own fleet would have cost more than the company was willing to pay. Then, as now, the company was strapped for cash.

Said Sam Walton in his autobiography, "Unlike both Kmart and Target, which contract out with third parties to delivery a lot of freight from their distribution centers, we've always felt that we needed our own fleet."[6] As of 1992, Wal-Mart had more than 2,000 tractors and more than 11,000 trailers.

Increasing the number of deliveries wouldn't have made a difference, however, because Kmart's information system was so far out of date that the company had little idea of what products were out of stock, which products were hot sellers, and which stores needed what when. "They (Kmart) would buy a million bouncing balls . . . and what people didn't buy they would put in the back of the store—or put in a truck in back of the store," says Marie Driscoll, a financial analyst with Argus Research. The company had a hard time matching the merchandise coming through its distribution system with the items it currently had on sale, says Driscoll. "They get people to the stores, and then they don't have what's advertised. It's hard to get people back once they've had a bad experience."[2]

But after only a short while in his position, Conaway claimed those practices were in the past. "We're now pulling products that customers need, rather than pushing products they don't need."[2] Although the statement might not have been totally true, given the real state of Kmart's information system, Conaway's statement indicated how serious he was about improving the company's supply chain record.

Shortly after he was appointed CEO in 2000, Conaway got rid of nearly 15,000 truck trailers full of inventory that had been sitting behind stores because there was no space inside. CEO number 6, Floyd Hall, had amassed the truckloads as part of his campaign to push inventory through the stores using advertising circulars. But perhaps because of the poor information system, the merchandise in the 15,000 trucks was unaccounted for; when it was discovered, few people seemed to remember that it had been there. After seeing firsthand the result of its antiquated system (the tens of thousands of trucks), Conaway allocated $207 million to improve its distribution centers— enlarging some, increasing the number of shipping and receiving doors, and installing new sorting equipment to speed the entire process.

Conaway also pledged a minimum of $50 million to building an entirely new supply chain and inventory management system, scrapping $130 million in outdated supply chain hardware and software along the way. If the system had worked, Kmart could have added $1.9 billion to its bottom line, says a retail technology guru. But instead of replacing the outmoded inventory management system, Kmart replaced Conaway.

Willy-Nilly Distribution

Kmart's distribution centers couldn't keep pace, suggests Professor Don B. Bradley III of the University of Central Arkansas. Whereas Wal-Mart and Target were building distribution centers nationwide to serve their retail stores, Kmart seemed satisfied with its old distribution centers. "In fact, in the Little Rock Kmart store, they were actually distributing stuff out of Fort Wayne, Indiana, and Detroit. That was their closest distribution center to Little Rock, Arkansas—about 700 miles away."

Alternatively, he says, "Wal-Mart, if they needed a distribution center, they'd build one in Florida, they'd build one in Texas, they'd build one in California." But even without the additional warehouses, Wal-Mart had the advantage of better information systems. "They knew exactly what was selling and what was not selling in the stores whereas Kmart was just staying with the same-old, same-old, and didn't bother to reinvest in its infrastructure logistics and inventory control.

As of January 2002, Kmart owned one distribution center and leased 17 others in the United States, with initial lease terms of 10 to 30 years, plus options to renew for addition terms.[7] A year later, the company decided to shut one down as part of its second round of store closings. The company also had announced a reconfiguration of the distribution center network, which involved replacing two aging distribution centers with two "state-of-the-art facilities," says Kmart. "The existing distribution centers were not properly fitted for soft-line distribution center operations and required significant investment to upgrade. Replacing the facilities is expected to enable increased throughput and quicker inventory turns and improve efficiency across all other centers. In addition, the distribution of slower-moving goods is being centralized at one newly designated center."[8] Certainly all steps in the right direction, just way too late.

Too Low a Priority

Back in 1987, Kmart had the opportunity to revolutionize its replenishment system with the help of a team of techies from Procter & Gamble (P&G). Instead, Wal-Mart, and not Kmart, ended up pioneering the continuous replenishment concept that would transform its operations. In the 1980s, Kmart's distribution team decided to investigate how the company could reduce its cost of acquiring Pampers diapers. So they turned to P&G, which had a prototype program it had developed and was willing to pilot at Kmart. As P&G's Ralph Drayer describes the project, "It was just a distribution project; it wasn't a strategic project to really, fundamentally change the trading relationship. It was just something that was run by the distribution people."[9] But it worked.

Kmart's CIO at the time, Dave Carlson, saw the potential. "My vision, that the technology would revolutionize the way we merchandise the stores was right . . . [but] Kmart wasn't ready. It could have generated, with the cooperation of the merchants, a far greater return" on that investment in equipment, he reflects in a *CIO* article.[10]

P&G's Drayer reports that Kmart "had dramatic improvements in landed cost, which could be reflected in lower pricing for diapers at the stores. Their in-stock was better, and they eventually saw continuous replenishment as something they wanted to extend to all their suppliers." Just not right away. Instead of pushing ahead aggressively to roll out the pilot across other product lines and with other suppliers, Kmart pulled the plug. Carlson suggests the technology was implemented at Kmart "probably three years earlier than it should have [been]."[10] P&G, however, saw the potential of the continuous replenishment system to change the nature of the supplier/retailer relationship. And when Kmart's "executive team didn't approve moving beyond the pilot stage. The rest, as they say, is history."[9] P&G went to Wal-Mart.

Drayer characterizes Kmart's no-go decision to be "one of those turning points where you can look back and say this is the one that missed the boat and this is the one that made it," although he concedes that Kmart did eventually implement a similarly revolutionary system with its suppliers in 1992 and called it the Kmart Information Network.[11] It just took longer.

Kmart's Collaborative Planning, Forecasting, and Replenishment Program

Another technology initiative that got sidetracked after significant upfront effort and success was Kmart's Collaborative Planning, Forecasting, and Replenishment program (CPFR). The system was designed to help Kmart and its suppliers collaborate on sales forecasts, promotional planning, and replenishment, copying a similar program that Wal-Mart had begun in 1995 with Warner-Lambert. In its program, Wal-Mart had boosted in-stock rates on Listerine mouthwash from 87 to 98 percent, had reduced the lead time for orders from 21 to 11 days, and increased sales by $8.5 million.[2]

Needless to say, having seen those results, Kmart was anxious to develop its own system, which it piloted with several vendors in 1998. Working with Kimberly-Clark, for example, Kmart saw a 14 percent increase in sales and raised in-stock rates from 86 to 94 percent without increasing inventory. And with Pharmavite, the vitamin maker, Kmart improved its sales forecasting accuracy by 36 percent so that it didn't have to buy as much product to satisfy customers. But other suppliers were also included, including Procter & Gamble, Colgate-Palmolive, and Bell Sports.[2]

By early 2000, Kmart was considering expanding CPFR from 48 suppliers to more than 200, but that never happened. Kmart decided to change the program's technical platform, perhaps because it didn't want to pay subscription fees that would have been required to stay with Syncra software, its provider, according to a Pharmavite project manager.[2] "To the chagrin of the suppliers, and to the chagrin of us, they just froze things," said Syncra CEO Jeffrey Stamen. "As far as I'm concerned, Kmart had a tremendous strategic advantage, they had a leadership position, and they gave it up."[2]

Shunning Supplier Involvement

Fast forward a year. Different products, same issues. Dan Hammond was a divisional vice president at Kmart, until his retirement in 2001, who was charged with trying to find ways to collaborate with the company's suppliers. At that point, however, Kmart was reacting to supplier pressure to develop a system similar to Wal-Mart's RetailLink network.[11]

One of Hammond's last projects at Kmart was an effort to share merchandise information with suppliers in order to better manage Kmart's warehouse operations nationwide. Hammond's project took aim at one of Kmart's ongoing challenges: ensuring that fast-selling merchandise, like bedding, towels, and underwear (soft-line products), is always available for customers. Hammond developed the capability to capture sales information at the cash register every time a soft-line product was sold, automatically update the on-hand inventory data to reflect the sales just posted, and then use a high-speed connection to report the sale to a central computer that suppliers could access.[12]

By accessing virtually real-time information on sales of their products, suppliers could then calculate how much product needed to be shipped to Kmart and when. "We established a very efficient program," said Hammond. "We had 29 vendors and suppliers up and running and were getting improved relationships with manufacturers and suppliers, and even had plans to bring the top 20 percent of the company's manufacturing partners into the program. We felt pretty darn good about it." But then CEO Conaway downgraded the project and announced a new hardware and software initiative in September 2000, outsourcing much of the work to be done, rather than keeping it in-house. A year later, Conaway reported that Kmart would write off $130 million in technology it had developed but wouldn't be using after all.[12]

In contrast, Wal-Mart's more than 10,000 suppliers have access to real-time data regarding product sales at the chain's 2,500+ stores, which process more than 10 million daily transactions, reports *Baseline Magazine* reporter David Carr.[12] "Wal-Mart has decided that sharing mission-critical information with its suppliers is in both their interest and the supplier's interest," said Joseph Andraski, a retail logistics expert. "Kmart has not been as aggressive in this area. Without timely, accurate information, errors will be made, and that means goods won't be where they need to be, when people are ready to buy."[12]

Involving suppliers in ordering, managing, and delivering the goods Wal-Mart needs at each store has continued to bring down costs and improve profitability. At Kmart, however, the company is still relying on warehouses to receive, store, and redeliver goods to its chain. Says Craig Winn, founder of now-defunct Value America, "Kmart's distribution system was antiquated and inefficient. Its buyers filled huge warehouses with inventory that then had to be reshipped to the stores. On the other hand, Wal-Mart's inventory management and distribution systems are much more efficient. Each store reorders from manufacturers on a weekly basis, based on what was sold the previous week. By keeping its inventory costs under control, Wal-Mart is able to offer better prices and that's what made it impossible for Kmart to compete."[13]

Ballooning Inventory

Claiming that he produced numerous reports for management identifying where change in inventory management was needed, former CIO Dave Carlson became frustrated at management's insistence on increasing its inventory when reductions were needed. Apparently, one such report showed that of the 13 toaster models Kmart stocked, the top two accounted for 85 percent of toaster sales[14]—a clear argument for a reduction in models carried.

Apparently, Kmart also liked to have a ready supply of some products, such as snow shovels. Liz Simpson reports that a Miami University marketing professor spent time at Kmart in March 2001 and found that instead of a four-week supply of snow shovels, the company was stocking 26 weeks' worth.[13] Given the seasonal nature of the product, as well as the size, it's surprising that Kmart would commit such valuable storage space to a product that can only be sold during the colder months, and only at some stores—Florida locations, for example, would have little need for shovels.

Crain's Detroit Business reports that Kmart did have an inventory control system, although outdated, that was maintained by its information technology (IT) department. However, the IT department's efforts to help the company better manage its swelling inventory were rebuffed, says Dave Carlson. He reported that senior management wanted to cut each inventory line by 20 percent by eliminating the worst performers and replacing them with new, trendier products that were forecast to sell better. But when Carlson produced a report demonstrating that store workers were ordering the new, trendier merchandise but not getting rid of anything, he was told not to produce any more reports, he said.[14]

As the strategy of paring back inventory was actually implemented years later, Kmart discovered it worked. According to Super Kmart district manager James Funk, quoted in a 2002

BusinessWeek article, culling inventory can actually boost sales. He reported that at a store in Bloomfield Hills, Michigan, he reduced inventory in the electronics department by 15 percent and sales grew nearly threefold.[15] Hopefully, this time Kmart can learn from its mistakes. Scaling back its inventory across the board could have a huge bottom line impact.

Peaks and Valleys

Kmart further challenged its inventory management capabilities by sticking to its promotions-driven business model—a strategy that relies almost exclusively on sales and special offers to get customers into its stores. Without advanced inventory management software to begin with, say the experts, its weekly advertising circulars, and their associated surges of inventory, make it even more difficult for Kmart to keep up with supply and demand at the local level. Stock outages were frequent because the system wasn't robust enough to keep up with the constantly changing inventory; customers frequently found sale merchandise out of stock. According to Eric Beder, formerly with Ladenburg Thalmann, the only way to effectively manage sharp peaks and valleys in inventory is to customize supply chain management software. But Kmart never built a supply chain planning and execution system to run such software.[16] Previous CEOs saw the need for better software, says Beder, but "never executed on that vision."

Thus, under Chuck Conaway's watch, Kmart bought new off-the-shelf logistics and proprietary merchandising software to improve the company's record of getting its holiday merchandise into stores on time. Conaway also purchased a custom version of TradeMatrix supply chain management software, but never implemented it because he decided Kmart first needed to do some work to improve supplier relationships. Another chick-and-egg situation for Kmart, brought on by the large number of critical changes that need to occur in short order. Where to start, however, may be less important than when. Kmart needs to take action now.

In 2001, Kmart paid an estimated $600 million for supply chain software from Manhattan Associates that was slated to help manage the flow of clothing, toys, auto parts, and other consumer goods. By tackling nearly 500,000 items, Conaway hoped to improve the company's back-end operations. At the same time, he wrote off millions in other supply chain assets, including some customized warehouse management software that was apparently too costly to maintain.[16] Beyond that, however, it appears Kmart will need to exit bankruptcy before it can make any other significant improvements to its supply chain systems. During bankruptcy it is unlikely that the judge will allow Kmart to buy more software to enhance its system, since it has operated so long without it.[16] Sadly, without improved supply chain capabilities, Kmart is likely to fail for good.

Back in 2000, following Kmart's announcement of its $670 million technology investment, analyst John Hutchins of AMR Research commented "There's been a lot of Band-Aiding, if you will, and the time has come. The have to make these changes in order to survive. In order for [Kmart] to synchronize their logistics and buying mechanisms, they're going to need to update their systems."[17] Hutchins also stated that Kmart has had "a significant problem with inventory control," as indicated by its stock outages on popular items. But one cash infusion was not going to be enough to cure Kmart's supply chain ills, Hutchins predicted. Instead, a "multiyear effort" would be required to develop an inventory management system to run parallel with its existing in-house–developed software.

Why Kmart would elect to develop "homegrown" applications is curious, however, given the size of its inventory. The answer is that typically prepackaged applications are not designed to handle hundreds of thousands of SKUs (stock-keeping units) in stores, especially in a chain as large as Kmart. And after investing so heavily to develop a custom solution, companies often become attached or dependent on them, unwilling to move on to something more robust. Explains Cathy Hotka, vice president of IT at the National Retail Federation, "Margins are slim, and there is a great desire to wring every day out of a product or service."[17] So Kmart holds on to what it has, even when it has outlived its usefulness.

Customizing Conundrum

On the flip side, sometimes Kmart goes overboard with customizing—modifying programs when modification may not have been necessary. Apparently, such was the case with its warehouse management system (WMS). Kmart bought software back in 1997 from EXE Technologies to help better manage its distribution but then scrapped it in 2001 as part of Conaway's technology write-offs that year.

The problem, according to Ray Hood, CEO of EXE, was not on his company's end. "When we cut that deal, Kmart's then-CIO made it very clear to the rest of the organization that they wanted the package to go straight in out of the box, so the company could benefit from the best practice embedded in the product."[13] But then Kmart took it through its Kmartization process, which caused problems down the line. Says Hood, "What ended up happening was that as soon as the project got turned over to Kmart's operations people, they went into an unnecessary 18-month customization fest and things got really out of hand. Kmart has a culture of 'we're big, we're proprietary, we're different from everybody else,' so they had this huge group of internal programmers working on modifying the code. The result was that 95 percent of the customization was pointless because all these things were already being done in the system, albeit in a different way."[13]

Kmart, however, elected to start over with a new system. That's par for the course, indicates Hood, who notes, "Kmart is into the big fix. You just need to look at how many times they've switched their Enterprise Resource Planning (ERP) software over the last 10 years to see how Kmart engages in this drunken walk from one strategy to another with no consistency of purpose."[13]

Although Kmart, under Conaway, aimed to methodically roll out a new supply chain management system starting in early 2001 and wrap it up by August 2002, the big fix didn't go so well. Kmart and its supplier, i2, ran into some problems, possibly around compatibility of systems. The upshot is that the work slowed down to a crawl as Kmart was forced to focus on generating short-term results. Gartner Group analyst Karen Peterson also surmised that Kmart may have underestimated the difficulty of the task at the start.[2]

Stuffed Stockrooms

A side effect of Kmart's behind-the-times supply chain system is its bulging stockrooms, full of inventory that has not yet been put out on the sales floor. Often disorganized, stockrooms and backrooms become piled high with boxes upon boxes of merchandise to be displayed. According to Gartner Group analyst Gale Daikoku, it was not unusual for supplier representatives to stop by stores to find out why their product wasn't selling as well, only to discover that product was not on the shelves but in boxes piled high in the stockrooms.[16] Likewise, deliveries often get jammed up at the warehouse, says Simpson, who estimates that it sometimes takes 24 hours or more before pallets that have been delivered are logged into Kmart's central tracking system at the warehouse.[13] If the warehouse takes that long to enter merchandise data, imagine how easy it is for deliveries to be delayed to stores.

In contrast, Wal-Mart has little need for large stockrooms because its vendors take responsibility for ensuring that product is in stores when it is needed. Its vendor-managed inventory system—RetailLink—puts the onus on suppliers to deliver product to Wal-Mart when they see that it is needed. Consequently, Wal-Mart doesn't need to stockpile merchandise in anticipation of upcoming displays or sales—its vendors take care of calculating the appropriate stock needed.[16] Wal-Mart also has the flexibility to deliver more or less frequently, as its stores require. The company used to make deliveries every day to 97 percent of its stores, until management discovered that the smaller stores didn't want as many deliveries. To meet their needs, Wal-Mart came up with a customized delivery program in which stores can pick one of four different distribution schedules. And stores that are within a short distance of a distribution center can receive deliveries within 24 hours if they need them.[18]

Claimed Walton in his biography, "The time savings and flexibility are great, but the cost savings alone would make the investment worthwhile. Our costs run less than 3 percent to ship goods to our stores, while it probably costs our competitors between 4.5 to 5 percent to get those same goods to their stores. The math is pretty simple: If we both sell the same goods for the same price at retail, we'll earn 2.5 percent more profit than they will right there."[19]

Buyer Cooperation

Although many of Kmart's problems originate with its outdated or insufficient technology, some are as simple as promoting cooperation and collaboration between merchandise buyers and warehouse staff. Says University of Florida Professor Bart Weitz, "The buyers just don't coordinate very well with the people working in the distribution centers. There's not a lot of teamwork and working together to figure out how to make the whole system work better."[20]

Working under one set of priorities, namely, to maximize the profit margin Kmart receives from product sales while trying to lower shipping and delivery costs, buyers may not realize that sloppiness in transit may actually be costing Kmart, says Weitz. By setting higher standards for shipment and delivery of its orders, Kmart's buyers could reduce the workload in its distribution centers, thereby helping to reduce costs. Wal-Mart has obviously learned this lesson and has called on its suppliers to pitch in to help keep its costs down. Kmart should follow their lead and ask for the same treatment.

Shrinkage

"Historically, Kmart has had a very high shrink rate. Usually, it is from stealing," explains analyst Ulysses Yannas of Buckman, Buckman, and Reid. "Typically one-third is because your information system is no good and two-thirds is from stealing—whether from the employees or customers." The industry average shrink rate, reports Yannas, is below 1.5 percent. Wal-Mart's is 0.0075 to 0.0100 percent. Kmart's is 3 percent. Lack of a proper information system, he says, invites stealing. Since employees know that the company is inaccurate when it comes to inventory tracking, the threat of being caught diminishes significantly and increases the chances that associates will try and get away with stealing.

However, under Conaway, the company dramatically reduced its shrinkage from 3 percent to 2.5 percent simply by selling off excess inventory that had been being stored in 15,000 truck trailers behind stores.[2] Undoubtedly, increased security in its stores could also help reduce the above-average shrink rate.

Split Distribution Creates Inefficiencies

As of the mid-1990s, Kmart still didn't have a unified information system. "Business analysts still couldn't generate one report that would give a complete picture of supply and demand—they had to run multiple reports, then bring the results together in a spreadsheet," states a *Baseline* article.[11] Because apparel sales were handled by a Kmart subsidiary, this and other soft-line products had their own distribution network that was not tied into the hard-line system, which handled products like appliances.[11] Maintaining two systems that couldn't share information was at least inefficient and at most damaging to Kmart's efforts to progress technologically.

The existence of two separate systems, which have been that way since implemented, it appears, is more evidence that Kmart has only been thinking about leveraging technology in recent history. When it first started introducing technology into the company, it obviously didn't think through growth and expansion issues that two systems would create. Or perhaps it couldn't foresee ever merging the two systems.

The Forrester Effect

Dr. Mohan Sodhi, a member of the Institute for Operations Research and the Management Sciences, states that Kmart's downfall was the bulldog or Forrester effect—a result of small fluctuations in customer sales that cause increasingly larger fluctuations upstream, where they are more difficult to manage.[13]

"As an antidote, you must have either an extremely responsive supply chain, including information systems that transmit sales information instantly upstream, or smooth out consumer sales through schemes like everyday low prices," according to Dr. Sodhi. Wal-Mart, of course, has both a vendor-managed inventory and everyday low prices, with much smaller inventory fluctuations, whereas Kmart has neither. "Fluctuations of orders upstream result in an inability to fill them fully, alternating with excessive inventory, and the result was that Kmart's shelves were full only 86 percent of the time, on average," Sodhi reports.[13]

One solution, under CEO Chuck Conaway's regime, was to increase shipping capacity from 900 to 2,000 trucks a day, he reported in December 2001. Another was reducing the percentage of merchandise being allocated to stores by central planners from 60 percent in 2000 to 40 percent in 2001, allowing product sales to dictate the other 60 percent. Finally, deciding that bulky items such as pillows would be held at distribution centers instead of in stores' stockrooms was an effort to free up space in the stores.[2]

Wal-Mart's solution was to own its logistics channel—the trucks, warehouse, and systems needed to transport merchandise from supplier to stores. "When you own and manage your distribution and logistics channel, you have a great competitive advantage over companies that rely on third-party suppliers. It automatically shortens your lead times, but also you can constantly look for ways to improve your operation and try to make it more efficient. . . . In our case, we generally know where things are in relationship to when we want them to arrive, so we can schedule and plan to move goods into the stores at the right time. That maximizes our in-stock positions, which is vital. You can't generate sales unless you have the product there when the customer wants it."[21]

Inventory Turns

In 2000, Kmart had an inventory turnover rate of 3.6 times per year, versus Wal-Mart's 7.3 times per year and Target's 6.3,[13] which would explain Kmart's losses of $244 million and Wal-Mart's profits of $6.7 billion that year. The more inventory you turn over, the more sales are occurring.

Gary Busek, president of IHL Consulting Group, estimates that Kmart could boost its bottom line by $1.9 billion if it could match Wal-Mart's inventory turnover. It wouldn't happen in 2002, however, as CFO John McDonald indicated that Kmart's turnover would be flat the following year, staying at the same rate.[2] Perhaps poor upfront planning on Kmart's part was to blame. Apparently, the company built distribution centers of 500,000 to 1 million square feet, servicing 200 stores each, with only 40 outbound doors. EXE CEO Ray Hood points out the bottlenecks that creates as workers try and get trucks loaded in a timely manner.[13]

Education

In addition to continuing to improving an insufficient supply chain system, Kmart also needs to address the people side of technology as it relates to inventory management. "Implementing technology is the easiest part," says Professor David Closs of Michigan State University. "The hardest part is the discipline and education needed to put it into place."[13]

Changing Kmart's culture from technology-averse to technology-dependent will not be an easy task. Unfortunately, without such a shift, Kmart's investments in any kind of technology will be for naught. Through leadership, role-modeling, and education, the company has a chance at making great strides toward a state-of-the-art operation. But implementing technology without education and training is a useless effort.

The Store of the Neighborhood

Senior management's announcement that Kmart would be handing off more of the inventory selection decisions to its local store managers—called micromerchandising—sounds smart in theory, but dangerous for a company like Kmart, as behind the times as it is with inventory management. Will its existing system be able to manage the added strain of further customizing product orders by store?

Over time, Kmart should be able to iron out any kinks in the system, especially since the company appears to be rolling out the process, rather than immediately implementing it nationwide. But how will the company handle requests for products distributed by companies other than its existing suppliers? Will Kmart be willing to negotiate new arrangements with new vendors? Or are stores only allowed to alter the quantity of the existing products available to them?

"Great companies are going to have to look to a local customer like they're actually a member of that community," said Chuck Conaway, which apparently means that Kmart is going to try and pay better attention to who is in its community. Customizing a store's inventory to the local neighborhood should result in new product offerings, especially in the Pantry, where groceries are featured. In apparel, changes also will be needed, with petite sizes being the rule rather than the exception in areas with a high proportion of Asian shoppers, for example.[22] And for shoppers whose native language is not English, directional signs will need to be changed to use icons and universal pictures.

Although these are small issues, the bigger issue is whether Kmart can afford to allow stores to make such changes? Can its systems support such store autonomy? Kmart has few choices but to try. But if it fails, it will lose more of its shrinking customer base.

Notes

1. "Coming around again: Kmart's new ideas bear a familiar ring," by Vicki Young *Women's Wear Daily*, October, 28, 2002.
2. "Code blue," by David Carr and Edward Cone, *Baseline Magazine*, December 10, 2001.
3. *Sam Walton: Made in America*, by Sam Walton with John Huey. New York: Doubleday, 1992, p. 208
4. Presentation to shareholders committee for Kmart, Atlas Partners & Watertown Capital, June 14, 2002.

5. "If you don't see it, we don't have it," by Anne Obarski, About.com.

6. *Sam Walton: Made in America,* p. 209.

7. Kmart's 2001 annual report, p. 8 of its online document, May 2002.

8. Kmart's 2001 annual report, p. 21 of its online document, May 2002.

9. "It all began with Drayer," interview, *CIO, Magazine* August 1, 2002.

10. "The benefits of hanging around smart people," by Emelie Rutherford, *CIO Magazine,* June 1, 2001.

11. "How Kmart fell behind," *Baseline Magazine,* December 10, 2001.

12. "Kmart missed the opportunity Wal-Mart found in technology," by Mike Wendland, *Detroit Free Press,* January 26, 2002.

13. "Kmart sings the blues," by Liz Simpson, www.lizsimpson.com, October 4, 2002.

14. "What ails Kmart," by Andrew Dietderich, *Crain's Detroit Business,* January 3, 2003. www.digitaldetroit.org/web/main/feb02-news/feb02-04.html.

15. "Commentary: Attention Kmart: Find a niche," by Joann Muller, *BusinessWeek,* February 4, 2002.

16. "Now in bankruptcy, Kmart struggled with supply chain," by Steve Konicki, *InformationWeek,* January 28, 2000.

17. "Kmart moves to catch up on IT," by Carol Sliwa, *Computerworld,* July 31, 2000.

18. *Sam Walton: Made in America,* p. 209.

19. *Sam Walton: Made in America,* p. 209.

20. Phone interview with Bart Weitz, Professor of Marketing, University of Florida, December 4, 2002.

21. *Sam Walton: Made in America,* p. 209.

22. "Is Kmart out of stock in answers?" by Constance Hays, *New York Times,* March 17, 2002.

8

Loss of Focus

"If Kmart had stuck to what it was good at, instead of trying to be like JCPenney, or whomever they were trying to be like, it would have been fine," claims Dartmouth Professor Paul Argenti, who worked with Kmart in the early 1990s. Instead, the company diversified through acquisitions, significantly increased its number of stores, and made a move toward the upscale segment of the consumer market, bringing in brand names like Martha Stewart to improve the company's prestige factor and attract higher-income consumers. It was that effort to expand its market, broaden its product lines, and increase its influence that ultimately led to Kmart's loss of focus, says Al Ries of Ries and Ries. Kmart's efforts of late to consolidate, contract, and change are a natural reaction to its earlier decades of expansion, he says. Branching out achieves growth, but it also can move a company further from its mission. "The urge to grow has caused companies to become unfocused," he has found.[1]

But what is focus, and why is it critical to Kmart's success? Because it is a vision for the future that drives the company's operations, it is the possibility of dominating a market, says Ries,[2] and it is what makes that company different and special. Many years ago, Kmart had focus. Today it does not. Today its focus is on surviving tomorrow any way that it can, rather than clearly defining how it will succeed going forward.

The late 1980s was when Kmart made most of its mistakes, says Dartmouth's Paul Argenti, or at least when the mistakes that were made that would prove catastrophic. There certainly were mistakes made prior to that point, but from then on the pace of business quickened so substantially that Kmart never had a chance to catch up. It was always five years behind the curve.

Losing Direction

Kmart began to lose focus when it started looking beyond its existing business for more sales—beyond its existing storefronts, beyond its existing customer base, and beyond its existing product lines. For Kmart, growth became its reason for being, rather than a means to an end. According to Ries, "While growth might be an admirable objective, the pursuit of growth for its own sake is a serious strategic error."[1] Kmart fell into that trap and was lured away from focusing on building and strengthening its core business—discount retailing.

However, growth in and of itself is not the sole cause of problems; losing focus seems to be a natural occurrence for most companies eventually, says Ries. "Over time, a company becomes unfocused. It offers too many products and services for too many markets at too many different price levels. It loses its sense of direction. It doesn't know where it's going or why. Its mission statement becomes a mess."[1]

What often starts this loss of focus? Success, apparently. Success creates "the opportunity to branch out in many different directions," Ries says. But it never happens as planned and things start to go wrong eventually. Customers start defecting, sales start dropping, and profits are few and far between. This is exactly what followed Kmart's expansion era in the 1970s—the loss of market share, dominance, and profitability in the 1980s. Instead of increasing its market dominance, shifting its attention away from serving its discount customer base caused Kmart to significantly lose market share.

Since then, Kmart has been floundering, in need of a long-term focus and strategy to get the company back on track. Of course, it has tried a number of strategies to regain focus, without much success. The cure is specialization, offers Ries. "The driving force in business is not growth, it's specialization." Accordingly, "When you try to be all things to all people, you inevitably wind up in trouble." Of course, Kmart's unwillingness to change when change was necessary and inability to differentiate itself from the likes of Wal-Mart and Target, which have their own specialties, are part of its problem. Whereas Wal-Mart specializes in the lowest prices on a wide range of everyday products, Target focuses more on fashionable, designer-branded home goods and apparel. Instead of narrowing its focus, however, Kmart seems to waffle between low prices and branded goods just as smaller dynamos like Kohl's are making headway its market.

Ries suggests that there is a direct relationship between the size of a market and the degree of specialization required: The larger the market, the more specialization is required to succeed. Similarly, "The smaller the market, the more generalized the companies," claims Ries, which means that efforts to expand a market should be met with a reduced product line—the exact opposite of what most companies, including Kmart, have thought.

As Kmart has expanded geographically, it has sought to increase the size of its stores to carry more goods, raising its costs and shrinking its profits as it has grown. Now, in bankruptcy, the company is reducing its inventory and is focusing more on the particular needs of its customers in urban markets. Fortunately, says Ries, "Size is not a determining factor in creating a profitable business. Focus is." This means Kmart's efforts to shrink the size of its operations may have a big payoff.

If Kmart can survive another round of industry closures, its likelihood of profitability rises. That's because "in a declining industry the few survivors can remain fabulously profitable," states Ries. "The reason is that a declining industry attracts almost no fresh competitors and there's always a market, however small, for almost any product or service." Just at look at the growth in the retail industry in recent years. The winners have been specialists—the category killers, in particular—rather than general merchandise stores like Kmart.

In other industries as well, the specialists are thriving while the mass marketers are hurting. Just look at Starbucks, which sells coffee; Williams Sonoma, which sells high-end cooking gear; Dell, which sells low-end personal computers; Red Lobster, which specializes in seafood restaurants; or Wegmans Food Markets, a premium, privately owned grocer that is a leader many supermarkets follow. These specialists have carved out a niche, defined clearly what business they are in, and identified which market segments they cater to in order to focus on being the best in the business—their core business.

So far, few experts are convinced that Kmart has a focus. To regain the focus it had at its founding, Kmart needs to determine how large its market is and how specialized the company needs to become, and then set aside the financial resources to sustain a long-term branding campaign that communicates that focus to consumers. Although Kmart may have started out selling everything to everyone, that strategy no longer works. Today, the company needs to choose one particular concept that captures the essence of Kmart and makes customers want to shop there again. With Wal-Mart and Target having staked out their focus, developing a compelling niche for Kmart is that much more challenging.

Based on its current operations, Kmart could focus solely on products and services moms need, for example, thereby deemphasizing its automotive and sporting goods departments and increasing its toys, health and beauty, and children's offerings. Or it could beef up its multicultural brands and narrow its focus to do more business with ethnic minorities. But whether its strategy to be the "store of the neighborhood" will help the company refocus is unclear. How exactly will the company's operations change in order to achieve that vision?

Cathy Halligan, a director at brand-building consulting firm Prophet, points out, "A neighborhood store could be friendlier, provide higher service, know the customer better. . . ."[3] Kmart has stated that inventory will change to better meet the needs of its local shoppers, but what else? Halligan says, "Kmart is not telling us the whole story" by simply stating that it will become the store of the neighborhood. Will it retrain its employees to provide better service, such as learning the names of regular customers? Will it start offering free delivery, as stores in larger markets sometimes do? Does that mean it will increase its food offerings? Tailoring its inventory is not a big enough shift to transform Kmart's market position and focus. Hopefully, management has more up its sleeve than it has communicated thus far.

Get in or Get Out

"Perishables—that's what got them in trouble," says Buckman, Buckman and Reid financial analyst Ulysses Yannas.[4] Kmart's dalliance in groceries is looking more and more like the distracting acquisitions binge of the 1980s. But in the end, can the company simultaneously pull Kmart out of bankruptcy and expand into food alongside the likes of Target and Wal-Mart and hope to succeed?

Don Longo, editor-in-chief of *Retail Merchandiser*, thinks not. "Kmart has always wanted to emulate Wal-Mart's supercenter success but hasn't been able to accomplish that because it did not have an efficient, low-cost way of distributing food and groceries to its stores. The Super K—Kmart's supercenter name—strategy was and is flawed because these super grocery/general merchandise store combos are scattered around the country. Wal-Mart, in its usual well-thought-out plans, built or acquired grocery distribution centers and built supercenters out around the distribution centers."

Also, Kmart's supplier agreement with Fleming Cos. was on shaky ground, until Kmart rejected a contract with the company in February 2003. Kmart was Fleming's biggest customer, accounting for about one-fifth of the company's revenue in 2002. Conversely, Fleming was Kmart's primary food and consumable supplier. But Kmart did not live up to its end of the bargain, says former Fleming chairman Mark Hansen. Instead of big increases in volume each year, as Fleming was promised, Kmart's purchases declined. Kmart's closure of hundreds of stores, including 60 supercenters, impacted Fleming's earnings significantly. Fleming expected revenues of $4.5 billion from Kmart in 2002 but received closer to $3.3 billion and analysts estimate 2003 sales to be even lower, at $2.5 billion.[5] If Kmart could show that an existing contract with Fleming, which they could not terminate until 2007 outside of bankruptcy protection, would be unprofitable for the newly reorganized company, the agreement could be voided. The bankruptcy court agreed with Kmart and gave its approval to end its two-year alliance with Fleming.[6]

In turn, Fleming filed suit, asking for $1.47 billion to compensate it for profits it believes it would have earned under the terms of the contract. However, two weeks later the two companies agreed to settle their differences in exchange for $400 million. Unfortunately, that wasn't enough to keep the company afloat and in early April, Fleming filed for bankruptcy protection as well.

Fleming's former CEO Hansen had hoped that Kmart would take business away from traditional grocers, thereby giving Fleming a larger piece of the grocery pie. Ultimately, Fleming could not withstand the sudden cash shortfall that occurred when Kmart filed for bankruptcy.[7]

Burt Flickinger III of Reach Marketing thinks that Kmart's deemphasizing of food and consumables, where Wal-Mart is strong, is the right way to go.[8] But with Target taking direct aim at Wal-Mart's expansion into food and pharmacy, Kmart may feel left behind if it doesn't join the fray. The problem for Kmart is that if both Wal-Mart and Target already have strong food operations, Kmart's addition of similar offerings does nothing to differentiate itself—as analysts, consultants, and academicians have advised the company it needs to do. Kmart, Wal-Mart, and Target are "trying to add a new dimension to [their] offerings and to [their] way of operating, which they hope will attract new customers from their competitors, as well as department stores," says Kurt Barnard, president and chief economist of Barnard's Retail Consulting Group, and publisher of *Barnard's Retail Trend Report.*[9]

Management's hiring of a new Kmart CEO with food retailing expertise, Julian Day, suggests the company has made a commitment to groceries. But "selling groceries adds a level of complexity to Kmart's already overburdened distribution system," points out a *BusinessWeek* article.[10] Not to mention the low margins that groceries generate. And with Fleming now out of the picture, Kmart may be planning to rely on internal resources to manage its grocery buying, adding additional strain. However, even as recently as 1999, food sales accounted for nearly $2 billion worth of revenue for the company through its Super Kmart stores. Chain-wide revenue for 1999 was $35.5 billion, of which $4.62 billion was derived from Super Kmart locations. Thirty-five percent of Super Kmart revenue was from food sales, which totaled $1.62 billion.[11] Food represents a sizable chunk of change that Kmart may not be willing to walk away from.

Is it smart once again to go head-to-head with Wal-Mart on another front, however? Will adding grocery items, even if they are priced in line with Wal-Mart, be a reason for customers to come back to Kmart? No on both counts, says Rob Gelphman, president of marketing communications firm Gelphman & Associates. First, Kmart can't afford to be in the grocery business with its 1 percent gross margin when, says Banc of America analyst Shelly Hale, "for the company to survive, it needs to deliver 4 percent on operating margins."[12] Believes Gelphman, Kmart does not have the operating capital to support the grocery business long enough to get its cash flow positive.

Second, "Kmart and food is an oxymoron, emphasis on moron," says Gelphman. With all of Kmart's problems keeping its stores clean and fresh-looking, buying food from the retailer seems an unlikely prospect. "If you had problems with Kmart's appearance and shoddy merchandizing when you shopped for clothing, picture frames, or coat hangers, wouldn't you hesitate when it came to food?" asks Gelphman. Until Kmart gets around to upgrading its stores, food should not be on its list of things to do. Additionally, an aggressive move to sell food may actually attract more low-end shoppers and discourage high-end shoppers Kmart wants to court, he says. Upscale shoppers are likely to be more interested in designer home decor products and hard goods than milk and potato chips, two of Kmart's biggest sellers.[13]

The one big advantage groceries have to offer is the customer traffic that comes with them. Being able to drive traffic into stores with consumables is exactly why Wal-Mart is pushing so hard to compete with supermarkets. By positioning groceries next to general merchandise aisles, shoppers frequently end up purchasing nongrocery items they hadn't planned to, boosting Wal-Mart's sales. Likewise, customers intent on getting in and getting out with general merchandise may breeze through the convenient grocery aisles for that extra container of ice cream or dinner fixings, since they're right there. Helping customers make fewer shopping stops drives up sales.

Wal-Mart has a big headstart on supercenter development. If Kmart decides to proceed with supercenter development as a way to grow sales, management will likely get distracted from its primary mission, losing focus once again at a time when focus is exactly what management needs. And as former CEO Jim Adamson queried, why challenge a competitor on its strengths? Why indeed, especially when, during Floyd Hall's stint as CEO, Kmart expanded into food with the Pantry format in its stores and ultimately failed, reports James Harris of Seneca Financial. What Kmart found then was that "food retailing is very different from general merchandise. The buying is done differently, and the distribution is particularly tricky." And since Kmart's distribution system track record is mixed, as Harris puts it, it would be reasonable to assume that the company's food distribution would be no better.

Floyd Hall expanded into food, which weakened Kmart's focus. The company has the opportunity now to refocus on discount retailing, but whether it will is unclear. Expansion has been part of the Kmart culture for so long that considering a retreat from a major market like groceries may be impossible for the company. Food is certainly not going to help the company get its focus back; it has low margins, growing competition, and does nothing to differentiate Kmart from its frequent competitors. But the company has to make a clean break in order to end the distraction and get back to working on its core business. Unfortunately, Kmart seems unwilling to do that, with a spokesperson saying that the cancellation of Fleming's agreement does not signal an end to Kmart's interest in the grocery business. "Kmart is committed to operating the remaining (50) supercenters," he said.[14]

Spreading Resources Too Thin

Kmart has tried just about everything to boost sales: expansion, investment, hiring, firing, sell-offs, sales, web site development—you name it. "They were just throwing resources at so many different things. Not doing any one of them well or consistently," says Professor Pete Fader of the University of Pennsylvania's Wharton School. In fact, Kmart has historically been willing to spend, spend, spend to get results. Unfortunately, throwing money at problems has sometimes caused more problems.

Its store expansion program took the company off course and stretched resources. Likewise, its acquisitions binge turned management's attention away from serving its customer base. The allure of sales growth was too strong.

Management's willingness to scrap existing computing systems has forced the company to start building a stronger information network from scratch repeatedly and has stressed its information technology department to the brink. Just look at its IT turnover rate—six CIOs in nine years.[15] And still its infrastructure is weak in comparison to the competition.

Kmart's weekly circulars also stress the company's structure, all the way from marketing, which designs and produces the circulars, to inventory management, which must ensure that sale products are in stock and on the shelves of its stores before the circulars arrive, to store personnel, who have to reorganize and restock the shelves every seven days. The time and effort required to support weekly circulars is a major drain on the whole Kmart system, and yet the company hasn't yet figured out the solution to weaning its customers from weekly sales.

Unfortunately, investing in systems and personnel hasn't necessarily improved Kmart's operations. Former CEO Chuck Conaway brought in heavy hitters from other leading companies, such as Wal-Mart, Coca-Cola, Deloitte & Touche, and Sears—as many as 500—raising administrative costs in an effort to better manage the company. But those new hires later cost the company millions—maybe billions—in high salaries and retention loans made to solidify the employees' commitment to the company. Of course, the company has since asked the execs to repay the loans, which were apparently made improperly to some managers, and those who do will receive severance packages.

Cost-cutting measures haven't hit the mark either. CEO Joseph Antonini did attempt across-the-board cost cutting during his tenure, but it didn't work. A 1994 initiative that sought to bring administrative and overhead costs more in line with Wal-Mart was essentially unsuccessful. By 1995 Wal-Mart's administrative and overhead costs were at 16.1 percent of revenues while Kmart's was 23.4 percent.

Trying aggressive cutting of capital spending and turning his focus to store operations, recent CEO Adamson has tried to rein in spending during the company's bankruptcy. But has he truly been interested in cutting expenses? His own $8 million pay package could weaken the company's financial situation if Kmart comes out of bankruptcy before July 31, 2003. Of course, the company's focus during its bankruptcy period has been shedding unprofitable operations and eliminating cash-draining lease obligations. Five hundred ninety-nine stores were closed during this effort and more than 50,000 employees let go. But now, after the pullback, is Kmart on more solid footing? Or just stretched even thinner than before?

According to Burt Flickinger of Reach Marketing in an Associated Press report, "As the company contracts, there's still no sign that it can make any money. There's so much uncertainty in what Kmart can do to solve its problems."[16]

Advertising Circulars-cum-Income Generator

Kmart was the pioneer of weekly advertising circulars it seems, shelling out millions to announce special prices on items each week in a multipage, full-color booklet, a strategy they continue to use to this day. The company, and its customers, are clearly hooked on this type of marketing to drum up business—just look at the disaster that occurred when Kmart pulled back on its advertising in 2001! Billions in losses.

Even Target now uses a weekly circular to advertise its specials, though generally Kmart's is thicker. Wal-Mart, on the other hand, distributes a newspaper insert once a month, not once a week. That's because Wal-Mart has everyday low prices, says Wharton's Professor Hoch. It doesn't drop prices on products for limited time periods—it works to keep its prices the lowest on a daily basis.

The reason for Kmart's use of the weekly newspaper insert goes beyond pure promotional needs—Kmart generates income from it. "Kmart used [its] feature advertising to try to make money," says Hoch. "They charge manufacturers higher costs for the advertising space than what [Kmart] pays," which is okay, he allows, except that "it suggests you are playing games rather than focusing on what you are supposed to be doing." Is Kmart in the advertising business? Hardly. So why has the company allocated resources to selling space in its circulars, as Hoch alleges? The answer has to be that the company simply is not focusing on its core objective—running a chain of discount retail stores. If the company were more effective at managing its stores, perhaps income generated from its circulars would cease to be a necessary profit center.

The Acquisitions Binge

Seeing Kmart's slowing growth, Bernard Fauber turned to acquisitions in the mid-1980s as a means of improving Kmart's performance. Diversification was the cure-all for slowing growth. The company couldn't achieve respectable numbers internally, so Kmart bought chains experiencing sizable growth on their own. In 1980 Fauber bought a 44 percent stake in a Mexican discount chain, created a joint venture with Daiei Inc., a Japanese retailer, and acquired Furr's Cafeterias. In 1984, Kmart purchased Waldenbooks and Builders Square, followed in 1985 by Pay Less Drug Stores Northwest, Inc. Then Kmart retreated in 1987 by selling off its Kresge and Jupiter stores to McCrory, as well as Furr's Cafeterias and Bishop Buffets, Inc. to Cavalcade Foods, Inc.,[17] and its stake in the Mexican chain. In the space of just a few years, the company was consumed with identifying potential acquisition candidates, evaluating each target, negotiating the deal, and then working to oversee the company's operations once it was part of the Kmart fold. That focus certainly wasn't good for the 2,000-plus Kmart stores.[18]

Subsequent CEO Joseph Antonini also embarked on an ambitious acquisitions strategy, seeking out and buying a bevy of smaller specialty retailers in the 1980s and early 1990s. In 1988 Kmart acquired a 51 percent stake in Makro, Inc., a warehouse club; formed a partnership with Bruno's Inc., a food retailer; and created Sports Giant sporting goods stores and Office Square office supply warehouses, followed by PACE Membership Warehouse in 1989 and The Sports Authority in 1990. The company also bought an ownership interest in OfficeMax in 1991[19] and acquired Borders in 1992.[17] Of the acquisitions, Hoch says "Kmart did that in desperation. For a while the company lost its focus."[19]

Looking back, such strategies seem questionable, but when Antonini began acquiring specialty retailers in the late 1980s, his strategy was appropriate for the times, points out Dartmouth's Professor Paul Argenti. Those were the years when the smaller niche retailers were poised for major growth. Antonini's hope was that with Kmart's resources, he could propel a specialty chain like Borders or The Sports Authority to become a major player. If he had succeeded, he would have been a hero for Kmart shareholders, who were looking for new revenue increases.

But the companies had little in the way of complementary products, services, or customers, proving difficult to merge with the Kmart culture or moniker. Antonini's strategy also demonstrated his lack of belief in Kmart's own growth potential. Instead of reinvesting in the company's operations to strengthen its position, Antonini felt he had to buy other operations with greater growth potential. To do so, he channeled funds away from store renovations, technology investments, and infrastructure improvements that would have served Kmart well for decades.

Antonini didn't know whether any of his acquisitions would actually grow faster than Kmart, but he was willing to take the risk. Part of the problem may have been his ego. Unwilling to be left behind, or to appear a follower rather than a leader, Antonini did what CEOs of that decade did—he bought smaller companies. Not to engage in such activities would have branded him conservative or, worse, a coward.

Sadly for Kmart, by the mid-1990s its growth was coming primarily from its acquisitions, mainly Builders Square, The Sports Authority, Borders (which Waldenbooks had purchased) and Pay Less Drug Stores, rather than from its core discount retail operations. So while its financials may have looked healthy, its business model was flailing. Was Kmart a discount retailer or a holding company for a portfolio of unrelated retailers? At that point, it didn't seem to know.

Wal-Mart had even gotten into the acquisitions game in the 1980s and 1990s, acquiring McLane Company and Western Merchandisers, adding to its prior acquisition of Mohr-Value stores, Hutcheson Shoes, and Kuhn's Big K stores. But Wal-Mart was different. Instead of acquiring companies purely for better financial numbers on its income statement, Wal-Mart looked for leaders in particular functional areas. PACE Warehouse clubs, which it acquired from Kmart, for example, was a well-run warehouse club that Wal-Mart aimed to merge with its own warehouse club, called Sam's Club, which had debuted in 1983.

Even in 2002, Wal-Mart was still buying companies to improve its own operations; the company sought regulatory approval to buy a California bank in order to reduce the high cost of processing debit card transactions.[20] And by incorporating the company's infrastructure into its own, Wal-Mart as a company was stronger. Same action, but for very different reasons. Whereas Kmart bought companies because of lack of confidence in its own ability to generate growth, Wal-Mart bought companies to ensure future growth and market dominance.

When Floyd Hall took over in the mid-1990s, he recognized that although the earlier acquisitions had beefed up sales, they had contributed less to profits than hoped, proved a drain on the company's focus, and needed to be sold off. At that point, two of the companies had already been disposed of—Pay Less Drugs and PACE Membership Warehouse—and the rest would be sold within a year for approximately $3.5 billion. Hall tried to get Kmart to focus once again on its core operations, rather than get distracted by new revenue opportunities outside its own field of expertise.

Too Much All At Once

A company often can get into trouble when it has too many irons in the fire, making it difficult to prioritize objectives or effectively manage ongoing operations. There have been several periods in its history where Kmart was trying to do too much. Right now may be one of them. Attempting to increase sales while closing stores and firing employees is a tall order—one that Kmart is still struggling with. Its sales fell from more than $35 billion in 2001, prebankruptcy, to $30.8 billion in 2002, during its bankruptcy, and are not expected to reach its prebankruptcy levels in the near future. By 2007, Kmart projects sales of $30.2 billion.[21]

Of course, the number of stores it has in its portfolio has dropped dramatically during its bankruptcy filing. It had around 2,100 stores prebankruptcy in 2001, which dropped to 1,509 during bankruptcy, and will rise again slowly to 1,579 in 2007. In connection with its store closings, Kmart also reduced its workforce from 234,000 when the company filed for bankruptcy to 167,000 during bankruptcy.[21]

Kmart's plan to exit bankruptcy by April 2003, little more than a year after filing, is truly aggressive. Between one and three years is more realistic, says one bankruptcy expert. Which means that Kmart may not really be ready, says investment research firm Morningstar's Mike Porter. "[Kmart] is pushing to get out of bankruptcy so fast that it may not be ready for it." Although management has been focused on arranging financing to enable the company to continue to function during and after bankruptcy, and taking steps to reposition Kmart in a way that is meaningful to customers, "the wild card is the morale of managers and employees," according to Porter. A critical issue for Kmart is whether management can rally its troops behind its plan for the future—where it intends to focus.

Kmart's plan for reorganization states that the company will become the "store of the neighborhood," mainly because it is strong in its 300+ urban markets—where it already is the store of the neighborhood. Its strategy for the next five years is to extend that across all of its stores, including the 1,200 that are suburban locations. Since the core of the "neighborhood" strategy is to tailor the company's inventory to its local market's purchasing preferences, Kmart needs a state-of-the-art inventory management system, which it doesn't have.

The company will also continue to pursue moms with children as its primary shoppers, although multicultural customers seem to have been pushed into the top spot in terms of focus. Figuring out what these demographic groups—and there are many of them—want and how best to provide it, without alienating other groups, is an added obstacle.

Finally, Kmart has developed a prototype of an upgraded, renovated store that management is studying, with plans to copy at least certain aspects to its existing store base. Experts see store upgrades as the most important step the company could take to improve its operations, but Kmart is taking it slow. Of course, that will necessarily extend the completion date of the chain-wide overhaul that is so desperately needed.

Can Kmart realistically prioritize its challenges and focus long enough to make significant headway on all of them? Don't count on it. Its success rate in executing complex programs is low.

Weak Follow-Through

To its credit, Kmart has always been willing to pay for advice when it felt it was needed. "Kmart has spent millions on great consulting firms," says Tony Camilletti of JGA, who has worked with the company. Unfortunately, even when armed with great ideas, Kmart doesn't always implement the recommendations. After paying top dollar for information and guidance, Kmart's typical approach is to bring the recommendations inside the company, run them through the Kmart review process, which only serves to dilute the power of the ideas, and then roll out the watered-down changes. Only, says Camilletti, the implemented ideas "end up not reflecting any real change." In the end, significant improvements are not made, leaving the company right where it was.

Even when consultants have advised the company on exactly what actions it needs to take, Kmart feels a need to adjust those recommendations to make themselves more comfortable. But if the company is not willing to take analyses, observations, and recommendations at face value—as they were intended—Kmart wastes time, money, and attention, and draws its focus away from critical issues. The company is not able, or not willing, to face up to its biggest challenges and address them *head-on,* it appears. Focus requires a level of persistence and commitment that does not mesh with weak execution. Unfortunately, ignoring expert advice is destined to result in weak execution.

Forgetting about Customer Satisfaction

Although Kmart has stated its commitment to satisfying its customers, as recently as 2001 it still hadn't figured out how to do that. According to data compiled by PlanetFeedback, a consumer feedback web site, Kmart's customer service was consistently ranked below its mass merchant competitors during 2001.[22] Of the more than 330,000 consumer letters PlanetFeedback tracked that year, nearly 20,000 were regarding leading discount retailers, including Kmart, Wal-Mart, Target, Costco, and Sam's Club. In addition, Kmart's customer dissatisfaction levels rose during the year, from 67 percent in January 2001 to 83 percent by December, says PlanetFeedback, putting Kmart squarely at the bottom of the pack in terms of the quality of the in-store experience. "All mass merchandisers faced challenging times this year, but Kmart experienced the highest levels of customer dissatisfaction of any of the major players," said Pete Blackshaw, PlanetFeedback's founder, in his report.[22]

Perhaps of greatest potential concern to Kmart is the impact those dissatisfied customers could have on other shoppers. PlanetFeedback reported that nearly 73 percent of all comments to Kmart at the Web site were "viral," meaning that consumers spread word of their experiences to others, and that nearly 32 percent of Kmart shoppers characterized themselves as "at risk" of switching to a competitor. That compares with 21 percent of Wal-Mart shoppers and 20 percent of Target shoppers.

Even as the company stated its intention to improve the customer experience, it obviously didn't channel resources to that end. If it had focused on customer's shopping experiences, issues like poor store appearance, lack of personnel, and out-of-stock merchandise would be improving rather than getting worse, as PlanetFeedback's studies indicate.

Certainly Kmart has been absorbed with the challenge of emerging from bankruptcy a stronger, smarter competitor, but during its ordeal, customers have been hearing far more about the Kmart of the future than the changes being made to improve the Kmart of today. Is Kmart so focused on its vision of the future that it hasn't yet worked out the details of implementation? What it needs to do to make some headway is to begin to communicate to customers what its new focus is. So far, what customers have heard has been vague.

Passive Board of Directors

If Kmart management lost focus on its mission, part of the blame has to rest on the shoulders of the company's board of directors, whose role it is to oversee management's activities. Working on behalf of shareholders and customers, it is the board's responsibility to set goals and monitor the company's progress. Apparently $4 billion worth of losses in the last couple of years wasn't enough to get the board's rapt attention.[23]

Unfortunately, Kmart's board seems to have been out to lunch when it came to noticing questionable behavior on the part of former managers, suggests *The Detroit News*. "It is clear that the retailer's previous management team engaged in highly questionable behavior—and that the firm's board of directors was too passive in granting department managers millions of dollars in 'retention loans' as the firm's fortunes plummeted," the newspaper reports.[23] In fact, *BusinessWeek* named the Kmart board one of the worst in the nation in 2002 and charged that the board should have been more active in overseeing its executives. One of the directors who later became CEO, Jim Adamson, claims that the board was out of the loop on some issues, saying "We weren't told everything. There are a lot of things that took place where I wish that the management team had been more forthright."[23]

By now it is clear that management under the Conaway regime did virtually everything in its power to mislead the board regarding executive activities, so its members can't be expected to have unearthed misdoings when it took two government agencies several months to sort it all out. Where the board can be faulted is in its approach to executive oversight. Believing that its role was to be reactive rather than proactive, the board waited for management to report problems rather than keeping a closer eye on the situation. What it felt the need to focus on is unclear. That the company is now restating three years of financial reports indicates that the board's audit committee "failed to keep track of management's accounting," says *The Detroit News*. Essentially, "The Kmart board waited too long to act."[23]

Even on more obvious issues, such as former CEO Chuck Conaway's failed attempt to beat Wal-Mart at its everyday low pricing claim in 2001, Adamson indicates the board had no confidence in his success going in. "We at the board said, it's logistically, humanly impossible to do. You put a sign up, your competitors change their price, and you have to put a new sign up. So you can't even manage it," states Adamson in a *BusinessWeek* interview.[24] This is why the board gave its approval only for a test run of 8,000 items. Conaway and Mark Schwartz, however, apparently took it on themselves to expand that test to more then 40,000 inventory items.[25] "That was the beginning of a flawed marketing strategy that wasn't aimed just at Wal-Mart." In fact, Target sued Kmart over the "Dare to Compare" campaign and the two companies settled out of court.

Calling it "mistake number two," Adamson describes the scenario of challenging Wal-Mart on price, as Kmart did. "You look back and say, when you're going to forge your competitive niche, you don't want that to be your competitor's strength. You'd like to look for their weakness. So it would have failed Day One to try to take them on, because . . . they'd just lower their price. You don't win that game."[24] This makes all the more puzzling that Kmart proceeded to do just that—taking on discount retailers that were far better positioned to win such a contest. Why did the board permit management to proceed with a strategy that was, by their own admission, obviously flawed?

As Adamson sees it, it is not the board's job to question a CEO's strategy. "At the end of the day, the board's job is to manage, hire, and fire the CEO, it is not to run the business. And it is not to micromanage his decisions. The day the board steps in and starts telling the CEO what to do, you might as well get a new CEO."[24] Kmart's newest CEO, Julian Day, with the backing of Adamson, decided to get a new board.

A year after filing for bankruptcy, the company decided to dump its existing nine-member board of directors and let its creditors choose a new one.[26] As part of the retailer's reorganization plan, Kmart has started over with a new board post-bankruptcy, with four of the directors to be chosen by its major investors, ESL Investments Inc. and Third Avenue Trust, which are providing as much as $352 million in exchange for stock of the reorganized company; two by bankers; and two by the unsecured creditors' committee.[26] One member of Kmart's management team, Day, also will join the board.

As the board begins to meet, however, Kmart needs to set some ground rules to tell its board where it is expected to focus its attention. Is it responsible for overseeing executive decisions? Should it be expected to ferret out corruption and fraud? To what degree is it expected to monitor executive activities? Just as Kmart the company needs to find its focus to be successful, its board of directors needs to learn where it should be devoting most of its time and attention. What is its focus? What is its role? And how can it best achieve its objectives?

Bankruptcy

By filing for bankruptcy protection, Kmart management hoped to be able to regain focus. Explains Professor Lars Perner of the University of California, Riverside, "Kmart had this vicious cycle, started spiraling downward and management presumably got tied up in a lot of fire fighting. They had to deal with the media problems, 'how do we meet our accounts payable,' and they had to worry about all the stores that were run down—all sorts of different things." Bankruptcy protection could take the pressure off to immediately solve the company's liquidity issues and allow management to focus on how to permanently repair the company's weaknesses.

Before getting to that stage, however, Kmart needed to focus on how to make the most of its protection from creditors. Evaluating its lease obligations and store performance was one issue, as was the need to carve out a defensible niche, which Kmart hasn't had for decades. Prior to emerging from bankruptcy, Kmart needed to identify what fires it was currently fighting that it could put out through the help of the bankruptcy court. Some experts question whether the hasty exit from bankruptcy protection actually gave the company enough time to identify and address those key issues.

For little more than a year, CEO Adamson was focused on finding a way to bring Kmart out of bankruptcy stronger than ever. Its filing of a reorganization plan in January 2003 was the culmination of his work to develop a plan for paying off its creditors, shedding unproductive assets without financial repercussions, and paving a way for the company to be profitable in an industry with three major players. Days before the plan was filed, Adamson turned over the reins to Julian Day, former president and chief operating officer, now president and chief executive officer, charged with returning Kmart to profitability.

The government investigations of former executives' misdeeds continues, however, even as Kmart struggles to move on. To try and refocus on current operations, rather than the past, Kmart has set up a litigation trust to pay for attorneys' fees in connection with any lawsuits that may be filed against former managers.[27] If federal or internal investigations yield evidence that managers acted improperly, Kmart intends to sue them to recover funds paid out while they were employees. Given the sizable signing bonuses, compensation packages, and retention loans, those numbers could add up quickly. However, getting beyond bankruptcy is Kmart's first challenge.

Finding Its Way

To develop a focus, which Kmart clearly has lost, the company needs an "all-encompassing vision"—a concept that synthesizes what Kmart wants to be, says Al Ries. He explains, "In the conventional view, strategy is a tent. You stake out your tent big enough so it can hold everything you might possibly want to get into," but not so big as to make your tent structurally weak. An "'everything for everybody' strategy is not going to work. Companies are going to have to refocus themselves on a single idea or concept," advises Ries.

Whether Kmart is willing or able to do that remains to be seen. Its current focus on its ethnic customers, urban markets, neighborhood store positioning, building its private label and licensed brands, and converting its stores to create a more satisfying environment for mothers of young children doesn't seem to be a focus at all. Rather, these seem to be several potential focuses that the company is trying out. But will Kmart ever be willing to choose one and only one differentiating factor and stick with it? It wasn't able to back when Harry Cunningham was in charge, but Julian Day may be a stronger leader.

The wild card is the external forces that pushed Kmart into bankruptcy in the first place: intense competitors, unpredictable consumers, and fluctuating product demand. Although Kmart once may have been arrogant enough to believe it could control or guide consumer purchases and overcome strong competitors, hopefully it has now learned the truth.

Notes

1. "Refocusing the corporation," by Al Ries, Poolonline.com, Spring 1999 issue.
2. *FOCUS: The Future of Your Company Depends on It,* by Al Ries. New York: HarperBusiness, 1996.
3. Phone interview with Cathy Halligan, Prophet, January 29, 2003.
4. "Redesign may be more modest," by Jennifer Bott, *Detroit Free Press,* January 25, 2003.
5. "Fleming says it may stop supplying Kmart," Associated Press, January 24, 2003.

6. "Grocery supplier out at Kmart," by Karen Dybis, *The Detroit News,* February 4, 2003.

7. "Kmart's ex-grocer files for bankruptcy," by Steve Matthews, *Bloomberg News,* April 2, 2003.

8. "Kmart mired in identity crisis," by Anne D'Innocenzio, Associated Press, January 23, 2002.

9. "Big discounters turn warlike in fight for customers," by Anne D'Innocenzio, Associated Press, August 25, 2001.

10. "Commentary: Kmart's shopping list for survival," by Joann Muller, *BusinessWeek,* March 25, 2002.

11. "Top 25 food retailers, 1999," www.producecareers.com, January 21, 2003.

12. "Kmart must cut stores, carve niche," by Andrea Lillo, *Home Textiles Today,* January 28, 2002.

13. "Kmart facts," kmartforever.com, May 6, 2003.

14. "Grocery supplier out at Kmart," by Karen Dybis, *The Detroit News,* February 4, 2003.

15. "Kmart looks within for CIO," compiled by Meredith Levinson, *CIO Magazine,* July 1, 2002.

16. "Kmart to close 326 stores and shed over 30,000 jobs," Associated Press, January 14, 2003.

17. "Kmart Corp.-History," Gale Gale Group Business & Company Resource Center file online, May 6, 2002.

18. Kmart's corporate timeline at its web site announced that Kmart had 2,000 stores by 1981, www.kmartcorp.com.

19. "Kmart's 20-year identity crisis," Knowledge@Wharton www.knowledge. wharton.upenn.edu, January 30, 2002.

20. "A study in contrasts," by Greg Jacobson, *Mass Market Retailers,* May 27, 2002.

21. "Kmart pins comeback on 'neighborhood' plan," by Mike Hudson, *The Detroit News,* January 26, 2003.

22. "What happened at Kmart? Customers knew things were going downhill," PlanetFeedback press release, January 25, 2002.

23. "Lax Kmart board compounded woes," *The Detroit News,* January 16, 2003.

24. "Kmart's new CEO: 'Who is Kmart?'" BusinessWeek Online, March 15, 2002.

25. "Schwartz attacked Kmart stores, assaulted rival Wal-Mart," by Bill Vlasic et al, *The Detroit News,* June 23, 2002.

26. "Kmart files plan of reorganization," Associated Press, January 24, 2003.

27. "The internal investigation," by John Gallagher, *Detroit Free Press,* January 25, 2003.

Strategy du Jour

In 1962, the year that the first Kmart and Wal-Mart both opened, the business models of both companies were the same—selling nationally advertised brand names at lower prices than department stores. Both companies were founded by charismatic men, Sebastian Spering Kresge and Sam Walton, respectively, who recognized the consumer's growing preference for discount goods, were committed to a national presence for their stores, and were frugal to the bone. Both came from dime and variety store beginnings, Kresge through his S.S. Kresge chain and Walton through his ownership of Ben Franklin locations; both took on early business partners; and both appeared to truly value the contributions of their employees, providing leading profit-sharing and benefit programs for workers. Wal-Mart has remained true to that vision, but Kmart has veered off course in a variety of ways, and at a number of times.

Wal-Mart clearly defined its business model—sell a large inventory at rock-bottom prices to customers in rural areas—and made significant investments in its infrastructure early on. Kmart, in contrast, decided to establish its stores in higher-rent urban areas and its blueprint for growth was opening new stores—an average of 200 a year. But opening new stores did nothing to grow sales at its existing stores, which languished.

Unfortunately for Kmart, its flawed business model worked for a while, lulling the company into believing it had a superior strategy—set up shop in most major metropolitan areas.

Kmart's second CEO and the true architect of the discount format, Harry Cunningham, had a vision for a chain that sold customers quality merchandise at prices lower than department stores. Although Kmart today is known more for its licensed brands, such as Martha Stewart and JOE BOXER, in the late 1960s it differentiated itself by selling nationally advertised brand names at lower prices, filling in its inventory with private label goods only when brand-name products were not available.

Even Sam Walton praised Kmart and Cunningham, stating in *Wal-Mart: A History of Sam Walton's Retail Phenomenon*, "I'll bet I've been in more Kmarts than anybody—and I would really envy their merchandise mix and the way they presented it. So much about their stores was superior to ours back then that sometimes I felt like we couldn't compete."[1] Cunningham's vision for Kmart, much like Walton's for Wal-Mart, was "mainly brand-name merchandise at discount prices all the time."[1] However, Kmart started to veer from the new retailing concept that Cunningham had developed and to which Walton stayed true.

Expanding Beyond Its Comfort Zone

Spying an opportunity to expand its new Kmart store format, management began its aggressive new store push in the 1960s and 1970s. This new strategy took the company off course in a couple of ways that would prove dangerous: its new store focus took attention off existing stores, which became shabby shopping environments, and its turn toward private-label goods to boost profits shifted away from name brands that consumers recognized.[1]

Another misstep when it came to expansion, says the author of *Wal-Mart*, Sandra Stringer Vance, was Kmart's abandonment of Cunningham's big-store format in favor of a smaller layout. "Cunningham's successor, Robert E. Dewar, started opening Kmart stores in towns with populations of 15,000 to 20,000, and he was convinced that these smaller markets required smaller stores."[2] Instead of opening 80,000-square-foot outlets, as Cunningham envisioned, Dewar chose to downsize to 40,000-square-foot stores, which carried fewer product lines and less inventory in general.

This strategy didn't last long, however, because within a few years, Kmart saw its profits plunge, moving from 3.1 percent in 1976 to 1.3 percent in 1980.[2] Wal-Mart, in contrast, stuck with its standard-size store, built them in smaller markets, such as those Kmart tried to enter, and did well. Its size and selection were far superior to existing retailers in the smaller markets, giving Wal-Mart a significant advantage.

Kmart's store upgrade program is a perfect example of weak execution by Kmart management, says Professor Paul Argenti of the Tuck School at Dartmouth. "It took Kmart five years to figure out what they needed to do and then it took too long to do it." At that point, Wal-Mart had blown by Kmart in size, market share, and customer base. "They were five years too late."

Private-Label Push

During the 1970s, Kmart started to change course from its initial mission of selling branded merchandise at lower prices, compliments of CEO number 3, Robert Dewar, who chose to replace expensive brand-name products with higher-margin private-label goods. It was during this time that the Kmart "K" was emblazoned on a variety of products, from garden accessories to housewares. Although private-label products have higher profit potential, they also require a much greater marketing and branding investment in order to position the brand name correctly. Any company hoping to establish a new consumer brand must be prepared to invest heavily in brand-building activities. Whether Kmart committed to making this investment is unclear, but what is clear is that putting a "K" on various products was not a successful means of boosting sales. However, Kmart wouldn't give up.

At the urging of apparel division president Joseph Antonini, in 1984 Kmart launched into merchandising private-label apparel as a means of enticing shoppers back into the store. The first new celebrity-branded clothing line was from former Charlie's Angel Jaclyn Smith, which helped boost apparel's sales significantly, making it the fastest-growing business in the company.[3] By the time he was named CEO in 1987, Antonini had expanded his branding strategy beyond apparel and into other areas of the store. He shifted the company's strategy again, choosing to improve the quality of its private-label apparel in order to shed its cheap image, buying TV ads to promote the improved quality, and signing on celebrities to stand behind the products' caliber. He recruited race car driver Mario Andretti to promote automotive accessories, golfer Fuzzy Zoeller for golf products, and caterer Martha Stewart for kitchen products and housewares. With the help of these celebrities, Kmart's profits rose 19 percent, hitting $692 million on sales of nearly $26 billion.[3]

Growth through Acquisitions

Boosting Kmart's ailing sales became Antonini's next challenge, which he addressed by resuming Bernard Fauber's acquisitions strategy of the mid-1980s. Despite the fact that Fauber had initiated and then retreated from buying smaller companies, Antonini obviously felt he could make the strategy work. He set out to identify and buy small specialty retailers that had the potential for sizable sales growth. The acquisitions essentially became Antonini's hedge against continued falling sales at Kmart. Although the acquisitions added dollars to the bottom line, they also required a significant amount of attention—attention that Antonini should have been paying to the Kmart corporation as a whole. Which is why, a few years later, Kmart decided to divest itself of the specialty retailers so that it could focus on its core retailing business.

Return to Discount Retailing

"Realizing that Kmart's future lay in its core retail business, the company began shedding non-core assets and sprucing up its stores," reports a company history prepared by the Gale Group. And so began the process of selling off the retailers it had worked so hard to buy. Acquisitions became more than a strategy at Kmart, they were a cycle.

What triggered the massive sell-off? It's unclear, but the spark may have been Wal-Mart eclipsing Kmart in sales and market share in 1990. Whatever the reason, Kmart was clearly focused on making up for lost time in cleaning up its act. One of the first initiatives was renovating all of its stores, which were sorely in need of a makeover. During the next four years, Kmart stuck to its plan and successfully rejuvenated its stores by the end of Antonini's reign, which was coming.

Back to Basics

Once chain-wide sales fell in 1994, Kmart decided that change was needed at the top and named former Target CEO Floyd Hall as Kmart's CEO number 6 in 1995. Hall continued the divesture, selling and spinning off remaining ancillary operations so that management could focus on rebuilding Kmart's market position. Drawing on his experience at Target, Hall proffered a new emphasis on merchandising with brands, consumables, convenience, and culture as his watch words. A new advertising campaign featured comedienne Rosie O'Donnell and director Penny Marshall pointing out the great bargains at Kmart.

Supercenters

Starting with one supercenter in 1992, Kmart laid claim to combined grocery and general merchandise operations, increasing its supercenter locations to 96 by fiscal 1996 year end.[4] Fueled by visions of dramatically increasing sales taken from supermarket chains, Kmart intended to open three supercenters per year. Or at least, that's what Joseph Antonini intended. But Floyd Hall let the supercenter strategy languish as he focused on repairing the broken existing stores. Says Buckman, Buckman and Reid financial analyst Ulysses Yannas, "Floyd fixed all of the stores, but he didn't expand the supercenters. He kept playing with it but he knew that he couldn't run the supercenters the way they were positioned, mainly because he didn't have the supply chain organized properly." He continues, "Supercenter means produce. You'd better be good at it and you'd better be capable of doing it efficiently."

The company's vision was also supported by a major individual investor, Ron Burkle, who met with executives to encourage the company to pursue its supercenter strategy. He saw Kmart, as well as Wal-Mart, competing with smaller supermarket chains like those Burkle once owned (he also owned Kmart shares). But what gave Kmart the advantage, he told them, was that many of Kmart's stores could be very easily converted to supercenters.

As a result, Burkle invested $50 million to buy 8.7 percent of grocery distributor Fleming, as Kmart negotiated an exclusive agreement with the company to supply grocery and health and beauty products.[5] The multiyear agreement was designed to allow Kmart to focus on building its general merchandise business while relying on Fleming for its consumables. However, analysts immediately questioned Fleming's suitability, citing delivery delays and too few warehouses as evidence that it wasn't a good match. Although Kmart did end up having some issues with delivery, what killed the Fleming alliance was management's obsession with Wal-Mart. According to Burkle, Kmart executives became obsessed with trying to beat Wal-Mart, "instead of sticking to the strategy he had outlined."

"They went out and hired hundreds of ex-Wal-Mart executives," he claimed in a *New York Times* article, including Mark Schwartz, who led the charge on Wal-Mart. How this was going to further Kmart's supercenter strategy was lost on Burkle, who said, "We became concerned that they had a Wal-Mart strategy rather than a supercenter strategy," especially when Kmart opened a supercenter in Bentonville, Arkansas, mainly to get Wal-Mart's goat, it seems.

Burkle became convinced that management's eyes were not on the supercenter prize, but were permanently trained on Wal-Mart, when he learned that Chuck Conaway had a dartboard with an image of Wal-Mart's CEO, H. Lee Scott Jr., hanging in the Kmart boardroom. Managers who furthered the company's mission of beating Wal-Mart at the local level earned the chance to toss darts at the dartboard.[5] "I would never back a company that wanted to beat Wal-Mart," said Burkle, "but I would back a company that wanted to take market share away from supermarket chains and drugstore chains," which was the original strategy.[5]

Ultimately, Fleming did end up having difficulty meeting the terms of its Kmart contract and was let out of the obligation in February 2003 as part of Kmart's bankruptcy proceedings. According to Gary Giblen of the New York–based research and equity trading services firm C. L. King & Associates, part of Fleming's problem had been that it "has had a very bad delivery performance for Kmart. They low-balled the bid and then they couldn't deliver."[5]

So where does Kmart go from here? Having rid itself of a costly distribution arrangement, some analysts suggest the company should get out of food altogether. Others think a move toward more food is the way to go. Shari Schwartzman Eberts, a retail analyst at J.P. Morgan Chase offered that "perhaps [Kmart] should focus more on food and consumables and less on general merchandise," although she also allowed that "another iteration would be to focus on general merchandise and less on the food and consumables."[5] The upshot is that Kmart should either divest itself fully of food, or pursue it with a vengeance. Pick a strategy and stick with it.

Everyday Low Prices

Chuck Conaway, CEO number 7, made a valiant effort to turn the company around with a strategy heavily reliant on promotions, even reintroducing the formerly popular BlueLight Special promotions of Kmart's early days. Unfortunately, the BlueLight almost meant lights out for the company. The BlueLight Always program of 2001 lowered prices on about 45 percent of Kmart's merchandise[6] in an attempt to beat Wal-Mart's "everyday low prices" claim. Former CEO Jim Adamson points out that the BlueLight Always campaign also took on Target and anyone else in the market with signs that compared prices—it "wasn't aimed just at Wal-Mart."[7] However, the move backfired and ended up costing Kmart dearly.

"As Kmart lowered prices on more than 30,000 products, Wal-Mart lowered its prices further, capturing shoppers that Kmart had hoped to snare," reported a *New York Times* article.[8] Not only did Kmart damage itself financially in the short term by engaging in a price war it could never win, but the company ended up causing irreparable long-term damage through its customer defections. It also realized a 1 percent drop in same-store sales in December while Wal-Mart saw an 8 percent gain,[6] not the results Kmart had hoped for.

"The only way I can explain the Conaway decision to discount prices is a desperate attempt to generate some quick cash to build liquidity," says James Harris of Seneca Financial. "There is no strategic reason that I can see to explain this decision. At the time, Kmart was losing so much volume to Wal-Mart and Target that they obviously felt they had to do something." "Bringing back the BlueLight was just a bad move," comments Mike Porter of Morningstar.

Exacerbating the problem for Kmart was its lack of merchandise replenishment system that was up to the task of tracking inventory levels on sale items. And management didn't plan ahead for sudden increases in demand. Comments a former employee, "Planning and execution must be done prior to the roll-out of a given strategy, not after the fact. This was the case with BlueLight Always items, which should have been pool-stocked, instead of being out for six weeks after the prices were lowered."[9]

Why did Kmart think it could out–Wal-Mart Wal-Mart? No one seems to have an answer. "You don't start a war where you have all the disadvantages," says Gary Giblen of C.L. King.[5] In fact, it seems pretty clear to most observers that Wal-Mart had signaled its intention to remain the low-price leader—no matter what. Says Wharton's Professor Stephen Hoch, "Wal-Mart has been very clear about indicating that they are willing to absorb the pain and that they can absorb the pain because they have got a much lower cost structure." Apparently, the "frat boys," as Conaway and his management team were called, mistakenly believed they had a higher threshold for pain.

Cutback on Advertising

If challenging Wal-Mart directly was Kmart's first mistake of 2001, slashing its advertising budget close to 50 percent was its second. When a promotional retailer suddenly changes course and cuts back on the engine that drives customer traffic into its stores, upheaval is next. And that's what Kmart faced as a consequence. To find cash in his $500 million ad budget for the $25 million summer BlueLight Always broadcast and outdoor advertising blitz, Chuck Conaway cut way back on newspaper circulars—as much as 50 percent in September and October of that year.[10] Conaway's "catastrophic move,"[11] as CFO Al Koch called it, resulted in lowered prices, lowered traffic, and lower sales—5 percent lower in October alone. Although weekday traffic remained the same or increased slightly, Kmart's weekend sales figures were way down.[10] Of course, Wal-Mart and Target took ample opportunity to beef up their own promotions once they saw Kmart pull back.

The reasoning behind the reduced ad budget was apparently a cost-cutting measure designed to offset "additional expenses for higher utility rates and employee compensation."[11] Unfortunately, the fall in sales cost the company far more than any potential savings. Of its $2.42 billion in losses for the year, due primarily to "strategic mistakes,"[8] nearly $1 billion was due to lower sales.[11] "They cut back mass advertising too quickly," says Frank Badillo, senior retail economist at Retail Forward, Inc. "Customers were expecting advertising circulars every week and reacting to them. Kmart needed to overlap strategies for a longer time,"[10] rather than suddenly shifting gears.

Beyond promotional circulars, one strategic mistake was not communicating the significance of the BlueLight. "Was BlueLight a business strategy or a communications strategy?" one executive who worked on Kmart advertising asked, commenting that the Blue Light positioning confused even those working on the campaign.[12] Obviously, if the folks working on a campaign don't know if it's a strategy or a marketing ploy, it's not a strategy—or at least not an effective one.

Web Marketing

If a focus on acquisitions was one of Kmart's big mistakes, then a lack of focus on the Internet would be another one. But at least the company was persistent. When Floyd Hall did initiate a corporate e-commerce site with the help of the experts, it was in

1999, years after the "information superhighway" had become a buzzword, and after two previous unsuccessful in-house attempts to build an Internet presence.[13] "There was one last chance to make this work," conceded David Karraker, Bluelight.com's spokesperson. "What we wanted to do with BlueLight is take the best of what Kmart has, bring that online, and then expand it."[13]

Kmart's online venture, Bluelight.com, debuted in 1999, a few months before Wal-Mart.com's official relaunch and four months after Target.com debuted.[14] Funded by Kmart, Softbank Venture Capital and Softbank Capital, and Martha Stewart Omnimedia, Bluelight.com raised $142.5 million in two rounds of financing ($55 million from Kmart, $75 million from Softbank, and $12.5 million from Martha Stewart Omnimedia)[15] to get underway in November 1999,[16] bringing in experienced e-commerce pioneers to run that part of its business, which was kept separate from Kmart corporate. But Kmart owned 60 percent of it.[17]

It started off with an innovative strategy—build a customer base by offering free Internet access in return for increased shopping at the web site. Working through Spinway Inc., Kmart offered free Internet access to subscribers, raking in more than 4 million subscribers after only nine months of operations.[18] It would have surely continued to grow if Spinway hadn't shut down a year later, forcing Bluelight.com to take over the service itself in December 2000.[19] One new difference, however, was that high-volume Internet customers—those who spent more than 25 hours per month online—faced a fee.[18]

To Kmart's credit, the site continued to grow, achieving an 823 percent increase in traffic from November 2000 to February 2001 and sales that grew 1,060 percent for November/December 2000.[20] Bluelight.com ran into trouble with costs rising too quickly, so Kmart bought the remaining 40 percent of the business from investors in 2001 and took a $120 million pretax restructuring charge to cover it.[17] After filing for bankruptcy, the company decided to sell off Bluelight.com to raise funds, netting $8.4 million from United Online, now headed by Mark Goldstein of the initial Bluelight.com team.[21] The reason? Kmart wanted to focus only on its core retailing business.[22]

Kmart continues to host its own e-commerce site at Kmart.com, where customers have access to a selection of Kmart goods online. Where the site now fits in its overall business strategy is unclear, but it appears it will play a role, albeit smaller.

The Quick Fix

Historically, each successive Kmart CEO has tried to cure its ills with quick fixes, rather than a thorough, long-term growth strategy based on a proven business model. Frequently, Kmart leaders were pressured to immediately show sales improvements before being allowed to develop long-term programs. Unfortunately, few were ever strong enough to avert their attention from the short-term panaceas to come up with larger visions for the company.

Antonini, for instance, decided it was easier to look beyond Kmart, to specialty retailers, for fast growth. But how those organizations were to be incorporated into Kmart's operating structure was never worked out, it appears, perhaps because there was no long-term strategy for its acquisitions. The strategy was growth by any means—fast. Next, Floyd Hall recognized that implementing a supercenter strategy was useless until Kmart got its supply chain organized properly, says analyst Yannas. As a result, neither supercenter growth or Kmart's supply chain really ever got sorted out completely.

In addition to a history of trying to cure its ills with a quick-fix strategy, a related Kmart problem is weak execution. Even when management developed and introduced a new approach, actual implementation was slow and plodding. Conaway overpromised and underdelivered on results, primarily because from the start of his appointment, the board made it clear that results were expected in short order. Consequently, he beefed up his staff, announced a sweeping overhaul of the IT infrastructure, decided that cutting costs would drive up sales, and then was replaced in less than two years when results didn't materialize.

Adamson was given even less time to get Kmart back on its feet, with a handsome, multimillion dollar incentive if he did it in record time. In just about 18 months, if he could take Kmart through a whirlwind bankruptcy filing and come out the other end without the baggage of money-losing stores and creditor obligations, he would earn millions. That's quite an incentive to try and shore up any company. Julian Day, Kmart's current CEO, hasn't been in place long enough to execute any strategies, but his recently signed multiyear contract gives hope that he'll be around long enough to develop and implement some longer-term fixes to Kmart's troubles.

Who's fault is it that Kmart has adopted a short-term focus? The board of directors, who approve the strategies and set goals in conjunction with senior management. Although board members rarely get involved in the minutiae of everyday business management, they nevertheless weigh in on which tactics should be tried and which should not.

Outsourcing

An outgrowth of its quick-fix strategy was Kmart's frequent use of turnkey suppliers—suppliers that assume control of the bulk of the activities for a Kmart department. Examples include Kmart's fleet of trucks, which are outsourced, its food distribution, which was formerly handed over to Fleming to manage, and some of its information technology development, which is frequently handed off to consultants and software development firms.

Although in the short term such agreements ensure that customer needs are met without major capital investments, in the long term, Kmart loses control over important aspects of its business. But because of its lower upfront costs, outsourcing has become an increasingly popular business tool. Unfortunately, companies can quickly become reliant on outsourced services and hand off critical responsibility to their suppliers, who may or may not have the companies' best interests at heart.

By outsourcing its fleet operations, for example, Kmart effectively handed over responsibility for timely deliveries to its supplier. Keeping its drivers at arms length was probably not the best strategy for improving its operations. Instead of being Kmart employees, committed and incentivized to help the company achieve higher levels of performance, the drivers' priorities are more related to speed and delivery quantities, rather than operational efficiency and continuous improvement. Just looking in the back of a Kmart delivery truck and a Wal-Mart truck provides an excellent peek at how the companies operate, commented one observer. Describing a tour he took of a well-run Kmart distribution center, Professor Bart Weitz of the University of Florida said that the manager of the center often sees trucks pull in that have half of the truck stocked with Wal-Mart merchandise and half stocked with inventory for Kmart. The manager commented, "I can't believe how well, how all of the Wal-Mart stuff is labeled and put on the pallets and our stuff is just thrown in there." It's a culture issue that Kmart is struggling with in other areas of the company as well. The upshot is that by hiring an intermediary to get work done, Kmart has no control.

Likewise, Kmart's ill-fated alliance with Fleming to provide consumable deliveries worked on paper, with Kmart avoiding major investments in its own trucks, personnel, and warehouse space. But when Kmart ran into cash difficulties, instead of being able to shuffle budget allocations around from department to department, Fleming cut the company off. Until invoices were brought current, the company simply stopped delivering product. But without product on its shelves, Kmart couldn't make the money needed to pay off Fleming. So it filed for bankruptcy.

Now Kmart is considering self-distribution as a way to reduce delivery turnaround time, control quality, and save money. And since supercenters may no longer be the cornerstone of its growth strategy going forward, a powerhouse supplier like Fleming may not be needed, say the analysts. "Fleming is critically important for supercenters," says Richard Hastings, retail analyst with Cyber Business Credit LLC, a business credit consulting firm. "Fleming is not as critical for general merchandise."[23]

Although technology outsourcing is more common, it, too, brings up issues of control and integration. With teams in-house and at consulting firms working on various aspects of Kmart's IT puzzle, there are bound to be issues of control, process, and implementation that arise. Although the company may achieve faster turnaround on projects by handing them off to outsiders, it may also lose time when it has to re-integrate them with the rest of the system. At a time when Kmart is struggling to gain control of its operations, outsourcing just seems to be the wrong strategy.

Consolidation

James Adamson, CEO number 8, was given the reins as chairman and CEO at Kmart shortly after the bankruptcy filing in 2002. What impressed analysts was his willingness to admit that he didn't have all the answers and to frankly describe the challenges the company faced. One of the first things Kmart did under Adamson's leadership was to announce store closings and layoffs, trimming the chain's locations to about 1,800 and its employee base to about 220,000. But the first round of cuts was not enough and in January 2003, an additional 326 stores were slated for closing with an associated 37,000 job cuts.

Although Kmart has never before faced such a drastic pullback, retail industry watchers agree with the company's strategy. Many suggest that Kmart simply doesn't have the resources or brand strength to continue as a national player and that consolidation into a regional player—such as in the Northeast—would be a wise move.

Urban Strategy

Although for years one of Kmart's strongest market segments has been urban customers, until recently the company has never capitalized on this fact. Some of Kmart's best-performing stores are in urban centers, where they serve a high proportion of African-American, immigrant, and Hispanic customers. So far, the bulk of its urban locations have been spared from store closings, either because their performance was above average, or they provide access to ethnic consumers, or both.

Because Kmart established itself early as an urban retailer, competitors have so far stayed out of its stronghold. Wal-Mart's preference for building its stores from scratch and its need for transportation access severely limit its ability to effectively penetrate a metro area. Mike Porter of Morningstar confirms, "Urban areas are one area Wal-Mart has stayed out of." Target, too, has mainly stayed in the suburbs. But that may be changing, as Wal-Mart has indicated plans to penetrate major cities.

Day's intention to target urban populations, who have a higher proportion of Hispanic and African-American shoppers, was actually one of Chuck Conaway's strategies. *Women's Wear Daily* reports that Conaway stated his intent to pursue those market segments back in November 2000.[24] However, it wasn't until Jim Adamson took the helm during bankruptcy that Kmart began moving solidly in that direction, signing a licensing deal with Latin pop star Thalia for an apparel line and hiring African-American and Hispanic celebrities to appear in upcoming Kmart commercials. It was also Conaway who had stated an intention to improve Kmart's logistics functioning so that the company could better tailor its inventory on a local level. But it was Adamson who finally allowed Chicago area store managers to determine how much consumables inventory should be ordered for their stores, as a test of the concept.

Bright Lights, Wider Aisles

New management's testing of a prototype store design, featuring bright lights, wider aisles, less inventory, and a layout that showcases its celebrity brands, although a move in the right direction, also harkens back to Floyd Hall's vision of the new Big K format. Back then, as now, Kmart aimed to shine the focus on its Martha Stewart Everyday line and entice shoppers back into its stores.

The good news is that the strategy worked back then. Sales rose steadily, from $31.4 billion during Hall's first full year as CEO, in 1996, to $37 billion in 2000, his last.[24] What's different about Julian Day's newly designed stores is that they do not represent a format change, per se. Yes, the stores look radically different, but because they are operating on the same footprint as the former stores, it could be argued the upgrades are not actually a growth strategy. Perhaps a survival strategy would be more accurate.

A Recurring Theme

It appears that Kmart may have become trapped in a feedback loop that it couldn't exit. From 1995, when Floyd Hall became CEO, to 2002, when Adamson took the lead, Kmart's key result areas—the issues the company recognized that it needed to fix in order to be successful—remained the same. In describing his strategy for turning the company around, Hall stated "We will do this through better merchandise assortments, improved in-stock positions, cleaner stores, and better customer service,"[24] which indicates that these were the company's biggest weaknesses at the time.

Once Conaway assumed the CEO post, he reported, "To assure continued progress in 2001, we're focusing on what we call our 'Big Five' initiatives: fixing the supply chain . . . , improving marketing effectiveness . . . , making food world-class . . . , reducing SG&A and improving our bottom 250 stores . . . ," which sounds like the same thing as Hall said, but using different words.

Adamson echoed what Hall and Conaway had presented as their priorities, explaining, "The issue is what we do inside the store from an execution standpoint for each merchandise category. We're trying to fix this company store-by-store based on the location [each] is in."[24] Changing strategies frequently is the sign of a poorly managed company, but repeating the same strategies and hoping for different results is just lunacy.

A New Day

When Julian Day, Kmart's president, was named CEO in January 2003, replacing Jim Adamson as the company prepared to exit bankruptcy, the move signaled a new era for Kmart. Already, during the company's bankruptcy Day has been instrumental in helping Kmart change gears, identify its strengths, work on its weaknesses, and move forward with a sense of urgency.

To help Kmart get out of its middle-of-the-road positioning between price-conscious Wal-Mart and style-focused Target, Day has pointed Kmart in the direction of community-based marketing and micromerchandising. Complementary concepts, both involve having Kmart stores tailor their inventories to the shopping preferences of their local audience. What Kmart is finally doing, as well, is facing up to the influence of its Hispanic and African-American customers, who have become an important market segment for the retailer, albeit previously ignored. But are they a lucrative enough market for Kmart to commit to serving them long term? Hopefully, yes. But if sales from ethnic consumers don't rise with Kmart's additional marketing efforts, we may see yet another strategy introduced.

Notes

1. *Wal-Mart: A History of Sam Walton's Retail Phenomenon,* by Sandra Stringer Vance. New York: Twayne Publishers, 1994, p. 61.
2. *Wal-Mart: A History of Sam Walton's Retail Phenomenon,* p. 62.
3. "Kmart Corp.-History," Gale Group Business & Company Resource Center file online, January 21, 2002.
4. Kmart 1997 Fact Book.
5. "Is Kmart out of stock in answers," by Constance Hays, *New York Times,* March 17, 2002.
6. "Kmart mired in identity crisis," by Anne D'Innocenzio, Associated Press, January 23, 2002.
7. "Kmart's New CEO: "Who is Kmart?" BusinessWeek Online, March 15, 2002.
8. "Kmart reports $2.42 billion annual loss," by Constance L. Hays, *New York Times,* May 16, 2002.
9. "Target vs. Kmart—a store-level view," by Rick Wingate, *DSN Retailing Today,* May 6, 2002.
10. "Kmart's 5 big blunders," by Joanna Krotz, Microsoft bCentral.com, September 24, 2002.
11. "Kmart loses $2.4 billion," by Karen Talaski, *Detroit News,* May 16, 2002.
12. "Kmart's bluelight dims," by Alice Cuneo, *Ad Age,* January 22, 2002.
13. "Bricks-and-mortar retailers go online," by Jonathan Burton, Ciscosystems.com, January/February 2001.
14. "Orbitz launch among best in e-commerce history," by Michael Pastore, Jupiter Research, July 10, 2001.
15. "Now web bargains for Kmart," by Christopher Heun, *Information Week,* August 21, 2000.

16. "Ominous news for BlueLight.com," by Miguel Helft, *Industry Standard,* May 24, 2001.

17. "Kmart, turned off by bluelight.com, renames Web site," by Amy Merrick, *The Wall Street Journal,* June 20, 2002.

18. "The strategy behind Bluelight.com," by Cheryl Cohen, Digitrends. net, February 1, 2001.

19. "Two more free ISPs bow out," ISP Planet, December 4, 2000.

20. "Churn," by Dan Verton, *Computerworld,* February 5, 2001.

21. "United Online posts first profit," by Julia Angwin, *The Wall Street Journal,* November 10, 2002.

22. "U.S. court approves Kmart sale of Bluelight.com," Reuters, October 30, 2002.

23. "Kmart to distribute groceries by itself," Reuters, February 5, 2003.

24. "Coming around again: Kmart's new ideas bear a familiar ring," by Vicki Young, *Women's Wear Daily,* October 28, 2002.

10

Repeating the Same Mistakes

"What mistakes didn't they make?" asks Rob Gelphman of Gelphman Associates, expressing the exasperation of so many consumers, analysts, and consultants who have watched Kmart through the years. Kmart seemed to zig when it should have zagged, changed when it should have hung on to its mission, stayed put when it should have pursued new operating strategies, and so on. Where its competitors moved from point A to point B to point C, Kmart opted to try some shortcuts that ended up putting them behind. And now that they're behind, it's unclear whether they'll be able to catch up at all.

Even if Kmart can iron out its problems, correct its deficiencies, and get on the right path, who's to say the company will be willing to stay on the straight and narrow? Time and again, Kmart has made decisions that seem to fly in the face of practicality or common sense. In many cases, the same mistake has been made more than once. Instead of learning from its mistakes, as strong companies do, Kmart seems incapable of applying the knowledge it has at its disposal. In other cases, the company has preferred to ignore useful information, frequently making questionable decisions as a result.

Going on Gut

During the 1970s, Kmart started to veer from its initial mission of selling branded merchandise at lower prices, choosing to replace name-brand products with higher-margin private-label goods. It was Robert Dewar's charter to reposition Kresge's Kmart stores as leading discount destinations.

In 1982, like Dewar, Kmart's next CEO, Bernard Fauber, launched into merchandising designer and branded apparel at a discount as a means of enticing shoppers back into the store and boosting its profits. Whereas Kmart's strategy in the 1960s and 1970s had been to sell nationally known goods that could be turned over quickly, Fauber would bank on higher-end, higher-margin, branded merchandise. A big gamble, said many analysts, especially since Fauber had no research to back his contention that customers wanted branded clothes from Kmart. Jaclyn Smith was the first celebrity brand to be signed, followed later by Kathy Ireland clothing and Martha Stewart housewares. What was surprising in this case, was that Fauber relied on his gut, rather than on any kind of data or research. Granted, little data was available at that point to either support or refute his decision, primarily because Kmart as yet had not invested fully in technology. But Fauber took a big risk in changing the company's entire business strategy on a hunch.

During Antonini's watch, Kmart invested $1 billion in technology but then chose to continue to rely on the gut feel of its merchandising managers, who had no idea which products actually were selling best, for merchandise buys. Apparently, the expertise of its managers was considered a better gauge of customer purchase preferences than true sales data.

Starting Fresh with Each New Management Team

Once Kmart began its revolving CEO door in the 1990s, new issues and problems crept in. Initiatives introduced by one CEO that might have worked were shuttered and discarded by the new CEO, forcing the company to start its recovery from square one. Between 1995 and 2003, Kmart has had four CEOs; that's the equivalent of starting from scratch every two years. Making any significant progress on business issues gets more difficult as change occurs frequently at the top.

"One step forward, another step back," says David Carr, who writes about information technology for *Baseline* magazine and was quoted in a *Detroit Free Press* article. "Every time a new executive comes onboard, there are new directions and new programs, and it seems like everything else is pitched out, and they have to start all over again."[1] Instead of building on a previous leader's strategy and initiatives, Kmart CEOs preferred to wipe the slate clean. However, in recent years the company really couldn't afford to start from scratch.

Take its store upgrade program, for instance. Joseph Antonini began and completed the renovation and overhaul of all of Kmart's existing stores between 1990 and 1995. But by the time the format changes were made, maintenance taken care of, and renovations concluded, it was actually time to start the cycle once again.[2] But that never happened, because that year Antonini was replaced by Floyd Hall, who had a new management team and a new set of initiatives. After Hall came Chuck Conaway, who seemed to place a higher priority on information technology than store upgrades; Conaway was replaced shortly thereafter by James Adamson, who gave up the top spot a little less than a year after stepping in to steer the company through the bankruptcy process. Julian Day emphasizes the importance of store upgrades in the company's reorganization plan, but there is no evidence of a plan to renovate the entire chain, or even a plan to do partial renovations on the entire chain.

Creating and maintaining a consistent brand image, strategy, and vision have been difficult, if not impossible, for Kmart. Competitors like Wal-Mart and Kohl's face an easier task maintaining a consistent strategy when its CEOs stay onboard longer than a few years. Wal-Mart's founder Sam Walton was involved in the oversight of the company until his death in 1992. Although Wal-Mart's current CEO, H. Lee Scott, has been in place only since 2000, he has been a Wal-Mart employee since 1979. And his predecessor, David Glass, who is now chairman, had been president since 1984 and CEO since 1988, clearly having a lasting impression on the company. The current CEO at Kohl's, Larry Montgomery, is also a long-timer, having been with the company since 1988.[3]

Kmart's board seemed to grow ever more impatient with each new CEO, giving him less and less time to initiate wide-ranging programs designed to return Kmart to profitability. But their impatience served only to make the situation worse, by setting the company's progress back each time a new leader took office.

Short-term focus has crept in as a related problem for Kmart managers, who are compensated based on the progress they make in achieving goals set by senior management and the board of directors. Unfortunately, to raise shareholder value quickly, executives have been given incentives that require short-term business strategies and tactics at the expense of smarter, longer-term investments.

Despite the fact that new CEOs have the best intentions of devising and implementing long-term strategic initiatives, companies in crisis may appear to need short-term stopgap measures to placate the board and shareholders. The problem is that short-term initiatives often become de facto business strategies.

Store Upgrades, or Lack Thereof

At Kmart, greater attention was always paid to putting up new stores than to renovating existing stores, which frequently were allowed to become dingy, dirty, and disorganized before a new CEO would promise to invest in improvements. Old stores were forgotten, essentially. And despite each CEO's promises to improve stores' appearance, there were always higher priorities. Even as sales started declining and customer numbers were dropping, the only CEO who completely upgraded the entire Kmart chain was Antonini. And that was in 1995. Given the poor state Kmart was in as of the late 1980s, and the subsequent major "renewal" program that former CEO Antonini introduced, one would think that Kmart would aim not to let that happen again. And yet it has.[4]

Fast-forward from 1990 to 2002, as then-CEO James Adamson stated the need for store upgrades and renovations on a large scale, just as Antonini did. Same-store sales have been falling, sales chain-wide are down, and the stores are looking older and more tired every day. The large jump in sales the upgraded stores experienced in the mid-1990s should have been reason enough for Kmart to push ahead with another round of renovations, but so far that hasn't happened. The company's bankrupt status limits the extent to which Kmart stores can be improved, although virtually all of them are once again in need of a makeover. And Kmart's reorganization plan makes no mention of a chain-wide overhaul anytime soon.

During his brief tenure, Adamson oversaw the creation of a store prototype that is being tested in White Lake, Michigan, but the company has no plans to immediately update its remaining 1,500 stores. Adamson stressed the need to monitor the results from its five prototype stores (one in White Lake, Michigan, and four in Peoria, Illinois),[5] with the intention of applying best practices to its other stores chain-wide. Not all of its practices, just the best ones.

But how effective will those changes be if they are undertaken in a run-down, unkempt environment? If customers don't want to step foot in the door of a cluttered, dirty Kmart location, the terrific limited upgrades installed will be worth little. Who is going to notice that more merchandise is in stock if the lighting is still dim and the color scheme is drab? It is time now for Kmart to step up to the challenge and renovate its remaining stores. The $300 million saved from its last round of store closings should be invested back into much-needed renovations. Given the dramatic rise in sales renovated stores experienced in 1995, it's a mystery why Kmart would be holding back in this regard.

Format Shifts

Another change during Antonini's watch was that Kmart began opening smaller stores when it entered smaller cities, thinking that its larger-format stores were overkill for the audience. Despite the fact that customers seemed increasingly to prefer bigger stores, Kmart management elected to save money on construction by staying with the smaller-store format. Eventually, customers decided to shop elsewhere, at stores that carried a broader selection of in-stock merchandise.

In 1992 Antonini determined that a new store format should be introduced—the Big Kmart, a combination traditional Kmart and supermarket under one roof. Reversing its previous small-store strategy, Kmart planned that by year end 1993, 90 Super Kmarts, averaging 170,000 square feet versus 112,000 for a traditional Kmart, would be up and running, with a target of 500 total Super Kmarts. Kmart seemed to be vacillating from from small to big in terms of store footprint, all based on the same data.

Kmart's next CEO, Floyd Hall, had his own format idea—the Pantry, containing lower-margin food and drug items located at the front of the store—to lure shoppers back into Kmart for everyday items in the hopes that they would pick up higher-priced items on their way to the checkout counter. This idea is puzzling given research he cited: that Kmart's core customer is 55 years old with $20,000 in annual income and no kids—customers unlikely to be roaming the Kmart aisles taking advantage of higher-margin products. But in 1997 Hall also developed and pitched his Big Kmart format, which were simply better designed, better lighted, and less cluttered stores.

New store formats were created and then abandoned when a new CEO took over, costing Kmart in higher expenses and lost customers who became frustrated with the company and elected to shop elsewhere. Recent rumors are that the smaller Kmart format may be coming back, to enable the company to enter smaller markets with inventory tailored for the surrounding neighborhoods—a smart move that some analysts are skeptical Kmart can execute.

Ignoring Employees

All the while stating its commitment to its customers, Kmart has repeatedly done absolutely nothing to get to the root of its customer service problem—lack of employee involvement. That is, the company has placed the burden of satisfying customers on the shoulders of its employees without giving them any tools with which to do this. Nor any incentives. Reported one former area manager in 2002, "It was my job to insure great customer service and sales. It was too bad that the company did virtually everything it could to insure that the exact opposite of that occurred."[6] Unfortunately, that sentiment has been around for a while.

States John Tschohl, president of Minneapolis-based Service Quality Institute, "In 1991, Joseph Antonini, then Kmart's chief executive officer, spent some $80 million on an advertising campaign to convince customers that he and the company believed in customer service. Few customers believed him, however, and Kmart's sales increased by only 3 percent."[7] The same year, Wal-Mart's sales rose by 26 percent. A couple of years later, the company spent $3 billion on capital improvements in a move to recoup some of its lost customers, says Tschohl. It didn't work, mainly because Kmart still hadn't done anything to improve the quality of service customers received. Sure, it had cleaned up stores and increased the number of ads consumers were exposed to, but once they got into the stores, the story was the same—indifference, long waits, and rude help, hardly reasons to continue shopping there. Suggests Tschohl, "If the company had taken just 10 percent of its advertising or renovation budgets and used that money to train its employees in the art of customer service, Kmart might have realized profits similar to those of Wal-Mart."

One area where the company could have invested is in labor budgets. Kmart stores are frequently understaffed, reports the former area manager and anyone who's been in a Kmart store in the last decade. Most stores are allocated payroll dollars to cover the cost of their employees. Lower payroll allocations means fewer employees in the store at any one time. And fewer employees means lower quality of service. Kmart is at the bottom of the barrel on both counts.

The former manager reported that corporate policy and store reality often clashed when it came to staffing. "The company policy was that there were to be no more than three customers in line before other cashiers were called. Great idea. The problem was more often than not, there was no one to call because of the low hours (payroll budget). We sometimes conducted 'phantom pages' over the intercom to try and appease angry customers. It was sad to do, but sometimes we had to. At least the customers thought we were trying."[6] Confirms Britt Beemer of America's Research Group, "[Kmart] has to work on the attitude in their stores. You're not going to get excited to give your money to someone if they're not even going to say 'thank you' when they take it."[8]

Thinking Advertising Was the Answer

"Another mistake that Kmart made was not taking a holistic, orchestrated brand view when launching its marketing communications push in late 2002," says Cathy Halligan of Prophet. The company invested millions in expensive ads to drive customer traffic into its stores without making any changes to the customer experience once shoppers got there. So while consumers may have been enticed to visit a Kmart store once again, once they saw the still-dirty, disorganized, run-down environment inside, the experience solidified the reason why customers should never go back. In the end, Kmart probably did more harm than good with its major promotional campaign. "To drive people to broken stores was a total waste of money—a mistake," she says.

This wasn't the first time Kmart thought advertising was the answer to its customer woes. During the mid-1990s, Floyd Hall stocked up on inventory in preparation for surging customer demand once its advertising campaign succeeded in bringing shoppers in. But Kmart's inventory management system wasn't up to snuff, so despite the increased traffic, sales didn't climb as hoped.

Missed Opportunities

Kmart has never been very successful at maintaining a consistent brand image, strategy, and focus. Not to mention its weakness at implementing change. As Wharton's Professor Pete Fader states, "There is a blend of being consistent but changing with the times where Kmart keeps missing the beat."

There have been a number of occasions when Kmart missed the beat, or the boat. One such occasion was in the early 1980s when it retreated from its expansion into Super K formats just as Wal-Mart was aggressively moving ahead with its own super-center format. Not sensing the strategic timing of its decision, Kmart lost out. Wal-Mart moved ahead and now owns the combined general merchandise/grocery format that Kmart once dominated. Although Kmart has considered pushing ahead with its own Super K outlets now, as it exits bankruptcy, whether that is realistic in the long term seems questionable.

Kmart also missed the opportunity in the mid-1990s to be dominant in the home goods arena, a high-growth merchandise category. "Kmart had a compelling brand in the Martha Stewart Everyday Collection, an asset which, if deployed and supported correctly, could have positioned Kmart to be the destination for home goods," claims Prophet's Halligan. But Kmart only thought of Martha Stewart as access to branded products to plug a hole in their home goods offering and not as a platform.

Target, in contrast, developed a brand platform and viewed the Michael Graves Design™ collection not only as access to a branded assortment, but as a potential silver bullet brand—a brand that significantly enhances the image of another brand through a partnership or other affiliation. The Michael Graves brand did indeed become a silver bullet that has enabled Target to be credible as a compelling destination for home goods.

As part of its reorganization plan, Kmart indicated its interest in carving out a niche in home goods, positioning Kmart as a destination for home fashions with its Martha Stewart Everyday and JOE BOXER home brands. But Kmart today is not perceived by customers as a destination for home goods—Target and Kohl's are more credible and compelling in this category. Kmart is now the follower rather than the leader. "Kmart doesn't have a point of differentiation or a unique positioning" that separates it from its competitors, says Halligan.

Part of the problem is Kmart's lack of a brand strategy. Brand strategy is the face customers see of a business strategy, which answers the key questions: Which and how many brands will support the business strategy and corporate objectives? What is each brand's identity and purpose within the brand portfolio? How do the brands within the portfolio interrelate?

Kmart was a once-powerful brand that lost its relevance. It's still possible for Kmart to change its image the same way that IBM changed customer perception of its brand from a big blue, mainframe box to a leading-edge innovator through the launch of its ThinkPad, or the same way that Miata energized Mazda and XBOX rejuvenated Microsoft. Kmart does have brand assets it could strategically deploy in its portfolio, such as the BlueLight, Martha Stewart Everyday Collection, and Jaclyn Smith.

However, whereas Target's brand strategy is to build brand platforms, such as Michael Graves designs, which stretch across merchandise categories, Kmart restricts brands to one category, says Cathy Halligan. As a result, there are multiple brands that are not deployed as a portfolio. Doing so would provide synergy, clarity, and leverage to Kmart, but, as currently marketed, they are simply a collection of brands. The downside to this approach is that all of the brands are not supported and do not achieve a cohesive and compelling brand strategy. Instead of allowing Martha Stewart to cross platforms into new categories beyond home goods, Kmart has used the Martha Stewart brand solely to fill its need for upscale home fashions, nothing more. Halligan asserts that the Stewart brand could be more. "The Martha Stewart brand is about inspiration and how-to information. If Kmart were to position Martha Stewart in its stores as more about inspiration and do-it-yourself (DIY), rather than just home goods, then she could be credible in a variety of categories," says Halligan. As a far-fetched example, Martha Stewart could even make it as an automotive brand, she suggests. With car kits, cleaning accessories, and DIY-related activities, there could actually be a Martha Stewart Everyday Auto brand. But don't count on it. Not because it wouldn't work, but because Kmart is not approaching its brand assets strategically. Until Kmart solidifies a brand strategy, however, it will continue to miss more opportunities and remain at a competitive disadvantage.

Ignoring Technology's Capabilities

For years, Kmart management neglected any kind of sizable investment in technology, perhaps as a means of keeping capital costs down and its financial results rosier. But such a short-term strategy damaged Kmart's outlook. In the end, lack of a good technology strategy seriously hampered its success. Every CEO since Kmart's founding in 1962 has had the opportunity to install and implement a state-of-the-art information system able to link the various functions within the company. Granted, the challenge has grown with each passing year, with the cost and complexity of such an undertaking appearing daunting. But few CEOs have even identified it as a corporate goal.

The problem is that it's a capability that every retailer needs today to stay in the game. Today, information technology is not a luxury, as it may have been decades ago, it's a necessity. No company as large as Kmart can afford not to have an enterprise-wide system that links the various aspects of its operations, facilitating store-to-store communication, data sharing, and inventory updates, as just a few examples. Kmart's history of ignoring technology's capabilities only digs the retailer a deeper hole. While its competitors build on and improve their own information processing, thereby driving down costs and improving the efficiency of their own operations, Kmart tries patch jobs. The company was listed on the 2002 *InformationWeek* 500, a list of the companies that invested the largest amounts in technology during the previous year. Kmart's position at 43rd on the list looks impressive, but is partly due to its efforts to play catch-up, rather than signifying a shift in strategy or policy.

Continuing to ignore the major investment that Kmart needs to make will only push the company further behind. But since Kmart has been behind for so long, it appears that ignoring technology is a mistake it is destined to continue to make.

Not Standing for Anything

As the discount retail pioneer, Kmart certainly had a niche during its early days in the 1960s. Being the market leader had its advantages, namely, that consumers had few other choices when it came to discount shopping. Although there were other smaller chain competitors, none at that time came close to the scope and breadth of Kmart. Positioning itself as "The Savings

Place," Kmart had customers who knew what to expect when they entered the store's doors mainly because there were few other competitors that were anything like Kmart. Not so anymore. Not since the 1970s and 1980s, when Kmart lost sight of its customers, has the company actually differentiated itself in any meaningful way. Because it remained in place as competitors carved out niches around it, Kmart is now stuck between Wal-Mart's "Everyday low prices" and Target's cheap chic. Today, Kmart doesn't give shoppers a compelling reason to visit. Unless a Kmart store is much more convenient location-wise, there is little reason for shoppers to venture inside.

With Kmart having been all over the board with promotions, ads, and marketing messages in recent years—perhaps as a side effect of frequent management turnover—shoppers' heads may be spinning when it comes to figuring out what Kmart has to offer. And that's not likely to happen until the new management decides where Kmart is headed. Does "the store of the neighborhood" provide a major benefit to suburbanites? How do Caucasians feel about shopping in a store that's pushing hard to be the discounter of choice for Hispanics and African-Americans? What is there for mom to love about Kmart? Until Kmart clarifies the benefits of its market position, it will continue to stand for nothing, which means it will continue to see eroding market share.

Eschewing Competitive Intelligence

Kmart could learn a thing or two from Wal-Mart founder Sam Walton. If truth be told, Walton learned a lot from Kmart. The fact is that Walton understood the value of competitive intelligence, or studying the competition on a regular basis. He made frequent visits to competitors to study their marketing and pricing tactics and then took the best for use in his own stores. Those information-gathering forays served the company well as it overtook Kmart years later in sales dominance.

Did Kmart ever develop or implement its own competitive intelligence system? It doesn't look like it. Or if it does monitor its competition, Kmart doesn't appear to act on the information that it collects. Says Steven Greenberg of The Greenberg Group, "You always need to get a look at your competition. When your competition is doing something great, you need to respect it and respond to it, and they didn't."

Successful companies that respond to shifts in consumer preferences, competitors, and economic realities are able to do so effectively because of internal competitive intelligence systems. Designed to cull information from public and private sources about a company's internal and external environments, competitive intelligence systems can yield valuable information about a competitor's changing business strategy, new pockets of opportunity, or customer buying behavior that may indicate an untapped niche. Using tools such as census data, credit reports, legal filings, want ads, local newspaper articles, customer and supplier interviews, and on-site observation, competitive intelligence professionals can uncover useful information to help companies like Kmart know when and how to move ahead to make the most of their resources.

If Kmart has been monitoring its competitors, then its problems lie not with the existence of a competitive intelligence system, but in the execution. What's the point of collecting information about your competitors if you're not prepared to take any action as a result? Whereas Wal-Mart has made a science of studying the intricacies of its competitors' operations, in the past Kmart was more likely to ignore the company, thinking that it would go away. But Kmart underestimated Wal-Mart and now may be the competitor that goes away.

Overconfidence

Another problem for Kmart has been its confidence in its abilities to achieve results when all other factors indicated otherwise. Despite having faced financial difficulties in the past, including a near-bankruptcy in the mid-1990s, the company has always believed it could turn things around. Repeatedly, Kmart experienced ups and downs with respect to its sales, market share, and inventory and always assumed it would come out on top. Even when all signs suggested that its goals were too lofty, its target too out of reach, the company assured itself and its public of its strength. "Kmart has always had the philosophy that they could turn more around than they actually could," says America's Research Group's CEO Britt Beemer.

Former president Mark Schwartz may have been the epitome of Kmart confidence, believing that he, perhaps even alone, could turn Kmart's failing health around. "There were more good things done in the last 12 months than there had been done in 15 years," he states after leaving Kmart. "The company was a mess. This place was a dump," he says, while refuting claims that he was in over his head.[9] In return for tackling its toughest problems, Schwartz apparently felt Kmart should spare no expense. "There was no budget as far as execs were concerned," confirms Phil Adams, a former Kmart store manager in Detroit.[9] Initiatives that Schwartz felt warranted spending were undertaken, it appears.

Described as "brash, egotistical, arrogant" by a former store manager, Schwartz was known for his fixation with Wal-Mart, his former employer. Obsessed with the notion of beating Wal-Mart, Schwartz began devising strategies for challenging Wal-Mart head-on. During regular Friday executive meetings, a video would be routinely shown containing film clips from old war movies where pilots dropped bombs onto targets, with the word "Wal-Mart" superimposed on buildings.[10] This was apparently an attempt to rally the Kmart troops to beat the enemy. Why this was so critical was less clear.

Conaway and Schwartz devised a marketing program to attract low-price shoppers to Kmart by lowering prices on thousands of items. The board gave the duo permission for a limited test run on about 8,000 items, but Conaway and Schwartz quickly expanded that number to 40,000, feeling confident that the win would be sweeter with more inventory involved. So confident were they that they spent $850 million on inventory for the blow-out, but they didn't bother to get the board's approval or to alert the company's financial staff of their actions.

They also spent millions to renovate an aging Kmart store located right across the street from Wal-Mart's supercenter in Bentonville, Arkansas, and brazenly rented a billboard directly across from Wal-Mart's headquarters that read "The BlueLight is Back." Of course, this probably only served to fuel Wal-Mart's determination not to let Kmart win on any front. And it worried investors, including Kmart's largest individual shareholder, Ron Burkle, who said, "Every time I heard them talk about Wal-Mart, I got nervous."[10] Confident of Kmart's superiority, Schwartz and Conaway moved ahead with plans to defeat Wal-Mart, seemingly oblivious to the fact that Kmart wasn't prepared for the battle. Shortly thereafter, the truth became obvious as the losses mounted and Kmart could not afford to cover them. Bankruptcy soon followed, as did Conaway's demotion and Schwartz's ouster.

Lavish Spending

Although executives at major corporations deal routinely with dollar amounts containing more zeros than most of us will ever see firsthand, access to millions of dollars does not necessarily mean that senior managers are authorized to spend it. Some executive at Kmart didn't see it that way, however.

Mark Schwartz, for example, who was in senior positions at Kmart from 2000 to 2002, had a history of lavish spending that should have been a warning to Kmart. While at Wal-Mart in 1996, Schwartz started a real estate investment firm, MPG Enterprises, Inc., which ended up filing for Chapter 11 bankruptcy in 1997. To help Schwartz return his focus to his obligations at Wal-Mart, the company guaranteed $1.1 million in loans to help Schwartz restructure the debt. But after being reassigned to Wal-Mart's Mexico City operations, Schwartz took the top spot at Hechinger Co. in 1998. It was there that his management style would emerge. Schwartz started by investing heavily in store renovations and spending extravagantly at a time when the company could ill afford to. A former executive reported to *The Detroit News* that Schwartz once called an emergency meeting of Hechinger's 270 store managers at a cost of $3 million, and characterized the CEO's spending as lavish.[11]

When money got tight at Hechinger, Schwartz moved on to Big V Supermarkets as CEO in February 1999, leaving Hechinger to file for bankruptcy protection four months later and to liquidate two months after that. While at Big V, Schwartz again started expanding the chain, which operated as ShopRite. Said Neil Madera, a former Big V senior vice president and general counsel, "He came into town like a circus caravan with all his people. He expanded stores and built stores that just didn't make sense" until he left for Kmart in September 2000. In November, Big V filed for Chapter 11.

Schwartz was promoted from executive vice president of store operations to president of Kmart in March 2001 but was fired in January 2002, the same month that Kmart made its own Chapter 11 filing. Said Big V's Madera, "This guy ran a great company into the sewer. I can tell you now, I saw what was coming at Kmart."[11] So if former executives saw what was coming, that Schwartz was prone to overspending, how is it that Kmart allowed it to happen again?

In the three months before Kmart filed for bankruptcy protection, the company paid nearly 100 of its top executives at least $7.4 million in salary and perks, and paid $46.7 million to 78 officers for all of 2001. Twelve executives received signing bonuses worth between $76,000 to $150,000 in the year before its bankruptcy filing, and 17 individuals received nearly $10 million in severance that same year.[12]

Even in 2002, investors began voicing their opposition to excess at Kmart. Stated one major bond investor about management's efforts to get Kmart out of bankruptcy, "If they're the right guys for the job, they should be flying coach."[13] But if executive compensation packages and performance bonuses are any clue, it doesn't appear that they are. Both Adamson and Day will earn millions by virtue of their senior management positions, and even more if the company hits certain performance targets. Lavish spending lives on, even during Kmart's bad days.

At Wal-Mart, in contrast investors seem to be getting their money's worth. Stated Burt Flickinger of Strategic Resource Group, "There has been a tremendous amount of really strident criticism on the supplier and bondholder side about how can Tom Coughlin, the CEO of Wal-Mart Stores, get a base salary of less than a million a year, but you're paying these guys (at Kmart) to compromise and ultimately crater the company.

When they arrived, the company was marginally increasing same-store sales. Not they're being paid several million apiece, just to walk off the field."[14]

Short-Term Focus

In efforts to lure customers back into its stores, Kmart CEOs have tried a number of quick fixes that ended up costing the company more money than they generated. These include shifting focus back and forth from branded to private-label apparel, spending heavily on advertising circulars without communicating inventory needs to its buyers, and hiring Wal-Mart managers in a play to best Wal-Mart at discount pricing, only to discover that Kmart needed original thinkers.

Part of the problem is the incentives Kmart offers its leaders, and presumably senior managers, for attempting short-term fixes. James Adamson, for example, will receive in the neighborhood of $8 million if the company is turned around in less than two years. Julian Day could receive millions as well for his part. But will employees share in that pot if Kmart successfully exits bankruptcy in record time? No. The poor morale within Kmart's stores, and which threatens its continued existence, is a direct result of management's short-term focus. "If the current management team were long-term oriented they would be doing more to deal with employee issues, such as visiting employees in the stores," says Beemer, of America's Research Group.

To that end, he says, "Kmart has got to get off of its weekly circular strategy. It puts too much strain on employees, who have to relay out and rearrange the store each week to feature the sale items." Weekly promotions cause extra work for employees, challenge the inventory management system, and could be replaced by a different approach. "Kmart could do something different in its circulars, rather than weekly specials, such as a '10 percent off everything in the store' announcement," rather than reducing the price of individual items, suggests Beemer. Although Wal-Mart also uses a newspaper circular to advertise specials, it distributes them on a monthly basis, which causes far less stress on personnel than weekly sales, claims Beemer.

Each successive Kmart CEO has focused on identifying a quick fix. Instead of crafting a thorough, long-term growth strategy based on a proven business model, Kmart leaders have been pressured to immediately show sales improvements before being allowed to develop a long-term program. Unfortunately, few ever came up with larger visions for the company. Management's lack of attention to long-term issues that impact the morale of its workforce does not bode well for Kmart, says Beemer, who guesses that the current management team will not be around long after Kmart exits bankruptcy. "Current management is focused mainly on getting out of bankruptcy than on solving long-term issues," he says. A short time after Beemer made this statement, then-CEO Adamson promoted Julian Day to the top spot, reinforcing Beemer's point about long-term intentions.

Price Cutting

Former CEO Chuck Conaway was lambasted in the press following his disastrous attempt to beat Wal-Mart on price in 2001. But what most people don't realize is that this is apparently not the first time Kmart tried, unsuccessfully, to become the low-price leader. In 1977, recalls an early Wal-Mart manager in Sam Walton's autobiography, Kmart tried the same maneuver, with the same end result: "Kmart really took us on in about 1977 . . . . They took us on there in North Little Rock, where store number 7 had been one of our better stores. They got aggressive, and we fought back. We told our manager there, 'No matter what, don't let them undersell you at all, on anything.' I remember he called me one Saturday night and said, 'You know, we have Crest toothpaste down to six cents a tube now.' And I said, 'Well, just keep it there and see what they do.' They didn't lower it any more than that, and we both just kept it at six cents. Finally, they backed off," reports Thomas Jefferson.[15]

The funny thing is that Jefferson also concludes, "I always thought they learned something about us at that store—that we don't bend easy—because they never came at us with that degree of price cutting anywhere else." Until 2001, that is. Apparently 24 years later, Kmart had forgotten how well Wal-

Mart could dig its heels in until the Kmart cried "uncle." And just as before, Kmart backed off.

Misguided Corporate Policy

"So many policies made very little sense," reported a former manager. "For example, most stores had no fitting-room coverage, no loss prevention during peak periods, no extra coverage in the garden shop during the peak planting season, not enough and sometimes no employees for carry-outs, no janitorial service, old and outdated cash registers, virtually no training beyond that of register ringing, peripheral computer equipment was often broken, and the list goes on and on." But instead of fixing chain-wide policies, corporate managers tried to find ways to better enforce them.

The BlueLight Special is a perfect example, says the former manager. Kmart spent $6,000 per store to reintroduce the BlueLight Special but didn't allocate additional payroll dollars to cover the cost of the additional personnel required to make the program work as designed. "This resulted in very few blue lights and very little enthusiasm because everyone was so overworked," he says. Instead of investing in its people, Kmart invested in new blue shopping carts, signage, fixtures, and decorations. But "the customer didn't care about the fluff. What they wanted was someone to help them."[16]

The company's continued reliance on weekly circulars, despite the fact that weekly fixture changeovers, merchandise movements, and signage updates tax an already overworked store-level staff, should be reevaluated, too. But since Kmart found out firsthand how tied its customer traffic is to its sales when Conaway curtailed advertising and saw sales plummet, it may be trying to learn from that mistake by continuing the way things have always been—with weekly newspaper inserts. But inserts aren't the problem; it's the merchandise promotions that cause the upheaval. Kmart could test across-the-board markdowns as a means of highlighting bargains without causing tremendous extra work within each store. One week the toy department could advertise 15 percent off, while the next week the sporting goods department could have the same type of special, without requiring major layout adjustments and merchandise moves.

Learning from mistakes doesn't mean never trying something new again, it just means adjusting strategies based on the new information you've collected. Kmart has new information, but sometimes it is unwilling to apply it.

Reorganization Redux

Kmart's long-awaited bankruptcy reorganization plan has some new strategies it hopes will pull the company out of the doldrums, but it also has some initiatives that are reminiscent of CEOs past. Kmart's intent to start over with a totally new nine-member board, consisting of directors selected by the various constituents involved in funding the company's emergence from bankrupt status, harkens back to Floyd Hall. When Hall became CEO in 1995, one of the first steps he took was to recruit new directors to the board, including James Adamson, who eventually became CEO for a time.[17]

Its new White Lake, Michigan, prototype store, viewed as a great step forward for Kmart, is also similar to Joseph Antonini's Big K format, introduced back in 1997. What made Big Kmart a standout was the wider aisles, brighter lights, and Martha Stewart branded merchandise prominently displayed. The funny thing is, those are the same features that make White Lake a standout, too.

Learning from Past Mistakes

Most companies allow their employees to make mistakes from time to time, in the interests of risk taking and innovation, in the hopes that they will learn from them and help make the company wiser and more successful. However, that description does not fit Kmart, where risk taking was probably not encouraged.

When Chuck Conaway took the top spot in 2000, he let former, experienced managers go and replaced them with people who thought like he did, losing the knowledge and hindsight that only experienced retail managers can provide; he specifically decided not to learn from the company's past mistakes. The key to learning from mistakes, however, is first acknowledging that mistakes were, in fact, made. Sometimes Kmart does not want to do that.

Although Kmart has had its ups and downs through the years, much like other struggling retailers, the company seems to want to rewrite history—or just forget about the downturns. Its "Corporate History" section posted on Kmart's web site details the company's rise to dominance in the 1960s and 1970s and then fast-forwards to its "Back to Basics" focus in the 1990s without any mention of the pivotal 1980s when its growth faltered.

Owning up to mistakes, evaluating them, and identifying the good and the bad that was learned are the first steps toward success. All companies make mistakes, but the good ones make more new ones than old ones.

Notes

1. "Kmart missed the opportunity Wal-Mart found in technology," by Mike Wendland, *Detroit Free Press,* January 26, 2002.
2. Phone interview with Paul Argenti, professor of management and corporate communications at the Tuck School at Dartmouth, January 10, 2003.
3. Kohl's web site, www.kohls.com, January 13, 2003.
4. "Antonini's long-term strategy was right for Kmart," case study featured on the web site of Joseph Antonini's consulting firm, JEA Enterprises, www.jeaenterprises.com/casestudy.htm.
5. "Kmart tests new look . . . ," by Debbie Howell, *Drug Store News,* November 4, 2002.
6. "Phantom pages and false impressions," www.retailworker.com/ modules.php, January 28, 2002.
7. "Kmart's failure," Service Quality Institute web site, www.customer-service.com, January 30, 2002.
8. "Kmart sweetens closeout sales to lure shoppers," by Karen Dybis, *The Detroit News,* January 31, 2003.
9. "Brash Kmart exec accepts no blame," by Bill Vlasic et al, *The Detroit News,* June 23, 2002.
10. "Schwartz attacked Kmart stores, assaulted rival Wal-Mart," by Bill Vlasic et al, *The Detroit News,* June 23, 2002.

11. "Retail wunderkind involved in several bankruptcies, lawsuits," by Bill Vlasic etc. al, *The Detroit News,* June 23, 2002.

12. "Kmart discloses top executives' pay," by Lorene Yue, *Detroit Free Press,* April 17, 2002.

13. "Greed-mart," by Nelson Schwartz, *Fortune,* September 30, 2002.

14. "Kmart inquiry is focusing on executives," by Constance Hays, *New York Times,* May 3, 2002.

15. *Sam Walton: Made in America,* by Sam Walton with John Huey, New York: Doubleday, 1992, p. 193.

16. Comment from worker at www.retailworker.com in Kmart employee forum.

17. "Coming around again: Kmart's new ideas bear a familiar ring," by Vicki Young, *Women's Wear Daily,* October 28, 2002.

Forgiveness for Its Sins?

Despite the litany of missteps, mistakes, and poor decisions, can Kmart get beyond its history? The general consensus is yes, but with a few caveats. "I think any company can be saved," says Wharton's Professor Pete Fader. "Part of it is realizing what they are good at and what they are not good at."

Despite emerging from bankruptcy in May 2003, after securing $2 billion in exit financing, to help the company proceed towards its goal of profitability, here are 10 recommendations for getting back on track.

1. Scale Back

"The only way Kmart can stage a comeback is to scale back more than they have," says Professor Don B. Bradley III of the University of Central Arkansas. "They have to go back to where they're profitable and get out of the areas where they're not profitable." This may mean retrenching and regrouping as a regional competitor first, says Bradley, rather than a national presence. "They should be in the regions where they're strong and can logistically handle what they need. I don't think they have the money and the capital intensity to be a national power anymore."

Trim the kinds of products that they carry, says Professor Fader, which is exactly what former CIO Dave Carlson advised the company to do years ago—focus on the most popular products rather than trying to stock multiple brands of a product not many customers are buying. JGA's Tony Camilletti believes that is happening, because the inventory in the prototype store seems to have been "edited" and less cluttered.

2. Carve Out a Niche

Kmart needs to carve out a niche that differentiates it from its competitors, who have staked a claim on the mass market. The only way Kmart can thrive is by narrowing its focus to the highest-value, highest-opportunity consumer for its particular brand image. That niche could be celebrity brands that no one else carries, it could be focusing on its urban stores, or it could be using micromerchandising to tailor its inventory precisely to its local neighborhood's purchasing preferences. All of these possibilities have been mentioned in its bankruptcy reorganization plan. It's certainly a start in the right direction.

3. Promote Its Brands

In the new prototype store, Kmart seems to have finally recognized the importance the Martha Stewart brand name now holds for the company, and that is reflected in her products' placement within the store. Her brand is being merchandised much more effectively in the White Lake store, Camilletti points out, which is a good thing.

Kmart's other private-label brands also need to be highlighted and showcased, since they are one of Kmart's major brand assets. Nowhere else can customers buy JOE BOXER junior apparel, Sesame Street toddler outfits, or Martha Stewart home goods. That fact should be highlighted in all of its marketing communications.

4. Expand the Store of the Future—Quickly

Kmart's prototype is a look at "what the new Kmart can be," says JGA's Camilletti, who sees a lot of Kmart's merchandising issues addressed and corrected in the chain's new store design and image. Observers report that the new design is an excellent start at implementing needed cosmetic and layout improvements within Kmart stores. However, Kmart can't wait to implement much-needed changes chain-wide. Customers need to see proof of Kmart's commitment to customer satisfaction. Investment in upgrades in all 1,509 stores should start within the next three years.

5. Get Ahead of the Information Technology Curve

Although Kmart won't ever catch up to Wal-Mart technologically, it can still narrow the gap, reduce expenses, improve communication, and improve its operational efficiency. However, unlike sweeping past initiatives, Kmart needs to approach the process methodically, not trying to achieve a total overhaul in one fell swoop.

The company also needs to give its CIO more authority to do what is needed with the entire IT system, as well as championing the cause of improved information functioning company-wide. The only person who can accomplish that is new CEO Julian Day, who can choose to be an IT champion or wallflower. What Kmart really needs is a champion.

6. Boost Employee Incentives

Even after Kmart improves its information systems, renovates its stores, and gets its inventory in stock 100 percent of the time, it still needs to address corporate culture issues. Employees needs to be shown that they are an important part of Kmart's rebirth, and to see it in their paychecks. For years, executives have been paid outrageous sums by Kmart while its store-level employees get little, or get let go. Employee incentives need to be expanded to benefit associates who come into direct contact with customers and, therefore, have the greatest potential impact on a customer's experience.

7. Stop Focusing on Wal-Mart

Watch Wal-Mart, yes. Study its practices in order to improve Kmart's. But don't become obsessed, as past management did, with besting Wal-Mart. Kmart, Target, and Wal-Mart can coexist as long as Kmart finds a way to differentiate itself from its competition. The same advice holds true for up-and-comer Kohl's or veterans Sears and JCPenney. Pay attention to what Kmart needs to do. Right now the one factor keeping Kmart from success and profitability is Kmart itself.

8. Find Out What Its Customers Want

In designing its Store of the Future, Kmart asked customers and employees for input, ultimately developing a layout and appearance that gets rave reviews from all who visit. So why not take the same approach with the rest of its operations? Ask customers directly what they like and don't like about Kmart's merchandise, its checkouts, or its in-store restaurant. What would they rather see? What changes would encourage them to shop more often at Kmart? Then do something about it! Don't sit on the information, and don't overanalyze it the Kmart way, just implement as many changes as possible. Then let customers know that the changes they suggested were actually implemented. In addition to encouraging additional feedback, it will endear them to the company and solidify brand loyalty.

9. Stick with a Strategy

Once Kmart fully develops its plan for the future, stick with it longer than a season, or a year, or a CEO. Wal-Mart's mission has been in place since 1962, guiding the company's growth and success. As soon as Kmart determines where it can compete successfully in the discount retail arena, define a strategy and commit to it long term (hint: that means more than a year or two).

10. Foster Creativity

Unless Kmart can develop and perpetuate creativity within the company, it is finished. The corporate culture needs to be adapted to allow for new thinking, new approaches, and new ways of doing business. Kmart needs to be willing to emerge from the conservative corporate mantle that has held it back.

Has Kmart outlived its usefulness? "There's a theory about companies—after about 50 years they cease to be really innovative contributors to the economy and they exist just to employ people," says Rob Gelphman. "That might be Kmart." Then again, Kmart's customers, creditors, and employees may not allow Kmart to fade into the distance.

Loyal Customers Will Fuel a Turnaround

Despite the fact that Kmart has consistently received low marks from customers on issues ranging from the cleanliness of its stores to the frequency of out-of-stock merchandise, there is still a loyal contingent of shoppers who rate it highly. Research that Leo J. Shapiro & Associates has conducted on discount retailers has identified a dedicated band of customers who see no evil when it comes to Kmart. Explains Leo J. Shapiro & Associates chairman George Rosenbaum, "People who have stuck with Kmart through thick and thin give it high marks," no matter what. Consumers who shop at Kmart more than other stores rate Kmart highly against the competition; those are the customers who "have a strong relationship to it," says Rosenbaum. And it is those customers who will help Kmart reestablish itself with jaded former customers. Even consumers who aren't loyal Kmart shoppers are eager for Kmart to survive, if only to keep Wal-Mart and Target honest, says Rosenbaum. Most consumers have at least two of the three stores nearby, promoting competition and helping to keep prices lower.

Progress

Already, Kmart has made some leaps forward. Said CEO Julian Day in a press release before exiting bankruptcy, "Kmart is positioned to emerge from Chapter 11 in April with a stronger balance sheet and liquidity position. We have regained the confidence of lenders, creditors and critical vendors, securing needed financing during the Chapter 11 reorganization and, most recently, a $2 billion exit financing commitment. As we approach the first anniversary of our Chapter 11 reorganization,

Kmart has achieved a discernible shift in the Company's internal culture and substantially completed a stewardship review of its former management team; repositioned itself as a high/low retailer of exclusive proprietary brands; launched JOE BOXER, Disney Kids and Martha Stewart Everyday Holiday; secured a new brand licensing agreement with Thalia; and restructured the store base and distribution networks to protect and strengthen Kmart's competitive position in key markets."[1]

Kmart has also repaid all its outstanding debtor-in-possession borrowing and has used just $326 million of its available credit for letters of credit with vendors, leaving $1.57 billion available as of mid-December.[2] Kurt Barnard, president and chief economist of Barnard's Retail Consulting Group and publisher of *Barnard's Retail Trend Report*, notes that Kmart's exit financing package is a "vote of confidence from the financial community."[3] Even before filing its reorganization plan, there was a hint of hope. For the five weeks ending January 1, 2003—essentially December 2002—Kmart reported its first profit since filing for Chapter 11. The company had net income of $349 million on net sales of $4.71 billion, which was 5.7 percent below last year's figures for the same period.[4]

A Look Back

Even as Kmart pushed ahead with its reorganization plan in early 2003, the Justice Department and the Securities and Exchange Commission wrapped up their seven-month investigation.[5] What the feds found was a pattern of "deceit, intimidation and unauthorized spending," according to Kmart.[6]

What shareholders, employees, and customers learned in early 2003 was that "2001 was the year that broke Kmart," says *The Detroit News*. And Chuck Conaway had a big hand in making that happen, according to Stewardship Review documents submitted by Kmart.[6] Until Conaway was hired in mid-2000 to replace outgoing CEO Floyd Hall, Kmart's problems were longstanding and well recognized, but not dire. The company was generally profitable, but being hurt by aggressive competition. Then Conaway took over, making it virtually impossible for the company to recover from his team's extensive compensation packages and depleting corporate coffers without filing for bankruptcy, which it did in short order.

The Reorganization Plan

Kmart's filing of its bankruptcy reorganization plan on January 24, 2003, was somewhat sudden. The company had been working on it for months, but when exactly it would be filed with the Chicago bankruptcy court remained a mystery until mid-January, when Kmart announced its intention to submit its plan.

In the plan, Kmart outlines its intention to become the "store of the neighborhood" by positioning itself as a smaller, more neighborhood-conscious retailer. In doing so, it hopes to carve out a niche smack dab in the middle between Wal-Mart and Target.[7] Of course, that is where it is currently stuck. What is different about its new plan is that its effort to serve major metro areas by being larger than a party store but smaller than a Wal-Mart, as Professor Arun Jain of the University of Buffalo advises, is intentional.[7]

What Kmart has that its competitors do not is a strong base of urban stores where it could conceivably succeed at becoming the shopping choice of consumers in its immediate area. Three hundred and eight of its 324 urban locations are in major metro areas, where it has the jump on Wal-Mart to establish itself as the clear choice for discount goods. By leveraging its strengths and making the most of its multicultural customer base, Kmart sees sales increasing nearly 20 percent in the next five years, rising from $25.4 billion in 2003 to $30.2 billion in 2007. To achieve its goal of 18.6 percent growth, Kmart will add 70 new stores to its current 1,509 locations, beginning in 2004. In 2002 Kmart closed 283 stores, followed by an additional 322 in early 2003, and reduced its workforce from 234,000 to 167,000.[7]

Whether Kmart can actually deliver is in doubt, however. "Their forecasts and goals are very, very ambitious," said Professor Jain.[7] And Kmart's record of executing on plan is weak, not to mention the fact that the company is banking on an economic turnaround and improvements in the retail industry, both of which are totally out of its control. What's working in Kmart's favor are their exclusive brands, which can't be purchased anywhere but at Kmart, and management's new willingness to push inventory decision making down to the store level.

Playing a major role in Kmart postbankruptcy is Connecticut investor Edward Lampert, his firm ESL Investments, which currently holds approximately $1.6 billion in Kmart debt, and Third Avenue Value Fund, which have together pledged at least $293.4 million to aid Kmart. Lampert has also promised an additional $60 million that could become available, depending on the company's needs. Together they own more than 50% of the new Kmart.

Is Kmart really ready to venture beyond bankruptcy? Opinions are mixed on this score. Some experts believe that Kmart needed to emerge from bankruptcy as quickly as possible in order to reduce the huge fees it had to pay in connection with its filing, as well as to reassure customers that it will be around for good. In an anonymous letter from a group of Kmart employees, which was sent on January 9, 2003, to local media and government investigators, the letter writers allege that Kmart is rushing to exit bankruptcy "under severe pressure from several of its most powerful creditors,"[9] although the company is not necessarily ready to operate outside the protection of the bankruptcy court. The employees also call into question Kmart's viability as a company, stating "Kmart's diminishing chances for survival very much depend on an honest disclosure of what went wrong at the company and what actions must be taken to allow it to truly turn around after emerging from bankruptcy protection."[9]

Others think Kmart rushed the process so as to allow its executives to enjoy the huge bonuses that will be paid if Kmart exits before July 31, 2003. As James Harris of Seneca Financial previously stated, his belief is that "Kmart is no more ready to exit bankruptcy than the day it filed," characterizing Kmart's current situation as a "classic pump-and-dump scheme," with management boosting its financial prospects in order to collect as much reward as possible before moving on. Says Harris, "I think the reorganization of Kmart has turned into a real mess. The process reminds me of the comment that was made during the Vietnam

War, 'Let's just declare victory and go home.' In this case, declaring victory involves paying out millions of dollars to people who haven't succeeded. It also involves representing to the vendor community that problems have been fixed when in fact they haven't." Emerging now from bankruptcy, if Kmart is not ready, may lead to bigger troubles down the line. Whether there are bonuses in place for *keeping* the company out of bankruptcy is unknown.

Even executives inside the company, including its turnaround consultant and CFO, warn that it will take time for Kmart to fully rejuvenate its business. After years of ignoring its glaring problems, including tired stores, poor customer service, and inventory control issues, it will take more years before Kmart can reverse its bad reputation. And its bankruptcy gurus, turnaround consultant Jay Alix and CFO Albert Koch, won't be there to guide them.

Better Than Ever

Although Kmart has been compared to Montgomery Ward and Ames[10], the company surely hopes that it fares better than the now-defunct retailers. Montgomery Ward declared bankruptcy in 1997, came back, only to declare bankruptcy and shut down three years later, in 2000. Similarly, Ames declared bankruptcy in 1990,[11] reopened, and then shut down for good in 2002.

Fortunately, there are success stories. Continental Airlines, for one, came out of reorganization successfully.[12] "Most retailers, if they come out of bankruptcy, come out with a stronger store base and better finances," points out Eric Beder, formerly of Ladenburg Thalmann.[13] Other retailers, such as Federated, have lived to tell about their troubles.

The Kmart of yesterday, and even today, will cease to exist eventually, but that doesn't mean that a new Kmart can't be created.

Notes

1. Kmart press release dated January 19, 2003.
2. "Kmart latest plunge: third-quarter losses balloon to $383 million," by Dan Burrows, *Women's Wear Daily*, December 24, 2002.

3. "Kmart to lay off 37,000 more," by Glen Creno, *The Arizona Republic,* January 15, 2003.

4. "Kmart logs first profit since bankruptcy," by Joan Villa, *Video Store Magazine,* January 14, 2003.

5. "Retailer's revelations didn't surprise feds," by David Shepardson, *The Detroit News,* January 26, 2003.

6. "How 'frat boys' drove Kmart to ruin," by Karen Dybis, *The Detroit News,* January 26, 2003.

7. "Kmart pins comeback on 'neighborhood' plan," by Mike Hudson, *The Detroit News,* January 26, 2003.

8. "Strategy includes new board, shares," *The Detroit News,* January 16, 2003.

9. "Corruption helps sink Kmart, say employees," by Karen Dybis, *The Detroit News,* January 16, 2003.

10. "Kmart struggles to find effective marketing strategy," by Alice Cuneo, *Ad Age,* July 29, 2002.

11. Ames corporation description at Monster site: company.monster.com/ames and www.ames.com.

12. "What about the Kmart scandal?" by Mark Scheinbaum, *Albion Monitor,* February 4, 2002.

13. "The future of Kmart (online interview)," with Eric Beder at Washingtonpostonline.com, January 25, 2002.

Bibliography

Altman, Dennis. "Creating an impact." Kentucky Business Online, www.kybiz.com, March 2000.

Angwin, Julia. "United online posts first profit." *The Wall Street Journal,* November 10, 2002.

Armas, Genaro. "Hispanics now outnumber blacks in U.S." Associated Press, January 21, 2003.

_____. "Attention online shoppers." *CIO Magazine,* October 1, 2000.

Beder, Eric. "The future of Kmart (online interview)." Washington postonline.com, January 25, 2002.

Bennett, Jeff. "Tough pro will run Kmart." *Detroit Free Press,* March 12, 2002.

_____. "BlueLight's second-round financing gets green light." *Forbes,* August 14, 2000.

Bott, Jennifer. "Redesign may be more modest." *Detroit Free Press,* January 25, 2003.

Burrows, Dan. "Kmart's latest plunge: third-quarter losses balloon to $383 million." *Women's Wear Daily,* December 24, 2002.

Burton, Jonathan. "Bricks-and-mortar retailers go online." Cisco Systems, http://business.cisco.com, January/February 2001.

Carr, David, and Edward Cone. "Code Blue." *Baseline Magazine,* December 10, 2001.

Chartier, John. "Kmart faces image issues." CNNMoney, February 23, 2002.

Cheifetz, Isaac. "When elephants learn to rock and roll." *Minneapolis Star Tribune*, April 7, 2002, linked on www.opentechnologies. com/CC040704.htm.

Cohen, Cheryl. "The strategy behind Bluelight.com." Digitrends.net, February 1, 2001.

_____. "Court OKs takeover of Kmart leases." *Retail Merchandiser*, September 25, 2002.

Creno, Glen. "Kmart to lay off 37,000 more." *Arizona Republic*, January 15, 2003.

Cuneo, Alice. "Inside look at the bluelight battle plan." *Ad Age*, April 9, 2001.

_____. "Kmart struggles to find effective marketing strategy." *Ad Age*, July 29, 2002.

_____. "Kmart's bluelight dims." *Ad Age*, January 22, 2002.

D'Innocenzio, Anne. "Big discounters turn warlike in fight for customers." Associated Press, August 25, 2001.

_____. "Kmart mired in identity crisis." Associated Press, January 23, 2002.

Davis, Scott, and Cathy Halligan. "Extending the brand." Prophet. com, from the June 2001 issue of *Target Marketing Magazine*.

Dietderich, Andrew. "What ails Kmart." *Crain's Detroit Business*, 2000.

Dixon, Jennifer. "Kmart's holiday appeal." *Detroit Free Press*, October 15, 2002.

_____. "Kmart plan to sell more food shelved." *Detroit Free Press*, October 23, 2002.

_____. "Dowdle pleads guilty to Kmart defraud plan." *Women's Wear Daily*, May 13, 1996.

Driver, Anna. "Wal-Mart, Target prosper from Kmart woes." Reuters, February 7, 2002.

Duff, Mike. "Kmart launches JOE BOXER line." *DSN Retailing Today*, August 12, 2002.

_____. "The Martha miracle takes root in L&G and blossoms in baby." *Discount Store News*, March 22, 1999.

_____. "Population paradigm shift mandates new marketing." *DSN Retailing Today*, May 20, 2002.

Dybis, Karen. "Corruption helps sink Kmart, say employees." *The Detroit News*, January 16, 2003.

_____. "Grocery supplier out at Kmart." *The Detroit News*, February 4, 2003.

_____. "How 'frat boys' drove Kmart to ruin." *The Detroit News,* January 26, 2003.

_____. "Kmart hustles to keep pizza." *The Detroit News,* September 20, 2002.

_____. "Kmart sweetens closeout sales to lure shoppers." *The Detroit News,* January 31, 2003.

_____. "Exec sentenced to six months in prison, ordered to pay $500,000." *Beloit Daily News,* July 30, 1996.

_____. "Fleming says it may stop supplying Kmart." Associated Press, January 24, 2003.

Gaffney, John. "The ad campaign to save Kmart." *Business 2.0,* April 2, 2002.

_____. "The buzz must go on." *Business 2.0,* February 2002.

Gallagher, John. "The internal investigation." *Detroit Free Press,* January 25, 2003.

Garfield, Bob. "Kmart's new ads are not bluelight specials." *Ad Age,* March 4, 2002.

Gelphman, Robert. "Branding and positioning: There is a difference." *PRWeek,* February 25, 2002.

Grant, Lorrie. "Kmart takes aim at 284 underperforming stores." *USA Today,* March 10, 2002.

_____. "Shoppers pick Wal-Mart, Target over Kmart." *USA Today,* January 30, 2002.

_____. "Troubles continue at Kmart, top management out." *USA Today,* January 18, 2002.

Halligan, Cathy. "Will Sears be more like Target than Kmart?" MarketingProfs.com, July 9, 2002.

Hayes, Read. "Retailers toughen ethics codes to curb employee abuses." *Stores,* July 1996.

Hays, Constance L. "Built on the working class, Wal-Mart eyes the BMW crowd." *New York Times,* February 24, 2002.

_____. "Is Kmart out of stock in answers?" *New York Times,* March 17, 2002.

_____. "Kmart inquiry is focusing on executives." *New York Times,* May 3, 2002.

_____. "Kmart reports $2.42 billion annual loss." *New York Times,* May 16, 2002.

Helft, Miguel. "Ominous news for BlueLight.com." *Industry Standard,* May 24, 2001.

Heun, Christopher. "Now web bargains for Kmart." *Information Week,* August 21, 2000.

Higgins, Jim. "Kmart execs upbeat." *The Detroit News,* September 26, 2002.

Hirsch, Lou. "Can self-service help Kmart beat bankruptcy blues?" CRMDaily.com, February 7, 2002.

Hisey, Pete. "Home Depot, Kmart, Sears focus on logistics." *Retail Merchandiser,* January 1, 2002.

_____. "How Kmart fell behind." *Baseline Magazine,* December 10, 2001.

Howard, Theresa. "Kmart's new ads pin hopes on minority customers." *USA Today,* March 24, 2002.

Howell, Debbie. "Improve the in-store experience." *DSN Retailing Today,* March 11, 2002.

_____. "Kmart testing image with new layout, decor." *DSN Retailing Today,* October 28, 2002.

_____. "Kmart tests new look . . ." *Drug Store News,* November 4, 2002.

Hudson, Mike. "Kmart pins comeback on 'neighborhood' plan." *The Detroit News,* January 26, 2003.

Hwang, Suein. "How one struggling firm hopes to improve morale." *The Wall Street Journal,* October 31, 2002.

Jacobson, Greg. "A study in contrasts." *Mass Market Retailers,* May 27, 2002.

Keegan, Paul. "The rise and fall (and rise again) of JOE BOXER." *Business 2.0,* December 2002.

_____. "Kmart con salsa: Will it be enough?" *BusinessWeek,* August 30, 2002.

_____. "Kmart copes with loss of customers." *Retail Merchandiser,* August 29, 2002.

_____. "Kmart eyes 300 store closings." United Press International, December 24, 2002.

_____. "Kmart faces more store closings." United Press International, December 11, 2002.

_____. "Kmart files for Chapter 11." *SNL Real Estate Securities Weekly,* January 28, 2002 (at www.snl.com).

_____. "Kmart files plan of reorganization." Associated Press, January 24, 2003.

_____. "Kmart: Martha Stewart still selling well." Reuters, November 18, 2002.

_____. "Kmart reorganization won't be cheap." Visualstore.com, April 5, 2002.

_____. "Kmart seeks 'neighborhood market' tag." *Gourmet News,* November 2002.

_____. "Kmart sees store closings costing $300 million." Reuters, January 28, 2003.

_____. "Kmart to close 326 stores and shed over 30,000 jobs." Associated Press, January 14, 2003.

_____. "Kmart to close 284 stores." *Retail Merchandiser,* March 8, 2002.

_____. "Kmart to distribute groceries by itself." Reuters, February 5, 2003.

_____. "Kmart: will continue newspaper ads." Associated Press, January 31, 2002.

_____. "Kmart's new CEO: 'Who is Kmart?'" BusinessWeek Online, March 15, 2002.

_____. "Kmart's 20-year identity crisis." Knowledge@Wharton.

Koch, Christopher. "It all began with Drayer." *CIO Magazine,* August 1, 2002.

_____. "Kohl's succeeds while Kmart fails, says report." *Retail Merchandiser,* March 29, 2002.

Konicki, Steve. "Now in bankruptcy, Kmart struggled with supply chain." *InformationWeek,* January 28, 2002.

Krippel, Julie. "Home furnishings and housewares." HooversOnline.

Krotz, Joanna. "Kmart's 5 big blunders." Microsoft bCentral.com.

Laberis, Bill. "Why do good CIOs have to be the fall guys?" *Computerworld,* August 7, 2000.

_____. "Lax Kmart board compounded woes." *The Detroit News,* January 16, 2003.

Leung, Shirley. "Kmart to dismiss 37,000 workers, close 326 stores." *The Wall Street Journal,* January 15, 2003.

Levinson, Meredith. "Kmart looks within for CIO." *CIO Magazine,* July 1, 2002.

Lillo, Andrea. "Kmart must cut stores, carve niche." *Home Textiles Today,* January 28, 2002.

Lundberg, Abbie. "Inside the world's biggest company." *CIO Magazine,* July 1, 2002.

Lundegaard, Karen. "For sales or lease: Kmart parking." *Baltimore Business Journal,* November 8, 1996.

Martin, Antoinette. "New Jersey retail space; in the market for shopping centers, buyers line up." *New York Times,* November 8, 2002.

McGraw, Dan. "Kmart pays a steep price: the discounter faces a crucial holiday season after a long slide." *U.S. News & World Report,* November 13, 1995.

Meltzer, Michael, and Brian Smith. "Site selection: How to play the game." *Canadian Retailer* at the publication's web site at www.retailcouncil.org/cdnretailer/cr2000i5_siteselec.asp.

Merrick, Amy. "Can Martha deliver merry?" *The Wall Street Journal,* October 8, 2002.

_____. "Kmart, turned off by bluelight.com, renames Web site." *The Wall Street Journal,* June 20, 2002.

_____. "Turning Red Ink to Green?" *The Wall Street Journal,* October 15, 2002.

Muller, Joann. "Commentary: Attention Kmart: Find a niche." *BusinessWeek,* February 4, 2002.

_____. "Commentary: Kmart's shopping list for survival." *BusinessWeek,* March 25, 2002.

Obarski, Anne. "If you don't see it, we don't have it." About.com.

O'Brien, Wally. "Walmart, Kmart, and the brand that lost its way." iaaglobal.org, May 1, 2002.

Passikoff, Robert. "The arrogance of 'blue light' research." *Brandweek,* February 4, 2002.

Plasencia, William. "It's a good thing." *Hispanic Magazine,* July/August 2002.

_____. "Q&A: Chief says Kmart needs patience, focus." *Detroit Free Press,* March 12, 2002.

_____. "Q&A: If you were the CEO of Kmart . . ." *Home Textiles Today,* October 11, 2002.

Ratajczak, Donald. "Surprise lenders." *Atlanta Journal-Constitution,* January 27, 2002.

Reda, Susan. "Despite economic slowdown, retailers press ahead with IT spending plans." *Stores,* July 2001.

Ries, Al. *FOCUS: The Future of Your Company Depends On It.* New York: Harper Business, 1996.

_____. "Refocusing the corporation." Poolonline.com, Spring 1999.

Roush, Matt. "Kmart shows integrity." *Crain's Detroit Business,* April 22, 1996.

Rutherford, Emelie. "The benefits of hanging around smart people." *CIO Magazine,* June 1, 2001.

Santosus, Megan. "A seasoned performer." *CIO Magazine,* January 15, 1995.

Scheinbaum, Mark. "What about the Kmart scandal," *Albion Monitor,* February 4, 2002.

Schepp, David. "Kmart: Death of a retailing icon?" BBC News, January 22, 2002.

Schwartz, Ephraim. "Statistics reveal incremental online shopping growth." *InfoWorld,* December 30, 2002.

Schwartz, Nelson. "Greed-mart." *Fortune,* September 30, 2002.

Seamonds, Jack. "Nickels and dimes no more." *Fortune,* June 29, 1987.

Sellers, Patricia. "Kmart is down for the count . . . and Floyd Hall doesn't look like the man to get it back on its feet." *Fortune,* January 15, 1996.

Shepardson, David. "Retailer's revelations didn't surprise feds." *The Detroit News,* January 26, 2003.

Sliwa, Carol. "Kmart moves to catch up on IT." *Computerworld,* July 31, 2000.

_____. "Kmart names new CIO." *Computerworld,* September 15, 2000.

_____. "Smarter, faster, more profitable." *Intelligent Enterprise,* October 4, 2001.

Smith, Hubble. "Las Vegas Kmarts benefit from fast growth, low rent." *Las Vegas Review-Journal,* March 9, 2002.

Stafford, Nicole. "Sights, sounds on the sales floor." *The Observer & Eccentric Newspaper,* July 15, 2001.

Stankevich, Debby Garbato. "Kmart hopes to see green in White Lake." *Retail Merchandiser,* December 1, 2002.

Stavro, Barry. "Mass appeal." *Forbes,* May 5, 1986.

_____. "Strategy includes new board, shares." *The Detroit News,* January 26, 2003.

Swartz, Jon. "Retailers discover leap to Web's a doozy." *USA Today,* December 18, 2001.

Talaski, Karen. "Kmart loses $2.4 billion." *The Detroit News,* May 16, 2002.

Taub, Stephen. "Can Kmart come back again?" *Financial World,* March 31, 1983.

_____. "Two more free ISPs bow out." ISP Planet, December 4, 2000.

Underhill, Paco. *Why We Buy: The Science of Shopping.* New York: Simon & Schuster, 1999.

_____. "U.S. court approves Kmart sale of Bluelight.com." Reuters, October 30, 2002.

Vance, Sandra Stringer, and Roy Scott (contributor). *Wal-Mart: A History of Sam Walton's Retail Phenomenon.* New York: Twayne Publishers, 1994.

Vargas, Melody. "Bluelight shaping up to succeed where Kmart's previous e-tail attempts failed." About.com.

_____. "Vendors stand behind Kmart-and its $2B bailout." *TWICE,* www.twice.com, January 24, 2002.

Verton, Dan. "Churn." *Computerworld,* February 5, 2001.

Villa, Joan. "Kmart logs first profit since bankruptcy." *Video Store Magazine,* January 14, 2003.

Vlasic, Bill, et al. "Brash Kmart exec accepts no blame." *The Detroit News,* June 23, 2002.

Vlasic, Bill, et al. "Retail wunderkind involved in several bankruptcies, lawsuits." *The Detroit News,* June 23, 2002.

Vlasic, Bill, et al. "Schwartz attacked Kmart stores, assaulted rival Wal-Mart." *The Detroit News,* June 23, 2002.

Wagner, Jim. "Bluelight.com sale goes before bankruptcy judge." Internetnews.com, October 11, 2002.

Walsh, Tom. "Emergency surgery may help save ailing retailer." *Detroit Free Press,* January 15, 2003.

Walton, Sam, with John Huey. *Sam Walton: Made in America.* New York: Doubleday, 1992.

_____. "Watch out for competitor roadblocks." *CI Magazine,* January 30, 2002.

Wendland, Mike. "Kmart missed the opportunity Wal-Mart found in technology." *Detroit Free Press,* January 26, 2002.

Wiener, Michael, and Howard Makler. "Surplus real estate: Causes, solutions." *Shopping Center World,* May 1, 1999.

Wingate, Rick. "Target vs. Kmart—a store-level view." *DSN Retailing Today,* May 6, 2002.

Yerak, Becky. "Kmart must find niche to compete." *The Detroit News,* January 23, 2002.

Young, Vicki. "Coming around again: Kmart's ideas bear a familiar ring." *Women's Wear Daily*, October 28, 2002.

Yue, Lorene. "A test in White Lake Township." *Detroit Free Press*, October 18, 2002.

_____. "Design War: Kmart stores often do not send a focused message." *Detroit Free Press*, February 12, 2002.

_____. "Kmart discloses top executives' pay." *Detroit Free Press*, April 17, 2002.

Zuber, Amy. "Ex-Pizza Hut vps plan big Little Caesar's franchise." *Nation's Restaurant News*, July 16, 2001.